RIVER WITHOUT A CAUSE

RIVER WITHOUT A CAUSE

An Expedition through the Past, Present, and Future of Theodore Roosevelt's River of Doubt

SAM MOSES

PEGASUS BOOKS

NEW YORK LONDON

RIVER WITHOUT A CAUSE

Pegasus Books, Ltd.
148 West 37th Street, 13th Floor
New York, NY 10018

Copyright © 2024 by Sam Moses

Images where credited to Carr Clifton are © Carr Clifton

Images where credited to Mark Greenberg are © Mark Greenberg

Narrative map of the Rio Roosevely and Roosevelt-Rondon Expedition
created by Michael Siegel

First Pegasus Books cloth edition March 2024

Interior design by Maria Fernandez

Library of Congress Cataloging-in-Publication Data is available.

ISBN: 978-1-63936-557-9

10 9 8 7 6 5 4 3 2 1

Printed in the United States of America
Distributed by Simon & Schuster
www.pegasusbooks.com

For the late Charles Haskell,

whose dream and ambition enabled this book,

and the late Dr. John Walden,

whose experience and calm wisdom

helped keep the expedition safe, and mostly sane.

Contents

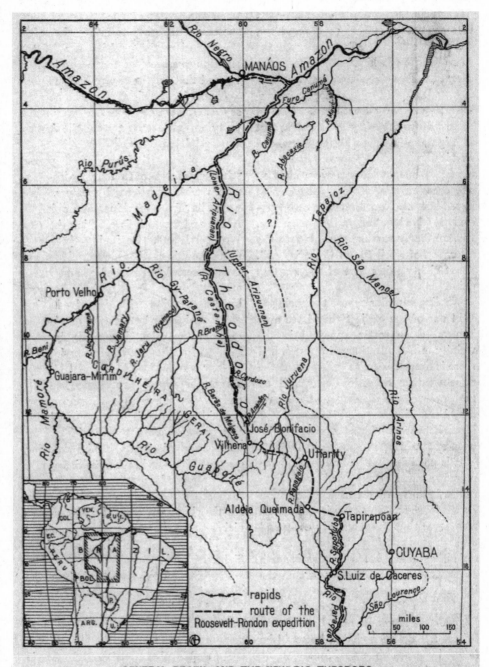

CENTRAL BRAZIL AND THE NEW RIO THEODORO

Sketch map of the south-central part of the Amazon drainage system, based on the surveys of the Brazilian Telegraphic Commission, showing the course of the Rio Theodoro and the route of the Roosevelt-Rondon expedition. Scale, 175 miles to the inch. The inset shows the location of the main map Reproduced by permission, in revised form, from the *Bulletin of the American Geographical Society* for July, 1914

Map Key for the Narrative Map of the Rio Roosevelt and Roosevelt-Rondon Expeditions

1. Madness in the jungle at night
2. Explorers open up the rainforest for farming and ranching
3. At the headwaters: Cabral the scientist stung by electric caterpillar
4. Kaminsky the kayak scout loses the tape for *Good Morning America*
5. Hither and thither
6. Tweed: "This is nothing!" Class III rapids
7. Graffiti at the entrance of the emerald forest
8. Diamonds at the foot of the falls
9. Resupply: gasoline-infused noodles washed down with icy Brahma
10. Steeper, deeper, faster
11. Captain Slade tells co-leader Beth she has to walk. She is pissed
12. A star is born: Kelley the "girl" boatman in Class IV rapids
13. Here lies poor Simplicio. Explorers raft over his bones
14. Joe Willie nails fast paddleboat run
15. Here lies poor Lobo, shot with long arrows. Good dog
16. *Aripuana* sinks at "camp of ill omen," camaradas on foot, stalked by Cinta Larga
17. Explorers corrupt the native children
18. The expedition that came for dinner. "Get bit by a snake and you're gonna die!"
19. Kermit gets a river, to make him feel not so bad after drowning Simplicio
20. Explorers look on wrong river for 78-year-old board that rotted to mulch 77 years ago
21. Mario attacked by vicious stowaways: red ants
22. TR gashes his leg
23. Chief Tatare gets hooked on whitewater rafting, in continuous Class IV
24. Slade and Beth duel with oars as their raft spins in a Class IV hole
25. Charlie and Beth attempt mutiny from the top down
26. Rondon tells TR he'll have to walk out
27. Kermit talks TR out of suicide by morphine
28. Julio murders Sgt Paixon with a shot to the heart
29. TR travels to Kubla Khan, out of his head with fever
30. Explorers portage around three 10-foot waterfalls, over a logging road; "Lucky it was there," says Charlie. Kermit's turtle soup brings TR back to the Duvida, now relenting.
31. TR, a would-be firing squad, takes aim at Julio but lowers his rifle. Let the Indians do it
32. Cinta Larga club three trespassing settlers to death, the previous year
33. Here roams the ghost of that cur Julio
34. An Indian matter: Chief Oitamina runs scared from Chief Jacinto
35. Airplane drops note in a bottle: "Do you need to be rescued?"
36. Mangrove maze: Candirus stick it to Captain Slade
37. Beer, spears, and guns at the party
38. Final search for a cause
39. Sam and Mario leave the expedition to follow the chiefs and the mahogany
40. The perfect dream: rafting trips down the Rio Roosevelt guided by Cinta Larga, ending at Muiraquita (magical frog, or big vagina) Eco Lodge

Narrative Map of the Rio Roosevelt and Roosevelt-Rondon Expeditions

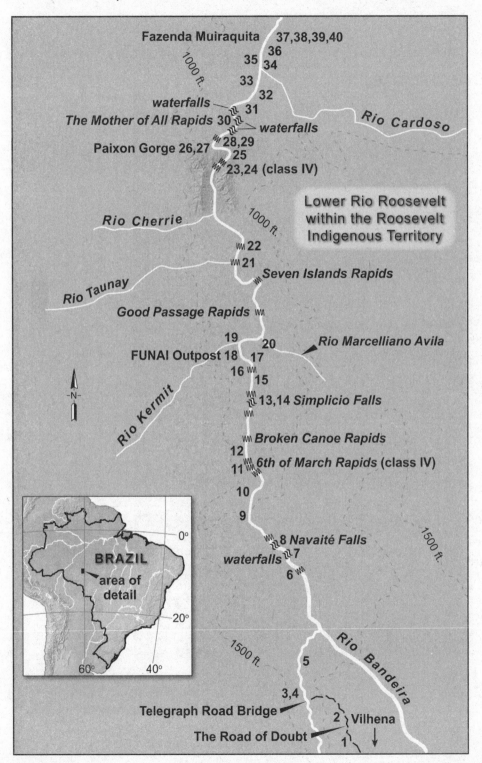

Fazenda Muiraquita   37,38,39,40
                          36
                    35 34
                  33
                      32
    waterfalls   31
The Mother of All Rapids 30
                      waterfalls
                    28,29
Paixon Gorge 26,27   25
                    23,24 (class IV)

Rio Cardoso

Rio Cherrie

Lower Rio Roosevelt
within the Roosevelt
Indigenous Territory

1000 ft.

1000 ft.

                    22
                    21
Rio Taunay   Seven Islands Rapids

Good Passage Rapids

                19
                    20   Rio Marcelliano Avila
FUNAI Outpost 18   17
                16
                    15
Rio Kermit   13,14 Simplicio Falls

                    Broken Canoe Rapids

                12
                11   6th of March Rapids (class IV)

                10

                9

                    8 Navaité Falls
    waterfalls   7

                6

BRAZIL
area of
detail

0°

20°

60°   40°

1500 ft.

Rio Bandeira

1500 ft.

                5

                3,4
Telegraph Road Bridge   2) Vilhena
The Road of Doubt   1

At the dedication of the Rio Roosevelt: the Vermont farmer, naturalist, and ornithologist George Cherrie, assigned by the American Museum of Natural History; Brazilian army doctor Jose Antonio Cajazeira, who would save Roosevelt's life with an operation on the jungle floor using the scalpel he carried in his jaguar-skin pouch; the loyal Lieutenant Joao Salustiano Lyra, engineer, surveyor, and astronomer schooled in geodesy in Germany, who charted the river by the stars; former president Theodore Roosevelt, the Great Man himself; Colonel Cândido Mariano Rondon, dirt-poor orphan caboclo with the IQ of a genius, uncompromising Positivist, one of the world's greatest explorers, legendary in Brazilian history; and Kermit Roosevelt, the president's 24-year-old son, Harvard graduate, reluctant participant, and savior of the expedition.

First they cut the trail, and then they pushed their dugout canoes weighing as much as half a ton, an uncounted number of times and miles over 48 days, all the while half-starving, watched from the forest by unseen Cinta Larga debating whether or not to kill them. Roosevelt died five years later, carrying the effects of the *Expediciao Scientifica Roosevelt-Rondon*.

PART I

REACHING THE RIVER

CHAPTER 1

The Promise

Yes, but why are you here?
—Brazilian journalist

C harles Haskell and Elizabeth McKnight hadn't even begun their expedition, and already they had some explaining to do. They were seated at a long table on the stage of a small auditorium at Universidade Federal do Amazonas in Manaus, Brazil, for what was being called a Round Table discussion. Haskell wasn't sure what it was all about, but he knew they should be there, invited by Silvio Barros, secretary of tourism for the state of Amazonas. Barrios got them the permits for their Rio Roosevelt expedition, a maddening process that had taken more than 18 months and five trips to Brazil.

The permits were granted on the condition that the expedition make a contribution to science, culture, education, and environment in ways that would be beneficial to Brazil. It would be a journey of nearly 2,000 miles by 20 people on four Amazon rivers, starting with 472 miles by inflatable rafts down the Rio Roosevelt, a ribbon of rugged whitewater winding north through the heart of the Amazon. They would retrace Theodore Roosevelt's first descent, then called Rio da Duvida, or River of Doubt. The river lies within 890 square miles demarcated by the Brazilian government as Roosevelt Indigenous Reserve.

In 1914 the ex-president had joined Brazil's greatest explorer, Colonel Cândido Rondon, to descend and chart the river that Rondon had discovered but not followed in 1909. It was a 12-meter-wide tributary to somewhere, drawn by Rondon on his map with a wiggly black line leading to the word *Duvida*.

Their *Expediciao Scientifica Roosevelt-Rondon* needed 56 days to reach the river, trekking over harsh highlands in a mule train, and 59 days to descend the river in one-ton dugout canoes, dragging them around unrelenting rapids. Three men died, from drowning, murder, and flight. Roosevelt nearly died from the effects of a leg gash with his 24-year-old son Kermit at his side, and risked death from a weak heart with each breathless step, stalked through the jungle by his lifelong asthma. He lost 54 pounds and never regained the vigor stolen by the Amazon. He lived five more years and died in his sleep, assisted by morphine for pains in his joints. Doctors today trace his death back to the leg wound in the Amazon.

He wrote his book *Through the Brazilian Wilderness* on the expedition, sent back in installments to *Scribner's Magazine*. Except for vivid descriptions of piranhas, he downplayed the drama, sidestepping Colonel Rondon's rigidity and his own anger and pain. He evaded comment on Kermit's rash action that led to the drowning, and never mentioned Kermit's talking him out of a decision to end his life with the vial of morphine he carried. The book avoids disputes and tense details, and reflects Roosevelt's positive attitude.

When the *New York Times* announced the ex-president's descent of this unknown river longer than the Rhine (named Rio Roosevelt during the expedition), cries of disbelief came from Europe, notably from British geographers. A former president of the Royal Geographical Society was incredulous. A famous Italian explorer of South America called Roosevelt a charlatan. An American explorer and geographer who'd been to the Amazon basin in 1907, Alexander Hamilton Rice Jr., insulted the ex-president until Rondon's charts brought an apology. But the negativity stained the expedition.

In 1926 the Roosevelt Memorial Association sent Commander George Dyott, a dashing American aviator who explored South America, down the river with two movie cameras. Dyott sent dispatches to the *New York Times* along the way. He confirmed Roosevelt's descriptions and praised their accuracy. He admired the fortitude and strength of Colonel Rondon and the late American president.

For the next 78 years there were only two known attempts to descend the river, one turned back after Indian attacks, the other vanished without a trace.

McKnight took the stage at the Round Table first, speaking words she'd used many times to introduce and outline the expedition in sponsorship pitches and permit applications. She and Haskell had formed a nonprofit they called New Century Conservation Trust, with "a vision to the future through exploration of the past," as its prospectus stated. The Rio Roosevelt expedition was its first project. "Through the eyes of a new generation, a team of Brazilians and Americans will conduct a biometric sampling, a ground observation, and comparison of the River of today versus 77 years ago," said the prospectus.

Charlie Haskell lifted his solid six-foot-three-inch frame out of his chair and spoke uncomfortably, as always for him. He told the audience what he had told the *New York Times*: "We hope to bring the 1914 spirit of Brazilian-American scientific cooperation alive to a new generation." He emphasized that seven of the expedition members were Brazilian, including two chiefs from the Cinta Larga tribe who would be guides through their reserve, the Roosevelt Indigenous Area. The team's three Brazilian scientists would be writing a paper for the upcoming United Nations Conference on Environment and Development in Rio de Janeiro, the Earth Summit, to be attended by 150 nations. All profits from the expedition would go toward the establishment of rainforest education programs in Brazil.

After McKnight and Haskell presented their dreams, Silvio Barros, the secretary of tourism, presented the problem. He was the moderator and interpreter, an environmental engineer and student of rainforest issues, including sustainable development.

"Tourism is a good alternative to farming and ranching in the Amazon because the product of the Amazon is nature," he said. "The world is trying to protect the Amazon, so let's bring them down to see nature the way it is. This is why I am very happy to see the Rio Roosevelt expedition here. They will go back with stories of how rich and beautiful is nature in the rainforest, and maybe more people will be excited about coming down here, and investing their money here to protect it."

After Barros's optimism, Professor Ribamar Bessa, teacher of Amazon History at the University of Rio de Janeiro, went long and dark, back to 1541 when the Ecuadorian conquistador Gonzalo Pizarro reached the Amazon. Pizarro went into the jungle with 220 soldiers and 4,000 Indigenous people, looking for the Land of Cinnamon that Columbus said was there. He came out with 80 men and no cinnamon, after building a brigantine and sending his Captain Francisco de Orellana and 55 men on a mission to find food. Instead, they found the Amazon River, and seven months later reached the Atlantic Ocean. Back in Spain, Pizarro accused de Orellana of treason.

The mission's padre, Dominican friar Gaspar de Carvajal, kept a journal and published a book. He named the river Amazon, for the fearless women warriors who attacked his ship, shooting arrows into musket fire, using slaves as warriors, who would be killed if they retreated. "These women are very white and very tall," he wrote, "and have hair very long and braided and wound about the head, and they are very robust and go about naked, with their privy parts covered, with their bows and arrows in their hands, doing as much fighting as ten Indian men."

Professor Bessa's message seemed to be that after the violation by Spaniards and 450 years of exploitation and decimation, the Amazon gets its revenge by eating explorers alive. Its many natural dangers, he said—namely jaguars, piranhas, anacondas, man-eating ants, and malarial mosquitoes—were God's way of telling people to stay out.

The professor was a tough act for Tweed Roosevelt to follow. But he was well prepared, having lectured many times on his great-grandfather's adventures and accomplishments. A Harvard graduate and consultant for a Boston financial management group, Tweed brought bona fide blood to the expedition, and like TR he had been interested in insects since he was a boy. As the American Museum of Natural History had sponsored the ex-president down the River of Doubt in 1914, they asked Tweed to bring back specimens from the Rio Roosevelt.

Tweed began by answering the question he said Brazilians always ask: Why would an ex-president of the United States go into the Amazon jungle, enduring its discomfort and risking its danger? Roosevelt's six children had asked the same thing. As Edith Roosevelt explained in a letter to daughter Ethel, "Father needs more scope, and since he can't be president, must go away from home to have it."

Roosevelt's seven-year presidency had ended in 1908. His enduring accomplishments are many. The greatest conservationist in history, he established 150 national forests, 51 federal bird reserves, 4 national game preserves, 5 national parks (including the Grand Canyon and Yosemite), and 18 national monuments on more than 230 million acres of public land.

His attempt to regain the presidency in 1912 as candidate of the new Progressive Party, called the "Bull Moose Party" after him, was a disaster. He split the Republican vote, handing the presidency to Democrat Woodrow Wilson. "Well, we have gone down in a smashing defeat," he wrote Kermit. For most of the next year, except for a trip to the Southwest where he visited Hopi Indians with sons Archie and Quentin and nephew Nicholas, he moped around the house on Sagamore Hill in Oyster Bay, Long Island. Then he got invitations for speaking engagements in Brazil, Argentina, and Chile, paying extremely well. He needed to put losing behind.

He'd done so before. When he was 25, his wife of three years, Alice Haskell Hathaway Lee, 22, called "Sunshine" for her disposition and athletic beauty, died in his arms on Valentine's Day from kidney complications after giving birth to their daughter Alice. Eleven hours earlier, his mother had died of typhoid in the same house. He ran from his grief to the South Dakota Badlands, leaving infant Alice to be raised by his older unmarried sister, Anna. For the next three years, with trips back to New York, he lived in the Dakota Territory, busting broncos, hunting grizzly bears, chasing cattle thieves, and getting in bar fights. He would write three books about his adventurous time as a cowboy.

Back in New York with a healed but scarred heart, he began courting his childhood semisweetheart Edith Kermit Carow, and soon married her. They raised Alice, while having five more children.

Roosevelt didn't allow self-pity, but revealed that he sometimes struggled with depression. "Black care rarely sits behind a rider whose pace is fast enough," he wrote. (Another genius, Winston Churchill, called his depression Black Dog, and ran from it by laying bricks.) Roosevelt rode into the Amazon to recover from the 1912 election defeat. "It rather diminishes the sum of my achievement," he wrote Kermit.

Edith was with him when he boarded the steamer bound for South America in October 1913, with other members of his expedition and five tons of equipment and provisions. After his speaking engagements, he planned to travel up the Paraguay River and into the Amazon basin on a scientific expedition with two naturalists from the American Museum of Natural History. The Paraguay was 1,675 miles long, flowed among four South American countries, and had 26 exciting tributaries, a paradise of specimens for the Museum. Roosevelt said it was "a little indefinite" about which tributaries they would explore.

But then Brazil's minister of foreign affairs, Lauro Müller, made Roosevelt another offer. Müller had asked Colonel Cândido Rondon, the renowned explorer, if he would take Roosevelt somewhere more exciting. Rondon said not if it was going to be a hunting trip like Roosevelt's safari in Africa. He offered five options, including Rio da Duvida, which he'd discovered in 1909 on an expedition that had nearly killed him, while cutting an 835-mile stretch of his Strategic Telegraph Line through the Amazon. Müller told Roosevelt that if he and Rondon were to descend the *Duvida*, it would be the first descent of an Amazon river of unknown length and difficulty, possibly the longest unknown river on earth.

It was a time of great exploration. The American Robert Peary had reached the North Pole in 1909; the Norwegian Roald Amundsen had reached the South Pole in 1911; and Irishman Ernest Shackleton was in the headlines planning his trans-Antarctic expedition. But the Amazon was literally off the map.

The night that Roosevelt lost the 1912 election, his oldest son Ted had sent a telegram to the next-oldest son Kermit: WHAT WILL OLD LION DO? This expedition with the great Colonel Rondon was the answer. It wasn't just his last chance to be a boy, as he said; it was his last chance to be a famous explorer. He "eagerly and gladly" chose Rio da Duvida, which presented "the greatest number of unforeseen difficulties," said Rondon. The Roosevelt South American Scientific expedition up the Paraguay River became the *Expediciao Scientifica Roosevelt-Rondon* down the River of Doubt.

When the president of the American Museum of Natural History got wind of the new plan, he sent Roosevelt a letter saying in effect that the Museum would have nothing to do with the likely death of a former president, and that it expected him to stick to the original plan. Not a chance, replied TR. He'd had a full share of life, and "if it is necessary for me to leave my bones in South America, I am quite ready to do so."

◆

The Round Table panel was completed by two of the team's three scientists from INPA, the *Instituto Nacional do Pesquisas de Amazonia*, or National Science Institute. Geraldo Mendes and Jose Cabral, seated at the end of the long table, watched their minutes to speak drift away.

Mendes was crushed. A shy and cheery ichthyologist, his passion for fish showed when he talked about them; he'd beamed in pride when Haskell chose him to be on the panel. But now, as the clock ticked, it seemed his assignment wasn't important enough to be recognized.

He wanted to tell the audience what he told James Brooke of the *New York Times*, in a second piece that ran while the team was in Manaus,

headlined IN T.R.'s FOOTSTEPS, SCIENTISTS EMBARK ON AMAZONIAN
EXPEDITION. "This trip is important because access is very difficult to
headwaters of Amazon rivers," Mendes said. "We believe that 40 percent
of the fish species in the Amazon have not been identified, and most of
them are in headwaters."

The other scientist who wouldn't get to speak, Jose Cabral, held a PhD
in pharmacology from the University of Mississippi. A rainforest cure for
cancer was one of his goals, along with treatments for everything from
headaches to AIDS. Cabral planned to spend his time on the expedition
interviewing Indigenous people and settlers, trying to learn more about
rainforest remedies, and maybe discover something new.

After about an hour, in order to speed things along, the program was
opened to questions, skipping the scientists.

It was a tough crowd. The purpose of the Round Table was to explain
the Rio Roosevelt expedition, but the attendees wanted it justified. "How
can this expedition benefit the Amazon?" was the first question, which
apparently hadn't been answered in its leaders' opening remarks. There
was a missing link or two between the plans of New Century Conservation Trust and stomachs in the Amazon. The audience got lost trying to
follow the anticipated profit from the expedition's media enterprises to the
conservation of Indigenous culture and land.

The prospectus stated it succinctly: "The purpose of the expedition is to
produce a book and film . . ." and that was how Haskell answered the question. But a woman in the front row, who appeared to be a journalist, was
persistent. She asked the question yet again: "Yes, but why are you here?"

"We're here for two purposes," replied Haskell, patiently. "To bring
the history of 1914 to 1992, and to introduce Americans to Rondon and
Brazilians to Theodore Roosevelt." Given that TR had his own bus line
around Manaus, the latter seemed redundant.*

---

*   The students also wanted to know about "biometric sampling." What did it mean? It
     sounded scientific but only meant the measure of change in the biology of something
     over a period of time. For the Rio Roosevelt expedition, it seemed enough to say that
     it meant a general comparison of the river and rainforest environment, then and now.

The Round Table discussion went as far as it could. The expedition's intentions were good but ethereal, and when Haskell was asked to please explain again about the goals, his repetitive answers floated out over the thinning room and were lost in the hollow crack of wooden writing trays falling on linoleum, knocked to the floor by the restless knees and shifting feet of the mostly female students. They might have been there on a class assignment until one and two at a time, they drifted out of their seats and up the two short aisles and out the doors. There were about a dozen people remaining at the end of the discussion, and Haskell had to go, to prepare for the flight to Porto Velho. But all told, he said, he thought it had been a pretty terrific conference.

CHAPTER 2

The Motive

I still remember the day when I was 16 and
wrote my name for the first time.
—Charles Haskell

C harlie's a really nice kid, but he's stupider, dumber than hell. He's just a little mongoloid." That's what Haskell remembers them saying about him when he was growing up. Born in 1943 into a powerful and intelligent Texas family, he grew up rich but unhappy. He had a maternal grandfather he loved, because he was kind to him, and a successful father he didn't, because he was not. Charlie was dyslexic, a handicap that wasn't understood at the time. He stuttered and couldn't read.

He says he believes his father thought he was "retarded." His very existence threatened his father, he says, and that's what made him mean. He says *The Prince of Tides* is his life story. "Dyslexia wasn't even a word then," he says. Actually, it's been a word since 1887, and for 10 years before that it was called "word blindness." In Charlie's case, it fit.

Charlie's handicaps were close to home. His paternal grandfather, Robert Henry Haskell Sr., was founder and head of a Michigan mental institution whose mission was to turn "morons"—it was a medical term back then—into upstanding citizens able to hold down a job, thus keeping them out of jail. "Idiots" and "imbeciles" were less of a concern, his institution said, because they were usually too passive to cause trouble.

Haskell Sr. was a brilliant doctor, valedictorian at Columbia in 1907, who ruled his Wayne County Training School until 1955. It's whispered that, with all good intentions, he might have performed brain surgery on developmentally disabled children.

Charlie Haskell's father, Robert Haskell Jr., was also an MD, but when he married Antoinette Marsh he gave up medicine to become publisher in the newspaper empire of her father. "My father was very bright, too, very bright," says Charlie, "and he just could not understand why I couldn't read. He would become so frustrated that he would call me names, which made it worse. But it wasn't only that. My brother and I both, we were not to be seen or heard. He would almost never play with us, and when he did, sometimes he would try to hurt us. There were lots of other things. Every hurt that anybody has ever had, I think I've had at one time or another."

It didn't help that Charlie and his brother Robert didn't really like each other. When friends asked Antoinette—smartest of all, turning her degree in literature from Vassar into matriarchal credentials—what was the difference between her two boys, she would say, "If I were to say I want the moon, Robert would say, 'Mom, you need to live with disappointment.' Charlie would say, 'Mom, I will get it for you.'" Years later her sons would be her business partners, until she and Robert voted Charlie out.

Charlie was tormented by other children because of his stutter. It was the South in the early 1950s. "The teachers would make me stand up in class and try to read, and all that would come out would be sputters and noises, and all the kids would laugh. It was extremely painful.

"When I was 12, my parents took me to be examined by doctors at Yale. They pried me, probed me, and had me do all sorts of stuff, and at one point they took all my clothes off and took pictures of me in the nude, looking for physical defects. You better believe that does something to a 12-year-old. It was tough. It was very, very tough."

But he had strength of character. He would not accept defeat. He had no fear of hard work. He had a sharp mind and learned by memorizing. He played well with other children and was good at sports. When they laughed at him, he didn't get mad. He learned to play the fool.

"You either become withdrawn, or you use it to your advantage. I said, 'Okay, this is another way of making somebody laugh,' and I became a clown. I was wild, real wild—and I became pretty popular.

"About the only thing I didn't have wrong with me was uncoordination, and that was my true salvation. I was bigger than most of the kids, so I worked very very hard to become extremely strong and very athletic so I could be able to have something that I could excel at and be respected for. I've always been a leader at sports, always the captain of my teams."

Charlie was clearly not headed for a life of crime, so he wasn't sent to his grandfather's training center for "morons." His parents enrolled him in a special prep school in Connecticut called Marvelwood, where he played football and lacrosse. He says for the first time in his life, he wasn't treated as if there were something wrong with him. He went to camp on a Massachusetts farm for kids with learning disabilities, and three summers there changed his life. "Those were probably the happiest years of my life," he says.

"Charlie was 17, and was a little old for our camp, but he was a very bright boy," remembers George Hayes, who owned the farm and camp with his wife Penny. "It took quite a lot of work, but he learned to read. He was just a joy. We had more fun with that guy—oh, he was a comedian. He used to fall down the stairs for laughs—he belonged on the stage, this kid. Penny and I never met anybody who was more delightful. Just the most marvelous kid. We had this old house, and the furnace needed cleaning, and Charlie just climbed inside and did it without anyone asking him. I still have the photograph of him covered with soot. He was just that kind of guy.

"We would turn upside down two or three times for this boy."

Until George Hayes taught Charlie how to write his name at 16, he had faked it. "I'd seen my name written enough to know that it started with a *C*, and then there was a loop, and in the middle there was another loop, and like that. So I'd do little scribbles and make the loops so it looked pretty good, but I didn't know what I was writing. I still remember the day I wrote my name for the first time."

Charlie idolized his maternal grandfather, Charles Thomas Marsh, a Texas oil tycoon and newspaper publisher who built the family empire. As he grew up he physically became Marsh, who was six-foot-three with a high forehead, beaked nose, and big bald head—they said he looked like a Roman emperor. He was warm, generous, and talkative, but with an explosive temper, and Charlie was like that, too. And sometimes Marsh spoke in "scattered and disjointed sentences," same as Charlie, although grandfather created order out of chaos, it was said; not vice versa.

Marsh's progressive politics were uncommon in his moneyed circles in Texas. His lasting legacy is the Public Welfare Foundation, which he founded in 1946 and has distributed more than $570 million in grants to more than 4,800 groups, according to its website. The foundation says it "focuses its grant-making in some difficult, and often overlooked, social justice areas where it believes it can serve as a catalyst for reform."

Charles Haskell got his ideals and money from Charles Marsh. His respect for the Public Welfare Foundation and admiration for his grandfather were carried by the intentions of New Century Conservation Trust.

As publisher of the *Austin American-Statesman*, Marsh discovered a hayseed, a young West Texas politician named Lyndon Johnson, and financed his career. Marsh's money and editorial voice lifted LBJ to the US Senate in 1948, via voter fraud in West Texas. For most of the rest of his years as a politician, LBJ used Marsh to further his career, as Marsh used LBJ to further his own ideas. One of Marsh's many obituaries said he had "erratic intensity," possibly suggesting the moment at age 44 when he left his wife of 20 years to pursue a willowy and brilliant 19-year-old from a small Texas town. Her name was Alice Glass, and Marsh would show his appreciation, admiration, and ardor with lavish gifts: diamonds, emeralds, paintings, a 100-acre estate in Virginia. She was an excellent horsewoman as well, "the only thing about her that was Texas," said one admirer. Marsh chased this free spirit for eight years, until she gave in and married him after his divorce.

Charlie's mother Antoinette grew up fast, watching it all happen, beginning when she was 17. When Charlie was born in 1943, the fabulous Alice Glass became his 32-year-old step-grandmother.

In 1953, on a trip to Jamaica to check on the Jamaica Inn he had built there, entertaining the writer Roald Dahl and his wife the actress Patricia Neal, Marsh was bitten by a mosquito carrying cerebral malaria and fell into a coma. He lived for 11 more years but suffered strokes that rendered him speechless. Haskell remembers with poignancy sitting as a teenager at his grandfather's bedside, meeting visitors like Adlai Stevenson and Sam Rayburn, as well as LBJ.

"He was a kingmaker," says Haskell. "He wanted to die absolutely broke, and he did. He gave it all away." Not quite. Like Theodore Roosevelt, Haskell had a trust fund.

Another Marsh obituary said he had "a knack for the vivid and colorful," which describes Charlie's favorite memory of him. The time when his grandfather and young gorgeous grandmother Alice stripped him down to his undies and threw him in a Washington fountain, and they all shrieked with laughter.

In *The Years of Lyndon Johnson: The Path to Power*, the first of three volumes in his definitive LBJ biography, author Robert A. Caro cites Marsh's wealth. "In Austin alone, his possessions included not only the city's largest newspaper, but much of the stock in its largest bank, all of the stock in its streetcar franchise, and vast tracts of its most valuable real estate. And forests of derricks pumped black gold out of the fabulous oilfields of West Texas for his sole profit."

Marsh had been a $25-per-week newspaper reporter in Oklahoma, with big ambition. He found partners, and bought more than two dozen Texas newspapers in seven years. Many of his readers were Okies like him, who had come to Texas during the Depression.

Marsh was a dedicated New Dealer. In 1940 he sold all but three papers in Texas, and went to Washington to support President Franklin Roosevelt. He focused on fighting Hitler, and financed an underground network to get Jews out of Germany. He lived near the White House, and was best drinking buddies with FDR's vice president, Henry Wallace. Every afternoon, walking home from the White House after work, the vice president would stop off at Marsh's four-story 19th century mansion for a few stiff ones, along with intense policy discussion. The Lend-Lease Act of 1941, FDR's controversial first step into World War II, came out of those sessions.

As for Alice Glass, "The first time Charles Marsh saw her, she was stark naked, a pale, shimmering goddess rising unexpectedly from the mists of his Austin swimming pool," according to Jennet Conant in the book *The Irregulars: Roald Dahl and the British Spy Ring in Wartime Washington*.

Besides being smart and beautiful, Alice Glass was idealistic, independent, and ambitious. Vice President Wallace liked her because, he said, "She seems to be the only person with enough imagination to know what I'm talking about."

The reason she held off Marsh's proposal for so long, said her sister, was because she was in love with Lyndon Johnson and believed he could save the world. It was Alice who ran the operation to get Jews out of Europe; traveling with Marsh in Germany in 1937, she had heard Hitler speak, and knew the threat was real.

Alice and LBJ had an ongoing affair while she was Marsh's mistress and LBJ was Marsh's protégé. LBJ was three years older than Alice but looked up to her for the sophistication he lacked—she made him look smart. Lady Bird Johnson knew about the affair but was stoic and silent. When Marsh found out, he unloaded his explosive temper on LBJ but soon forgave him. "My father and LBJ didn't let Alice come between them," Antoinette Haskell told Jennet Conant. "Men in power like that don't give a damn about women. They were not that important in the end. They treated women like toys. That's just the way it was."

Enter Roald Dahl. He, Marsh, and Glass were a threesome on the Washington social circuit in the early part of the war, and shared Marsh's flat in London at times. Dahl was a young RAF pilot who'd been shot down over Egypt, then sent to Washington, with a bad leg, for a vague job at the British Embassy. In fact he was a spy for Winston Churchill's team, the vast ring called BSC, British Security Co-ordination. Their mission in America was propaganda, to move public opinion toward the war. Churchill's spying on FDR was desperation—Britain was doomed without him. Dahl's assignment was to learn what FDR was thinking, and what he was being advised.

Dahl made Marsh his mentor. Dahl was young, tall, handsome, and articulate, with a fast and racy wit. He was so much of these things that his arrogance, rudeness, and occasional cruelty were accepted. He made himself a magnet for gossip. One way to get it was to sleep with influential older women, which was remarkably easy for him.

Few knew what FDR was thinking better than Marsh, thanks to his whiskey-and-ryes with Vice President Wallace, and the many dinners and lunches that Marsh and Alice hosted in their townhouse mansion. Marsh told Dahl everything, which got back to Churchill at least once within the hour. Eventually Marsh knew but didn't care (and FDR knew, but it was a game to him). He financed the beginning of Dahl's writing career that produced dozens of dark, hilarious, brilliant, and beloved children's stories.

Albert Einstein, Leonardo da Vinci, and Walt Disney were dyslexic. "Dyslexia" and "dumb" aren't medically connected. Charlie could listen to a teacher and perfectly repeat his or her words. "I'd tell myself, 'If I'm so damn stupid, how the hell can I do this?'"

Taking oral exams, he got into the University of Massachusetts but didn't last long. "When I would have to read, I would lose it. The classroom becomes such an alien thing, you overload and break down. Eventually I flunked out."

It was 1964 and 21-year-old college dropouts like him were doomed to be drafted for Vietnam, unless they were married; he married his girlfriend. He worked in the family newspaper business in Kentucky for three years, and at 24, using his inheritance, bought a newspaper as grandfather Marsh had: the *Dade City Banner*, deep in the Florida panhandle. When it failed, he went into marketing and sales, heading the "vitality division" of an orange juice company in Dade City, followed by a stint as a car salesman at a Buick dealership in Tampa.

That's when he joined the army so he could fight in Vietnam, he said, adding that he was a platoon leader. He wouldn't talk about his time in country, other than to say he didn't know what hit him. One day he was leading his men in the jungle, next thing he knew he was waking up in a military hospital in Kentucky. He said it was too painful to talk about.

When his father died in 1970, he inherited 25 percent of the business that included four papers—Antoinette got 50 percent and his brother Robert the other 25. He became associate publisher of the *Mt. Sterling Advocate* in Kentucky, where he had trained for the business. He was mayor of Mt. Sterling for 27 months. According to his résumé, during that time he obtained more than $13 million in state and federal grants for downtown development, street improvements, and recreation; built a new sewer and water plant; changed the city government from a city council to city manager structure; started a tourism and recreation board; obtained National Registry status for the downtown district; and restructured the fire and police departments.

In 1973, after eight years of marriage and three children, too much like grandfather Marsh (and Marsh's father, a Cincinnati lawyer who left his wife and six children), Haskell left his wife and three children to be with the former babysitter. He married her and fathered a fourth child, his daughter Antoinette.

In 1989, at age 46, separated and soon to be divorced for the second time, Haskell sold his share in the newspaper business (now seven papers) to his brother Robert. He says he got out because his mother and brother didn't have faith in his abilities. Now, with the Rio Roosevelt expedition, he had a chance to prove himself to his mother.

"The motivation that I've had to succeed in life was motivation that I created," he said. "That's how I grew up: saying, 'By God, I'm gonna do it.' And I'm going to continue to do challenging things that way. It's a whole lot more difficult for me, but that's why it's enjoyable; the tougher it is, the more I like it. Because that proves to me that I'm capable of doing more than I actually think I can do.

"I don't let anything put me down. Again, you have a choice. To be able to say, 'Oh, poor me,' or say, 'I've seen that happen so I'm not going to let that happen.' The good news is it made me much more sensible about people, and wanting to listen to what others have to say, so it was a plus. Everything in life I've learned, I've learned from people. People are my books. That's why I listen so intently.

"When my daughters were growing up, I could read them children's books, which I enjoyed because I was reading them for the first time myself. I can read now, but it's very difficult. I read very, very slowly, and I can only read about two pages at a time. I get very, very tired. I miss a lot.

"When they came out with books on cassettes, I bought everything. I spent $3,000 on tapes the first year I discovered them. My mind was insatiable; I couldn't wait to get back in the car after work. I'd put a book on the tape deck and become one of the characters in the story; pretty soon I'd be racing along at 85 miles an hour and not even know it. I had to start using the cruise control. Now I think I probably get more out of books than people who can read, because I *listen* to these books, and my mind and my imagination just goes whoosh, zoom, it just goes crazy for learning.

"You never get over dyslexia. There are always things you wish that you could do. Even today. For example, my youngest daughter's name is Erin Antoinette Haskell, and I don't know how to spell Antoinette. I can't write my daughter's name. The letters all come like jumbles," he adds, his voice cracking and eyes misting.

"When you're told your whole life that you're not capable of doing something, when you're told that you're a failure, when you're told that you're stupid, you're an asshole, the whole nine yards, even though you were a mayor of a town, even though you were successful in working with people, you still never thought that you were a success.

"This expedition is a personal triumph for me, for someone with a learning disability, who had trouble reading and writing, to get national recognition. Why not do things that can help more than yourself?

"I really, honestly, believe that Beth and I are doing something worthwhile, something that will be beneficial to people. And I believe that now I know where I'm going."

CHAPTER 3

The Plan

Can easily adapt to variable and complex
situations with relative ease.
—Elizabeth McKnight

C harles Haskell and Elizabeth McKnight met on a tundra buggy spotting for polar bears on a photographic safari in Manitoba, British Columbia. She asked, "Don't I know you?" and he replied, "Yes, I was at your wedding—you married my best friend from prep school."

"Ah," said Beth.

She lived in Vermont, he lived in Maine—off to a start. The environment gave them more to talk about. Beth had been on ecotours: an Earthwatch trip to Sarasota Bay with a dolphin research team, a bird-watching tour to the Outer Hebrides islands off the Scottish coast, and a three-week Wilderness Travel camping safari in Tanzania and Kenya, including Nairobi.

She'd worked for an engineering firm, acquiring permits for building projects, weaving through regulations and red tape. She quit after a few years when she realized she was helping developers, she said. The sight of a green Vermont hillside wiped out by condos did it, she said, suggesting it was her firm and she was part of it. She began working for an architectural design group.

Earlier that year, Haskell had been a delegate of the National Wildlife Federation at the Altamira Gathering, in the Amazon. Sting was there. The Kayapo wanted to stop a dam from being built on their Xingu River by bringing attention to the issue and presenting their case, which included the Brazilian government's history of atrocities directed at Indigenous people over development. For five days there were presentations, press conferences, displays, and interviews with 500 Kayapo and another 100 Indigenous from other groups.*

After the Gathering, Haskell hired three Kayapo guides and traveled down the Xingu River for two weeks. It was his boyhood dream from the time he saw films of the Amazon made by a friend's grandfather. "It was everything I thought it would be," he said. "*Exactly* like it was supposed to be. The bugs, the Indians, everything."

In June, he and McKnight flew to a village 300 miles north of Manaus, and took a riverboat with two guides up the Rio Negro for about 100 miles. Afterward she bought him Theodore Roosevelt's *Through the Brazilian Wilderness*, and he barely put it down for a month. Teddy Roosevelt was his hero (along with Chuck Yeager). In the book, he found his mission: retracing Theodore Roosevelt's descent of the River of Doubt.

But how? You couldn't just hire a guide to take you down the river, remote and wild. It hadn't been descended since 1927. And the Cinta Larga didn't allow White men on their Rio Teodoro, as they called it.

Beth was perfect. Intelligent, cheerful, intense, game for outdoor adventure. She knew how to get things done, starting with permits. She quit her job and moved in with Haskell, into his rented house in Boothbay Harbor, where he'd settled after his separation—he was headed for Alaska but a

---

* The Altmira Gathering was a logistical tour de force by the organizers, a hugely successful media event. The World Bank pulled out of the project, and the Kayapo held off the government for 22 years before construction on the Belo Monte Dam began. The final turbine went operational in 2019.

friend talked him out of it. They formed New Century Conservation Trust and began looking for funding for their Rio Roosevelt expedition.

"In the beginning all we wanted was $250,000," she said. "Bare bones, two or three rafts, six or eight people." They hired a professional fundraiser who came up empty-handed after being paid $75,000, she said. They approached the literary agent Peter Riva, who had steered the successful nonstop around-the-world flight of the Voyager with Dick Rutan and Jeana Yeager. Riva suggested a book, made a deal with a publisher, and found a writer, me.

In September Haskell borrowed $250,000 to keep the project alive. "It suddenly became a major expedition with tremendous responsibility, which we just never envisioned," said McKnight, in Manaus. "And that's a big, big burden. The expectations of people have grown, the stress has grown. And it has taken its toll. It's been a tremendous strain, because Charlie and I aren't only working in a professional situation, we're working in a personal situation, and the two don't mix. But it's very difficult to separate them."

She began writing proposals, climbing mountains and navigating rivers of administrative work. She read the mail to Charlie, who dictated letters, made financial decisions, and pitched the project. The hardest part was getting the permits.

The phone rang from morning till night. They used the speaker phone so they could talk together. Charlie liked Beth to listen with him.

"When Charlie and I listen to people, he will hear one thing and I will hear another," she said. "I sometimes think he doesn't listen very carefully. He gets what he wants to hear, but he doesn't get it all, because he'll discard what he doesn't want to hear. I think many dyslexics do that, although I don't thoroughly understand dyslexia.

"It's important that I don't make Charlie feel uncomfortable, and I don't make him feel like he can't do it on his own. I have to be careful that I don't hurt his feelings. He's so sensitive about it. I think that might be a problem for him in business. That's partly why I've taken on this whole administrative thing myself. But cumulatively this stuff just piles up on me, and I can only handle so much.

"When he was in publishing, his secretary was an ex-Marine, and she was really tough. He thought she was great. She organized his whole life. I just don't want to be in that role."

McKnight wasn't worried about hardship or pain on the expedition. She'd been there. Born with a bent spine, she needed surgery before she could walk. At age nine she got polio and was paralyzed for 10 days. "I've experienced some terrible, terrible pain," she said. "Discomfort doesn't bother me. There won't be anything on the expedition I won't be able to deal with."

In 18 months they'd made four trips to Brazil, and Haskell made a fifth, shortly before the team left the States—to Manaus, Brasilia, São Paulo, and Rio de Janeiro, searching for audiences with vague bureaucrats and elusive tycoons. Lost in the Brazilian way, the relentlessly circuitous approach around a problem, they bounced between the offices of FUNAI (Indigenous), IBAMA (environment), INPA (science), EMAMTUR (tourism), EMFA (armed forces), and CNPq (international cooperation). They dealt with the US Embassy and the Brazilian army, navy, and air force. The potential catches were exhausting. "We had to make sure that the expedition wouldn't get stopped in the middle of the Amazon for lack of a document," said McKnight.

On their second trip they went into the state of Rondônia to see the river. They brought along an experienced river guide, Jim Slade of Mountain Travel Sobek, a California company known for bold whitewater rafting trips on the world's wildest rivers. Over 20 years, Slade had guided some 30,000 river miles, in Pakistan, China, Indonesia, and Africa. He had a go at Mount Everest, carrying loads for 25 days between camps at 21,500 and 23,000 feet. He guided a group of Harley-Davidson riders around Russia.

Joining Haskell, McKnight, and Slade were Mark Greenberg, a photo-journalist, and Mark Baker, whose Boston company, Ecotour Expeditions, which specialized in Brazilian projects, had been contracted to help with documents and logistics. Baker had already steered New Century Conservation Trust around one problem with the permits. An early application was rejected, but he rewrote it to get accepted. It required the expedition to make promises that would be difficult to keep.

The five flew to Manaus and boarded a twin-engine Piper Navajo that Baker had hired to follow the route in reverse, south along the Madeira River for about 1000 miles, then over the Aripuana Territory and Rio Roosevelt for 935 miles to Vilhena. But they had trouble tracking the river as it disappeared under the rainforest canopy, once for 150 miles. In Vilhena they were met by the farmer Jose Anselmo, who said there was an affluent on his land that was one of the streams comprising the headwaters.

Anselmo had a lean jaw, a pencil-thin mustache, and a gold tooth winking at the gold chain around his neck. His shirt was open to his potbelly, a machete at his hip. He said his farm had been Colonel Rondon's original telegraph station. There was another route to the river, he said, over the old trail that led to the telegraph bridge where Roosevelt and Rondon began their expedition. It was more authentic and scenic, but it was uncleared.

It was late in the day and the airplane was due back in Manaus, but Anselmo said his farm was only about 5 miles from the river, over pasture land, so they piled in the back of a flatbed truck driven by Anselmo's 16-year-old son and shoeless 12-year-old nephew, who lived primitively in a squalid shack behind the house. They left the farm on a muddy road with livestock grazing between charred stumps. It was a lot farther than five miles. The truck got stuck in the mud a lot. Sometimes it got hung up on stumps and big roots, and the older boy, who was sick and vomiting, would order his barefoot cousin to crawl in the slime on his belly and chop away whatever bound the undercarriage.

They reached the stream at twilight. There was a farm at the riverbank, and pigs wallowed in the shallow water.

On the way back the truck sputtered and died in the dark, its gas having leaked away on the jungle floor from a puncture in the tank. Mark Baker and the older boy began hiking out for gas and tools to fix it, and walked most of the night, 20 miles back to Vilhena. The others spent the night in the back of the truck trying to sleep, slapping relentless mosquitoes. At daybreak Jim Slade began walking out, and about an hour later Haskell,

McKnight, and Greenberg followed, leaving the 12-year-old with the truck. At the road they caught a bus back to Vilhena, while Baker and the teenager went back and fixed the truck. The airplane was a day late getting back to Manaus, costing Haskell a fortune.

"Can easily adapt to variable and complex situations with relative ease," said McKnight's résumé, being tested.

By October the team was chosen. The expedition had grown to 19 people: two coleaders, one Roosevelt, four professional boatmen with inflatable rafts, three Brazilian scientists, two Cinta Larga guides, a FUNAI agent, a photojournalist, a landscape photographer, a cameraman kayaker, a writer, a son/communications technician, and an American doctor who practiced in Ecuador and was expert in tropical diseases.

New Century Conservation Trust brought most of them to Boothbay Harbor for a three-day orientation that included presentations by Dr. Robert Carneiro, curator of South American ethnology at the American Museum of Natural History; Dr. John Gable, executive director of the Theodore Roosevelt Association; and Dr. Howard Rosenfield, a psychiatrist who spoke on the "Psychological Effects of Working in a Close Environment." There was also a filmmaker shooting a documentary for the PBS *Nova* series, and an interviewer from a public relations company hired to publicize the expedition.

Mark Baker of Ecotour Expeditions wasn't there. After the trip to Vilhena, he'd withdrawn from the project, uncomfortable with the connection between promise and execution.

The final few days before the expedition left the States were especially challenging for McKnight. Her résumé didn't account for a coup d'état in Venezuela. The freighter carrying the expedition's three Jeeps, sponsored by Chrysler's international division, was stuck in Caracas as Hugo Chàvez's rebels attacked the palace. But the coup failed, and the freighter was freed to steam to Miami, where the Jeeps were flown to Manaus and carried by barge up the Madeira River to Porto Velho, arriving on time.

Then she got a call from Stair Cargo, the company shipping two tons of equipment from Miami to Manaus. Customs wouldn't let the gear on the plane because it wasn't properly packed. So Chip Haskell, Charlie's 26-year-old son and the expedition's communications tech, flew down from Boston, joining Sobek boatman Mike Boyle to repack everything. The aerosol insect repellent had to be put in a fireproof container, as did the canisters of Mace that Beth brought for snakes.

Next, Joe Kaminsky called from Chile, where he had just gotten off the Bio Bio. Kaminsky was a whitewater video cameraman and accomplished kayaker, so he had two big jobs: shoot the film for *Nova* and scout the rapids in his kayak. He said it was going to cost $4,200 to ship his kayak from Santiago to Manaus. So McKnight called Varig, the Brazilian airline providing 15 round-trip tickets from Miami, who gave the kayak a free ride to Manaus.

The visa crisis took the expedition down to the wire. The applications were at the Brazilian Consulate in New York, awaiting approval from the office of the minister of foreign affairs, which needed a fax approving them from CNPq (international cooperation) in Brasilia. McKnight's office assistant spoke some Portuguese, but no progress could be made with CNPq over the phone. Desperate, Beth called her contact at the American Embassy in Brasilia, who found the expedition's visa applications in a basket on a desk at the CNPq office, neglected when a secretary took a few days off. The visas were processed, and McKnight flew to New York to pick them up and FedEx four of them to team members in Central and South America.

She had pulled it all off, using her "expertise in problem solving, quality control, and procedure implementation."

The report from Brazil was that the affluent at the pig farm did not appear to flow into the Rio Roosevelt, which was not a surprise. On Haskell's solo trip to Brazil he'd made a second flyover with a fellow named Fabio Bueno Netto; they'd followed the stream on Anselmo's farm to what Anselmo had said were the Rio Roosevelt headwaters, but it was a maze of swamps. So Haskell bought a GPS and sent it down to Fabio.

Fabio was a surgeon-turned-travel-agent who lived in Manaus and was a cousin of Silvio Barros, the Amazonas secretary of tourism. When Ecotour

Expeditions quit the project, Barros had recommended Fabio as the man for the job of guiding the expedition in Brazil—he'd twice handled logistics in the Amazon for the Camel Trophy, an event contested in remote locations around the world by teams in Land Rovers. Fabio was a likable wheeler-dealer who knew the way around roadblocks in his country. With the GPS, he flew over the river a third time.

Fabio called from Vilhena with the news. He found a good put-in spot for the expedition, but it was 30 miles from the road and there was no trail. Anselmo could cut one, for $2,500 plus expenses. "Do it," said Charlie to Fabio. Anselmo hired a few young men with machetes and a chainsaw who began working as the expedition team converged on Miami and Manaus. All told, Haskell said the week had cost him $70,000; that's $350,000 spent on the expedition so far, he said.

Twelve team members met at the Miami airport and flew with 4,000 pounds of gear to Manaus. We checked into the elegant Tropical Hotel on the Rio Negro and put on our best clothes for the expedition's opening event at Teatro Amazonas, the magnificent Amazon Theatre,* built during the rubber boom at the end of the 19th century.

Mark Greenberg had done a photo shoot for a German magazine of the Polish virtuoso pianist Voytek Matushevski, and had asked him where in the world he would most like to perform, and when Voytek replied Teatro Amazonas, the idea was born. Voytek told McKnight he would do a concert for the expedition for $8,000 plus expenses. McKnight said she only had $4,000 and would try to find a sponsor for the other four. When none turned up, she told Voytek she would take the other $4,000 from ticket sales and sent Voytek and his young Italian manager plane tickets to Manaus.

---

*   Teatro Amazonas was built by German rubber barons, taking millions of dollars out of the forests in latex from trees to make tires to feed the automobile. Cost was no object. It had pink Italian marble stairs and columns, steel walls from Scotland, and a mosaic dome with 36,000 decorated ceramic tiles from France, glazed in the Brazilian national colors of yellow and green. There were mahogany staircases, velvet seats, and 198 Italian chandeliers. The labor came from slaves stolen from the Congo (Brazil was the biggest market for slaves in the world at that time), along with Indigenous slaves from the Amazon.

Advance ticket sales did not go well. In order to fill some of the 700 seats in the theater, tickets were given to friends and sponsors—Banco Económico, Varig, and the Tropical Hotel. At showtime, Voytek wanted his $4,000. McKnight called Peter Riva, who had already gotten a call from Voytek's lawyer. Riva told McKnight to pay the four grand. Banco Económico had just signed on for $15,000, so the money could be covered.

The audience enjoyed the performance, and Voytek looked resplendent in white tux with tails. He got his cash backstage at intermission.

The bill for Voytek and his young Italian manager at the Tropical Hotel included nearly $2,000 for room service, laundry, tours, and phone calls to New York. At checkout Voytek told the front desk that McKnight would cover it, and left. She said no, and hotel staff chased Voytek to the airport and confronted him, with no success. McKnight asked Fabio to fix it, and he paid the Tropical out of the money New Century Conservation Trust was paying him.

When her résumé declared that she was "able to interface with a cross-section of people," that might not have included prima donna pianists, nor Indian chiefs, coming next.

CHAPTER 4

The Adventure

Would a rich guy do this for fun?
—Charles Haskell

F ive miles over the Amazon in the dead of night, Charlie Haskell sat alone near the back of the Varig jet, staying awake as if to watch over his team. He took the role of protector seriously. Six-foot-three, barrel-chested, and hard as stone, he'd been training for the expedition by pumping iron. And if his muscles weren't enough, his shotgun would be. Like Roosevelt and his Springfield, Haskell had a favorite gun, a six-shot stainless-steel Winchester 12 Gauge (there was also a .44 Magnum pistol in baggage that would be taken by customs upon landing). The Brazilian army had suggested that the expedition carry firearms. There was a history of trouble along the Rio Roosevelt: desperate settlers, lawless *garimpeiros* (gold miners), angry Indians.

There had been talk of encountering Indians that had rarely, maybe never, seen White men. Dr. Carneiro, the expert from the American Museum of Natural History, said that if you surprised some Indians, and they didn't immediately kill you, they might shout, make faces, and jab spears, but ignore them. Look right through them. Don't run, don't show fear. Slowly, very slowly, reach into your pocket and pull out a kazoo. *I wish I was in Dixie* might be good.

Haskell said if Indians attacked the expedition it would be their big mistake; he had the Brazilian government's permission to be there. Anyhow it was unlikely, because there would be two Cinta Larga chiefs along. As for the shotgun, "Better safe than sorry," he said, narrowing his eyes.

"Here I am, 49 years old, taking on a challenge, doing something that could snuff out my life in a New York second," he said, belted into his seat on the jet. "It's been a little scary, but there's nothing wrong with being scared."

He said he'd been scared in the past, hinting that it was in the Vietnam jungle, but he had no fear of failure. "When I started this program I said, come hell or high water, I'm gonna do it. There was absolutely no time I wasn't. You have to have a mindset like that. That's how I've done everything in my life."

Haskell had heard that someone at Mountain Travel Sobek had called him a "rich guy on vacation," and it bugged him. He and Beth were doing something good for the world. Rich guys don't take scientists along on their vacation. When things would get hot and dirty, he would shout with a grin, "Would a rich guy do this for fun?" He liked his own tag: "the boy's home adventure."

That was as close as he would come to comparing himself to his hero Theodore Roosevelt, who said his own trip down the River of Doubt was his "last chance to be a boy."

"Anybody that can sit there and say, 'Walk softly and carry a big stick,' you gotta love," he said as the plane carried him deeper into the dark.

◆

Theodore and Edith Roosevelt left Brooklyn bound for Barbados aboard the SS *Vandyck* on October 4, 1913. TR was dashing in a soft gray three-piece suit with a flower in his lapel, and Edith was comforted by family, including her niece Margaret, son Teddy Jr. and his wife, and some women friends. Roosevelt had six members of his expedition team with him. He climbed the steep gangway from the pier to the upper deck and waved to his fans. "The decks of the ship were packed with admirers of the colonel," reported the *New York Times*.

The cargo holds carried the gear for Roosevelt's expedition up the Paraguay River for the American Museum of Natural History. Equipment had been purchased by the expedition's quartermaster, an explorer from Brooklyn named Anthony Fiala, called "Thermos" for his love of gear and gadgets. There were five tons of food and supplies, gear and gadgets. As it dwindled, it would follow them to the headwaters of Rio Duvida, stacked on the decks of half-sinking sidewheel steamers; poled up twisting rivers on flatbottom barges; carried by starving oxen and mules over parched plateaus; hacked through the jungle; and pulled across fast-flowing rivers on ferries made of planks over dugout canoes.

Edith was hesitant about going to South America, but she knew Father needed her. She wanted to see their son Kermit, a few days shy of 24, who would meet them in two weeks in Bahia, 600 miles north of Rio along the Atlantic coast. For more than a year, Kermit had been building railroad trestles and bridges in the Xingu Valley of northeast Brazil, working for the Brazil Railway Company and Anglo-Brazilian Iron Company, in conditions much like Colonel Rondon had faced building the telegraph line, including Indian snipers with long arrows. TR wrote to him from the campaign trail in 1912, "I am very proud to think of you living in a boxcar and bossing the steam-shovel gang way off in Brazil."

Kermit was in the Xingu when he got the news that his father had been shot while campaigning, so mortality was on his mind. The would-be assassin's bullet was slowed by TR's folded speech in his breast pocket; he spoke for 45 minutes, the bullet nudging a rib near his heart and oozing blood onto his white shirt.

That summer Kermit was riding a steel joist suspended by a derrick, 35 feet over a ravine, when something slipped or snapped. The joist nearly crushed him on the way down, but they carried him out with only two broken ribs, two knocked-out teeth, and a dislocated knee. "He was practically all right again when he started with us," said his proud father.

Roosevelt, too, was practically all right again, leaving politics and the Progressive Party behind. There was dancing on the boat at night, and the ex-president got roars of approval for his sailors' hornpipe to fiddle and flute, a dance known as "the jig of the ship." How about that, they said in bed that night; the Bull Moose can dance. Special guests at Sagamore Hill already knew.

When they reached Bahia on October 18 there were thousands of Brazilians on shore to greet them; the Brazilian ambassador had set up the grand welcome. Kermit was there, waiting on a launch in the harbor.

Kermit Roosevelt didn't appear to be much like his father. He was thin, sensitive, and introverted, moody and sometimes brooding. His father, the stocky, thick-skinned extrovert, controlled his moods by force of will. But they had the same brains; Kermit graduated from Harvard in two-and-a-half years,* could speak Spanish, French, German, and Portuguese, and read Latin and Greek. Like his father he was an insatiable reader, carrying a book of Kipling poems on the river. (He'd been a guest in Kipling's house.) Like TR he was hooked on adventure while being tough, determined, and driven by relentless energy.

And they had the same romantic soul. As Theodore had married Alice when he was 22 and she 19, and thought his life was over when she died so young, Kermit had fallen for Belle Wyatt Willard, a socialite and heiress, "the fair one with golden locks," as Edith described her. She hoped her son, "the boy with the white head and black heart," would be happy with Belle.

The summer before Kermit left to work in Brazil, they'd spent flirtatious time together, not quite a romance. But they fell in love through correspondence, as Belle's spirit fit into the Roosevelt family. "I have thought of two other things I want to do," she wrote. "Wolf hunting in Russia, and tiger shooting from elephants' backs in India!"

---

* Kermit had promised his father that he would graduate from Harvard on schedule, if TR took him along on his year-long African safari. He kept the promise.

When Belle's father, a hotel magnate, was made ambassador to Spain by President Wilson, she lived in Madrid and traveled to London and Paris. Her letters on fancy hotel stationery arrived at the Xingu River, where Kermit was building a railway bridge. Beyond smitten, he was awed.

He proposed in a letter he wrote on the boat north on the Xingu to the Amazon, a sweetly rambling missive so innocent and intimate it seems almost wrong to repeat the next-to-last line here: "I've wished and prayed so much that you might love me, and perhaps you might tho' I can't seem to believe that you could." She said yes, in a letter that ended, "I love you, Kermit, I love you." He replied, "If it's a dream I want to stay asleep forever."

When Kermit left the Xingu he didn't know he'd be going down the River of Doubt. It was a shock when TR told him in Bahia. He thought it was too dangerous for his old father, who thought it might be too dangerous for his young son. Kermit just wanted to go home and be with Belle. But it came down to one thing: Edith felt that Kermit was needed to look after his father. "She's dreadfully worried about him, and there's nothing for me to do but go," he wrote Belle.

◆

It took a day in Porto Velho to collect the Jeeps from the dock on the Madeira River, and two days to move Haskell's team 420 miles down the highway to Vilhena. Nine explorers rode in a chartered Mercedes-Benz tour bus while six more piled into three Jeeps and sped down BR-364, the highway that began as Rondon's telegraph trail and now spears Brazil for 2,700 miles like a long arrow through a jaguar. Since the beginning of its construction in 1960, BR-364 has opened the Amazon to civilization and progress, while taking countless thousands of Indigenous lives largely through epidemic. The two-lane blacktop has enabled the settlement and development of Rondônia, over millions of acres of rainforest.

The Jeeps were led by Fabio Netto, driving the short black Renegade with chrome wheels. He screamed down the treacherous highway like it was La Carrera Panamericana (the Mexican road race that killed 24 drivers and spectators during the 1950s). Enjoying the ride with him was Charles Haskell Jr., the communications tech, carrying gadgets and gear that bulged over the sides of the Jeep: the single-sideband radio, the walkie-talkies, the GPS, the Emergency Position Indicating Radio Beacon (EPIRB), and the big Magnavox satellite phone.

The red Wrangler, the classic Jeep, was driven by photojournalist Mark Greenberg, known for the book *Bhagwan: Twelve Days that Shook the World*, featuring his photos of the infamous cult leader Bhagwan Shree Rajneesh at his commune in Oregon. His striking images of the flight of the *Voyager* appeared in *Life*, *Time*, the *New York Times*' front page, and covers of *Newsweek*, *Paris Match*, and *Stern*. His passenger in the Jeep was Carr Clifton, a landscape photographer whose 1986 book *California, Magnificent Wilderness* had drawn high praise. *Outdoor Photography* magazine called him "the most rapidly rising 4x5 star" of his time. He hoped to bring back another great coffee-table book.

Relaxing in the bed of the Comanche pickup, the fastest of the three Jeeps, catching some 90-mph rays, was Joe Kaminsky, the ponytailed kayaker, one-man camera crew, and codirector of the documentary. Behind the wheel was a former *Sports Illustrated* senior writer, author of the race-driving memoir *Fast Guys, Rich Guys and Idiots*, and expedition journalist who, with two partners, had put a first ascent up the 3,000-foot wall of remote Puncak Jaya in Papua New Guinea, assigned to write this book. That was me.

Driving the Comanche in the middle was maddening. Greenberg couldn't keep up and Fabio wouldn't slow down. We pulled over to talk about it. Greenberg said the Wrangler was unstable over 70 mph, adding that Fabio and I were irresponsible maniacs. He said all our lives were in danger already, and blamed Haskell for not ordering Fabio to obey the speed limit. His codriver and fellow photographer Carr Clifton got behind the wheel, but backseat driving maintained the stress in the cabin.

Haskell had put the four-man media contingent in the Jeeps to do some research along BR-364: photojournalist, landscape photographer, video cameraman/director, and author/newspaper reporter/codirector. *Good Morning America* was expecting live satellite phone calls from the river along the way.

Taking pictures and shooting video, we made it about two-thirds of the way by dusk, spending the night in Ouro Preto d'Oeste, once a gritty gold town, now a gritty lumber town. Driving BR-364 at night would have been madness, a nightmare under the bright lights of teenage truckers on speed, so we checked into a motel. Fabio called Haskell at the hotel in Vilhena, where the tour bus had just arrived. Charlie was furious that the Jeeps weren't there, and accused us of playing around all day. He wanted to speak to me. "You *will* be on the road by 6:00 A.M., and you *will not* stop until you get to Vilhena," he said. I was dumbfounded. Chip whispered in my ear, coaching me on how to deal with his father. When I got Charlie to allow 90 minutes in the morning for a smoky sunrise shot for television, Chip offered a high five for my tightrope-walking, something he said he'd been doing all his life.

"The great thing about this expedition," he said with a grin, "is that this is the first time I've been on a boat trip with Dad that he hasn't been able to threaten, 'If you don't stop that, I'll turn this boat around right now and we'll all go home!'"

Fabio shrugged it off, but the rest of us were stunned by Haskell's lack of reason and faith.

When we arrived at the Hotel Mirage in Vilhena the next afternoon, the greeting was tense. Beth's jaw was set. She said that because the Jeeps had gotten there late, "It might hold us up a week." I didn't see how but didn't ask. "We were just trying to capture some images of destruction in the rainforest," I said, meekly.

"We're not here because of the destruction of the rainforest," she snapped, to my astonishment. It was the permits. We were there to paint a pretty picture.*

Haskell immediately called a meeting with the Jeep crew, dubbed "Sam's Bad Boys" by Tweed. He was still steaming. He said he needed the Jeeps to check out the trail that was being cut to the river. He and Beth had worked 18 months on the expedition and he'd spent $300,000 out of his

---

* It took 30 years to figure this out.

own pocket, he said. He added that he was most mad at me for not getting Chip and Fabio there yesterday.

Huh? Wasn't Fabio the leader? Fabio was Brazilian, knew the road, knew the laws, and was being paid to handle logistics. And there he was up front, driving the lead Jeep.

I suggested to Charlie that his miscommunication to us and lack of knowledge of the road contributed to the lost hours—and besides, the Jeeps had gotten a late start after spending half the morning waiting while the Mercedes tour bus was being loaded. He could have sent us down the road.

Kaminsky was less diplomatic. He told Haskell that he didn't care much for his attitude because they were working hard to save his ass and keep him from looking like a rich guy on vacation.

Charlie took Kaminsky's insults and simmered down. Everyone knew it was critical that the meeting erase the bad vibe that had hung over the group for the past 16 hours, so it ended with vows for better understanding all around. There were handshakes, and hugs from Beth, who was greatly relieved. But the incident again raised the question of the expedition's cause, left hanging at the Round Table.

CHAPTER 5

The Revolutionary

In him, everything is united, nothing is lost.
—Diai Nambiquara, activist and sociologist

It was Colonel Rondon who pounded the first nail of civilization into the heart of the Amazon, in 1910 at the telegraph station he built in Vilhena, naming it after his chief engineer. For its first 50 years only a couple of families lived there to operate the telegraph, surrounded by jungle and harassed by Indians until BR-364 came through.

Rondon knew his telegraph brought a future with downsides, that assimilation could destroy Indigenous culture. He knew he was "delivering his charges to evil," as one lieutenant said. But he saw a big picture, connecting the country—literally, by wires—and bringing cultures together. He believed in the long run it would be worth the damage to the Indigenous people, and devoted his life to minimizing it.

"All told, Rondon participated in more than a score of expeditions through Brazil's northern wilderness, traveling more than 25,000 miles by foot, over water, and on horse or mule as he surveyed his country's hitherto-unknown territory, mapped its borders, built roads and bridges, founded settlements, and made the initial, peaceful contact with dozens of Indigenous groups," writes Larry Rohter, in *Into the Amazon, the Life of Cândido Rondon.* *

In his 2004 book *Stringing Together a Nation*, the only published biography of Rondon in English until Rohter's 400-page tome in 2023, author Todd A. Diacon reveals another side. "Brazilian scholars criticize the legacy of the commission's telegraph line through the Amazon, seeing it as the first salvo in a war of environmental destruction and ethnocide that continues to this day," Diacon wrote.

After living in the jungle with Rondon and nearly dying there because of him, and after furious disagreements with him, Theodore Roosevelt called Rondon one of the four greatest explorers in history. Upon his return from the River of Doubt, TR told the press, "I never saw, nor know of, a project equal to the Strategic Telegraph Lines Commission headed by Colonel Rondon." He called it a "cyclopean achievement," and praised "the work of Rondon—scientific, practical and humanitarian." That work, especially the humanitarian, would continue for another four decades.

Before Rondon's death in 1958 at age 92, writes Rohter, "The commission bearing his name published over 100 scientific papers, addressing disciplines as varied as anthropology, astronomy, biology, botany, ecology, ethnology, geology, herpetology, ichthyology, linguistics, meteorology, mineralogy, ornithology, and zoology." He would "lead troops that quashed a military revolt against civilian rule, mediate a conflict between Colombia and Peru, help

---

* *River Without a Cause* was in its final month of fact-checking, when *Into the Amazon* by Larry Rohter was released on May 30, 2023, just in time to get Rondon right. It was a godsend. Its details fill out my portrait of Rondon, and I used some of Rohter's hard-researched quotes from documents he found in Biblioteca Nacional do Brasil in Rio de Janeiro, where he was bureau chief for the *New York Times*. His select bibliography includes 140 books; visits to 21 archives in both Brazil and the US; 42 documents, diaries, and official reports; 65 theses, dissertations, and academic articles; and 27 newspapers and magazines. I counted. I am in awe, as well as appreciation.

convince Brazil to support the Allies during World War II, and establish his country's first national parks."

Cândido Mariano da Silva was born in 1865 in the far-off Mimoso rainforest on the vast Mato Grosso, in the first year of the bloody Paraguayan War, begun when Paraguay invaded Mato Grosso. (In that war 60,000 Brazilians would die, most of them slaves who had been freed to fight.) Cândido Mariano was a caboclo, a Brazilian with mixed Indigenous and European blood. His father, Cândido Mariano da Silva, was of Portuguese, Spanish, African, and Indigenous Guyanese descent; he died of smallpox before the child was born. His mother, Claudina Maria de Freitas Evangelista, youngest of 10, was Terena and Bororo, the two predominant tribes in Mato Grosso. She died when he was two.

His Portuguese blood came from *bandeirantes*, who came to Brazil in the 1700s to capture and sell Indigenous slaves. One of them was his great-great-grandfather, Gaspar da Silva Rondon, who married a Guana princess, daughter of the chief of a tribe taken by bandeirantes.

"In him, everything is united, nothing is lost," says Diai Nambiquara, the Nambiquara activist and sociologist.

After his mother died he was raised on a dirt-poor cattle ranch by his widowed Bororo grandfather and da Silva godmother. "By the time he was six," writes Rohter, "Rondon could already ride, shoot, set traps, hunt, fish, and track. He knew which berries, fruits, and mushrooms were edible, and which were not. From local Indigenous folklore, he learned about the medicinal qualities of the roots, bark, and leaves of certain trees and plants."

The boy was clearly gifted with intelligence as well. A local rancher called him a "child prodigy." Since school in Mimoso ended at a very young age, he was sent to the town of Cuiabá, no longer occupied by Paraguayan soldiers, to continue his education. He lived with his Uncle Manoel, who carried a note from Candido's father written on his deathbed that said, "If the child we are expecting is a boy, don't leave him in Mimoso. Send for him, to save him from the sad ignorance to which Mimoso's children are condemned."

The child prodigy was denied a scholarship to the private school in Cuiabá because he was caboclo, discrimination that would drive him the rest of his life. He called his next 10 years there "sad and solitary," as they shaped his beliefs. He saw slaves being sold on the streets, making him an abolitionist; and watched soldiers there kill Indians, making him a pacifist and protector. He spent most of his time studying, excelling in math, science, and geography. He learned about the stars from Bororo mythology, stories built upon constellations, leading him to a lifelong study of astronomy. When he wasn't studying he worked in his uncle's store, and for fun swam in the Cuiabá River, showing off by walking there on his hands. Across the river lived a band of Guana Indians, and he was comfortable with them, being one-eighth Guana.

At 13 he began taking courses to become a teacher, and by 16 was teaching elementary school. But he wanted to further his education in Rio de Janeiro, and to see the world that he studied in geography. There were only two ways to get there, the military or the seminary. "He makes his choice," says Diai Nambiquara, "rather warrior than priest." He joined the army at the outpost in Cuiabá.

Since many of the Brazilian army's 13,000 men came or were dragooned from the dregs of society, and many were recently freed slaves, this disciplined young man with a spotless past and exceptional education was unique and special. They put his brains on a riverboat for the monthlong sea voyage to the military academy in Rio.

Cândido Mariano da Silva arrived at the Academy in 1882, a fresh-faced caboclo boy who looked Indian. at a wiry five-foot-three. The Indigenous population in Rio de Janeiro was just 0.3 percent, so he stood out. The city was booming to more than half a million people, one-third of them slaves, sometimes flogged at whipping posts in the public squares. It was so crowded, filthy, and ridden with cholera, smallpox, and yellow fever that it was called the "City of Death." It was also the nucleus of fast change in Brazil, with the rubber boom, ending of slavery, and founding of the Positivist Church, formally the Church of the Religion of Humanity, brought to Rio de Janeiro in 1881.

Positivism burst from the remarkable brain of the French philosopher, author, and guru, Auguste Comte, who wrote the six-volume *Course on Positive Philosophy* and founded the Religion of Humanity. He created sociology, and first used the word "altruism," from his expression *vivre pour autrui*, or "live for others."

Positivism promised progress, discipline, morality, and freedom from the tyranny of Catholic theology. It was carried home to Brazil in 1881 by the young Brazilian Miguel Lemos, who had paused his engineering studies for a trip to Paris, where he stayed four years and never returned to engineering. Lemos argued that faith should be demonstrable and founded on seven principles: it must be real, useful, right, precise, relative, pleasing, and organic.

These points became the guiding tenets of the Positivist Church of Brazil. Out of Comte's metaphysical ideas came a pragmatic religion. The popular Positivist platform argued that there were three barriers to national progress: slavery, the Catholic Church, and the monarchy.

The Temple of Humanity, Rondon's church in Rio, was built to worship and spread Positivism, whose saints included the Jewish prophet Moses, along with Julius Caesar, Shakespeare, and Dante. Its beliefs were years ahead of their time. Positivism lobbied for labor laws and animal rights; women were valued and venerated as central to the spirituality of mankind, for their goodness, affection, and power to shape family values.

Comte's words, L'AMOUR POUR PRINCIPLE ET L'ORDER POUR BASE; LE PROGRESS POUR BUT (Love as a principle and order as the basis; progress as the goal) are inscribed over the doors of the Temple of Humanity. The philosophy—*ordem e progresso*—continues to fly on Brazil's national flag, where it was stamped when Brazil became a republic.

When Cândido Mariano tried to enroll at the Academy, he was told his diploma from Mato Grosso wasn't adequate, and that he would have to go to school in Rio for three more years, starting next year. He lived in the army barracks next to the Imperial Palace, with recruits from Rio, some

illiterate and/or criminal. The barracks were filthy, the toilet was unspeak-
able, the food was rice and beans, and the opportunity was golden. His
unit commander was Captain Hermes da Fonseca, a Positivist who would
go on to become president of Brazil, at the time of the Roosevelt-Rondon
expedition. Da Fonseca took the brilliant young caboclo under his wing,
supporting his enrollment at Colégio Pedro II, Brazil's best private school,
a progressive institution chartered to "serve both the sons of the elite and
the destitute."

At 19, Cândido Mariano took extension classes for a year, rising at
4:00 A.M. to swim in the ocean and study in the barracks by whale-oil lamp.
He asked to take the final tests of the three-year program—completely
impudent, he was told with a wink of approval—and he aced them, with
a perfect score in math. "As a boy, I had only one dream in life, to study
so as to properly serve mankind," he wrote in his memoir, *Historia da
Minha Vida*, published as an e-book in Portuguese, 61 years after his
death.

At the Academy he studied engineering, mathematics, geography, and
astronomy, along with German, French, and Italian. His notes, copious
because he couldn't afford textbooks, were in elegant handwriting. In the
library, he devoured the writings of naturalists Charles Darwin and Alfred
Wallace, and called Alexander von Humboldt his hero, for charting not
only the earth but also the cosmos. (In fact, he named them, in his 1845
volumes *Cosmos: A Sketch of the Physical Description of the Universe*.) Humboldt believed in racial equality and the wireless, as well.

Positivism was all around him, in the best, brightest and most compas-
sionate. The faith was abolitionist and pacifist, its goal world peace through
acceptance of Humanity (the word was always capitalized). Rondon was a
perfect fit. Positivism was based on secular and empirical values, described
as "Christianity without Catholicism" by Thomas Huxley ("Darwin's
bulldog"). It attracted intelligent and orderly people who believed the
numbers, not the imagination, and military mathematicians were three-for-
three. Rondon's dream and the Positivist dream were one and the same: to
"transform the Earth into Paradise, for all mankind, without distinction of

race, belief, nation," he wrote in one journal "—banishing the specters of war, misery, and disease."

For the rest of his life Rondon would be true to Positivism. It ruled his every professional move, shaping the lives of millions of Indigenous people and thus Brazil. Positivism gave him conviction and spiritual strength. Its ideals "have constituted the key to my successes with Indians during the last 20 years," he said in 1910.

Not incidentally, Positivism advocated an end to the monarchy. In 1889, Rondon's last year at the Academy, the government was overthrown in a military coup d'état driven by Positivism. Until Rondon's *Historia de Minha Vida*, his role in the coup that deposed the emperor was vague. He never spoke about it, and historians said only that he was "involved," or that he "took part in the founding of the Republic." But pieces pointed to what Diai says, that Rondon was the "right-hand man" of the coup that ended the Brazilian Empire.

Rondon was the star student and protégé of Lieutenant Colonel Benjamin Constant Botelho de Magalhães, a bookish teacher of math and engineering, with a passion for Positivism that commanded a following. He moved his curriculum from math to faith, not without resistance from the Academy. Rondon would name his first son Benjamin.

On the Saturday night of November 9, 1889, Constant gathered a large group of officers to the Military Club, founded the previous year by army officers who objected to being ordered to chase runaway slaves, in an elegant and successful petition made on humanitarian grounds. In a meeting that lasted most of the night, the officers made the decision to overthrow the Monarchy. Constant justified the break with Positivist pacifist doctrine by adding an asterisk for "extreme cases," in this case rule by "men without reason or discretion." He argued that an armed coup was necessary, to end the inhumanity of slavery.

As Constant fired up his charges for revolution, 5,000 of Rio's elite, invited by the Monarchy, were dancing, drinking, and eating the night away at a ball, on an island ringed by lanterns around artificial palm trees. The menu included pheasant, turkey, shrimp, lobster, wine, champagne, cognac, and beer. Rondon had been at the ball with other cadets, and had raced to the meeting at midnight. As Diai, the Nambiquara activist and sociologist says, "In him, everything is united, nothing is lost."

The next day Constant asked the wild-eyed conservative Marshal Manoel Deodoro da Fonseca, author of that beautiful abolitionist petition (and uncle of Captain Hermes da Fonseca who was Rondon's patron and commander), to lead the coup, which he reluctantly agreed to do. A declaration was drawn and signed by 57 officers, including Rondon.

Rondon was almost late to the coup, out at a party with his sweetheart Chiquita Xavier, the smart 17-year-old daughter of a professor—he'd been chasing her for a year. "I felt myself divided between my ardent desire to be at Chiquita's side and my worries about remaining alert," he would write in his memoir, hilarity unintended. He was summoned to the barracks late that night and given a top secret assignment by Constant, a midnight ride on horseback with another cadet to deliver a letter to the chief of the navy, asking his intentions. He galloped through the city to the Navy Club, knocked on a thick wooden door, passed the letter through a slot, and awaited his fate—game on, or arrested for treason. He received an envelope back through the slot and galloped back to Constant, arriving at daybreak. The admiral would not interfere. Constant assigned an artillery unit to Rondon, moving with a few hundred officers and soldiers to the army headquarters, next to the palace. People watched and wondered from sidewalks. The general in command of the soldiers there was ordered by the emperor's cabinet to stop them, but he refused. "Here, we are all Brazilians, and I will not fire on my brothers," he said.[*]

Cadet Rondon, the caboclo who looked more like an Indian, stood at the side of Marshal da Fonseca and Lieutenant Colonel Constant as they informed the emperor's cabinet that the 58-year Brazilian Empire was over. When Rondon finally revealed the details of his involvement in his

---

[*]   General Floriano Peixoto, hero of the war with Paraguay, no relation to boatman
       Mario Peixoto, far as he knows.

memoir, six decades later, he said it was an honor to have played a role in what he called "The Revolution of 1889."

◆

Charlie Haskell began loading things into the Renegade parked in the red dirt against the Mirage Hotel. He and Fabio were going on a night mission to find the headwaters. Darkness would make it difficult and dangerous, but he said he had to regain the day that the media crew lost him. So they raced off into the black jungle to pull an all-nighter. They bounced, spun, slogged, sweated, slapped, hacked, pushed, winched, cursed, and yelled until 2:00 A.M., when they turned around and did more of the same to get out, arriving back at the Mirage at daybreak.

Charlie was haggard at the 8:00 A.M. meeting, having had not one wink of sleep, he said. He was confronted by Kaminsky, who demanded the $5,000 he was being paid for his camera work, immediately, or else he was out. Reason prevailed when the others told Joe he was behaving like an idiot.

The main topic at the meeting was the "Road of Doubt," as the trail to the river had been dubbed. Fabio figured they'd gotten maybe two-thirds of the way, with 22 more kilometers to go; Anselmo's crew was still working on that final bit. The Jeeps had four-wheel drive with off-road tires, but they couldn't carry all the gear, so Fabio was trying to hire two 4x4 flatbed trucks with local drivers.

The other big topic was weight, and its effect on the handling of the 16-foot inflatable rafts. More than two tons of gear had been checked at the Manaus airport, not including food. Three of the boatmen, Sobek's Mike Boyle and freelancers Mario Peixoto and Kelley Kalafatich, flew ahead from Manaus to Vilhena, sent by head boatman Jim Slade to buy groceries. The canned goods, including canisters of cheese the size of cannonballs, were stacked in the carport behind the Mirage Hotel.

Slade believed there were at least six places where the rapids would be too big to run, based on his careful reading of *Through the Brazilian Wilderness*. Gazing in dismay at the stuff stacked in the carport, as if he had nothing to do with it, he said each person would have to carry six or seven loads at each portage, over unknown terrain. Mike Boyle, very good at worst-case scenarios, said, "When you have to slog through slimy waist-deep water, with mud grabbing you at the knees and sucking your shoes off, 60 or 70 pounds on your back, insects biting and stinging you wherever they can find skin, and do this for hours, maybe days . . . well, it's enough to reduce a grown man to tears." Beth, whose first question at the meeting had been about maid service at the Mirage, was the only one to laugh.

We debated the necessity of stuff. I kept myself out of it as much as I could, walking a weird and wobbly tightrope between participant and reporter. There was general disdain for the heavy Magnavox satellite phone, bigger than a breadbox with a collapsible dish antenna. Its main job was to call the media from the jungle, namely Charlie Gibson and Joan Lunden at *Good Morning America*, so the question of its importance got to the cause of the expedition.

Haskell believed the sat-phone was necessary in case of emergency. We could call the Brazilian Air Force. In Manaus, we'd taken a bus to the air force communications headquarters to learn the procedure; Charlie wanted everyone there, to show the expedition's appreciation. He knew the fellows at the Brazilian air force; for months he'd tried to persuade them to fly the expedition to the headwaters in a cargo chopper.

About 16 explorers were led into a small classroom by an air force captain, and given instructions in Portuguese about who to call, under what conditions, at what times, and what color smoke bombs and flares to send up depending upon the nature and degree of the emergency. The system appeared to be made up on the spot and changed during the discussion, and no one understood a thing. Much was lost in translation, despite being ably performed by the boatman Mario Peixoto, a Brazilian who worked in Oregon for Outward Bound.

Luckily the Brazilian Air Force would not be needed. Chip Haskell called them a few times from the river, just to check in, but there was never an answer.

The issue of weight included the Yamaha generator that powered the sat-phone, charged the batteries for Kaminsky's two video cameras, and provided light to draw insects for Tweed's collection. And the generator needed gas. A lot of weight could be lost if the phone were left behind.

Haskell's big yellow McCulloch chainsaw was a sacred cow, its symbolism lost on him. "The first time we come to a fallen tree blocking the river we'll be glad we have it," he said. The 19 purse-sized canisters of Mace that McKnight brought for snake warfare didn't seem excessive, weight-wise. Tents vs. hammocks were discussed, along with how many machetes, and baby wipes. Beth had mailed a memo suggesting them; but three per day per explorer would weigh as much as the satellite phone. I did the math but didn't need to present the numbers, as no one got on board with baby wipes. It went on.

Fabio had found the two Indigenous people that FUNAI required the expedition use as guides. Charlie had brought a nine-foot inflatable raft for them, believing they could handle it in rapids, but whatever Fabio might have said about their boating skills was lost in translation and dyslexia. There was also an inflatable canoe they might have used, easily carried around rapids, but Haskell nixed it. "I was afraid they would get hurt," he said.

Slade said it was not possible to squeeze everyone and everything into four rafts. Haskell said he would like to leave the Indians behind, but couldn't do that. He told Chip to set up the sat-phone by the hotel pool and call Mountain Travel Sobek in California, to send another raft and boatman, which they quickly did for $10,950 for a six-week rental and the boatman's wages.

Waiting by his phone in Atlanta was Joe Willie Jones, a freelance boatman who'd been next in line to join the expedition. Kelley Kalafatich, with 15 years' experience loading people and gear into rafts, had told him to expect a call from Charlie or Beth and be ready to get on the next plane. He would fly to Miami and meet the raft coming from California, fly with it to São Paulo and Cuiabá, where he would heave the 110-pound giant rubber python on his broad back and throw it on a bus for the 12-hour ride up BR-364 to Vilhena.

Three Cinta Larga chiefs arrived the next morning. They drove up to the Mirage in an emerald-green turbocharged Ford Bronco with mag wheels

and all-terrain Pirelli tires, tinted windows, black upholstery, personal-
ized plates, stereo with a stack of country-western tapes, and a hammock
hanging from the rearview mirror like Amazon fuzzy dice. Chief Piu
was behind the wheel, with Chief Oitamina, aka Roberto Carlos, riding
shotgun; the tribe's junior chief, Tatare, was in back. Piu pulled the chrome
bumper of the Bronco up to the front porch of the Mirage, where I was sitting. He stepped out and brushed the red dust off his white slacks, as gold
buckles on his black patent leather faux Pierre Cardin loafers flashed in the
equatorial sun. A Carlton dangled from thick lips under dark shades, and
when he pulled it out to flip it in the dirt, a front tooth glimmered gold.

The chiefs got there just in time for the meeting. They'd been called
down from their homes in Riozinho, 210 kilometers up BR-364, to discuss
a problem and iron out a detail or two. Piu said he'd done a pre-run of the
river in a raft made of oil drums and logs in order to recon the rapids and
clear out garimpeiros and seringueiros (rubber tappers). He wouldn't be
going on the river with the expedition, but he made the deals.

The agreement between New Century Conservation Trust and FUNAI
was for Oitamina and Tatare to be paid $20 per day for their services as
guides, and for the tribe to receive $5000 in medical supplies after the
expedition.

Sitting in a semicircle on couches in the hotel lobby were Haskell,
McKnight, Fabio, Tweed, the scientists Geraldo Mendes and Jose Cabral,
and the FUNAI agent Assis. Kaminsky filmed the meeting, catching
Haskell and McKnight with intense scowls as Piu told them that some
Cinta Larga downriver were resisting the expedition passing through their
territory because they believed it was more about gold and diamonds than
science or history; after the White men found the gold they would buy the
land from the Brazilian government and try to evict or kill them. Piu said
it was these same Cinta Larga who had recently killed five miners who
wouldn't leave. Clubbed them to death, he said.

The discussion was in Portuguese, between Piu and Fabio and Cabral.
The young chief Tatare sat at the end of the couch appearing uninterested, distracted, with one eye on the television in the corner showing

commercials for Carnaval with lithe women shaking their bare butts at the room. Haskell sat on a couch and squirmed, anticipating a demand for money to settle the issue.

Meanwhile, Chief Oitamina, a short fellow in jams and tank top, with chubby cheeks, dark almond eyes, and a front tooth with more gold than Piu's, went outside to his $30,000 truck and came back carrying a black case. He placed it on the floor, snapped it open, and like a pool hustler with his custom cue, lifted out his video camera. Kaminsky stood dumbstruck as Oitamina switched on the camera's strobe and began filming the filming, circling Kaminsky and the drop-jawed others on the couches. The talk faded into shrugs, the Brazilian way, issue aired, nothing changed, issue resolved. Fabio proved his worth as a fixer, Piu didn't ask for more money. Charlie made a short speech thanking the great chiefs Piu, Oitamina, and Tatare, saying the Rio Roosevelt expedition was privileged to be permitted to pass through Cinta Larga territory.

CHAPTER 6

The Indian Agent

A monstrous inversion of facts, reason, and morality
—Cândido Rondon

After the coup, Rondon was rewarded with a double promotion to full lieutenant, even before graduation. With a big raise in salary, he proposed to his sweetheart Francisca "Chiquita" Xavier, after the proper courtship that began when she was 15—they had never been together unchaperoned. Rondon was already like family to the Xaviers. Francisco Xavier was a prominent physician, director of the hospital, and teacher at Colegio Pedro II—he'd taught Rondon geometry, when he was a hungry caboclo fresh off the Mato Grosso, a teenage prodigy, budding atheist. Clearly the Xaviers believed he was good enough for their daughter, who carried her own brains into the relationship. Colegio Pedro II didn't accept women, a rule the headmaster couldn't change, so he personally tutored Francisca.

But Rondon's proposal came with a catch: first he would have to leave her. He had army orders back to Cuiabá for an important engineering assignment, finish the telegraph line in Mato Grosso—the monarchy had started it but couldn't finish it. They set the wedding date for February 1892, two years away.

He'd left Cuiabá with nothing, eight years earlier. He was now a military academy graduate, army officer, and engineer, "returning happy," he said. To honor his Uncle Manoel who raised him, now an old man with few years left, he took the surname Rondon, carried five generations from his great-great-grandfather the bandeirante.

For 125 harsh and desolate miles east across Mato Grosso, followed by 250 miles through hostile Bororo territory, a 120-foot-wide swath for telegraph poles was cut. Rondon's commander was another Positivist, Academy graduate, and engineering teacher who would become Rondon's third consecutive powerful mentor, after Hermes da Fonseca and Benjamin Constant. Lieutenant Colonel Gomes Carneiro was 20 years older than Rondon and his role model—he taught him how to make wine out of palm-tree sap. Carneiro posted a notice on his telegraph poles: HENCEFORTH, WHOSOEVER ATTEMPTS TO KILL INDIANS OR DRIVE THEM FROM LANDS THAT ARE LEGITIMATELY THEIRS WILL HAVE TO RESPOND FOR THAT ACT TO THE CHIEF OF THIS COMMISSION.

After a year there, Rondon got called back to Rio by Benjamin Constant, now education minister of the Republic, to be professor of astronomy and celestial mechanics at the Academy, a job that involved research at the National Observatory, including a study of Brazil's climate. Constant and Carneiro fought over Rondon, who was torn himself. The assignment gave him time to marry Chiquita, and time to miss the backlands. He enjoyed the intellectual challenge of the job and the convenience of living in Rio, but he was an explorer, not a scientist. When Carneiro—Rondon's best man at the wedding—asked him to come back to Cuiabá he said yes, and took his 19-year-old bride with him. It was a Catholic wedding, a small compromise of faith that expressed his love for Francisca.

Things happened fast the next couple of years: he was promoted to captain and Carneiro was sent south to subdue an uprising against the Republic, where he was killed, making Rondon chief of the commission.

Their first daughter was born, Heloisa Aracy named for Benjamin Constant's daughter, followed by their only son, Bernardo Tito Benjamin. In June of 1894, with babies of 2 months and 18 months, Chiquita moved back to Rio for better health care, into a small house near her parents at the edge of town. She and Rondon would live there, on and off, over the next six years.

Rio was safer for Chiquita and the children. There were uprisings all over the country. That March, nearly 300 civilian and military insurrectionists were executed at the 300-year-old fortress of Santa Cruz, and 100 soldiers court-martialed and sent to Mato Grosso, most of them to work for Rondon. "I gave myself over to resentful reflections on the fact of undisciplined men still in the stage of forced obedience always being sent to me to work in the Commission," he said. There were rebels within his ranks, the same rebels who killed his father-figure Carneiro. So, as he put it, "I resorted to the only means of maintaining discipline in the wild among men removed from the duties in Rio precisely because they were insubordinate."

"In desperation," "against my religious principles," and "deeply pained," he began having the "bad elements," including deserters and drunkards, tied to a post and whipped with branches or bamboo. They plotted to kill him, and he had the ringleader tied to the flagpole in front of his tent and left to rot in the sun for a week, before sending him to a penal brigade. One man died when the bamboo cane he was being flogged with snapped and punctured a lung. Rondon got back to see Chiquita when he was ordered to Rio for a court martial, demanded by a rival captain.

The War Ministry, with its own executions of bad elements fresh in memory, was sympathetic to Rondon's plight. They called the charges against him "unfounded," and furthermore he should be "commended and thanked for services rendered."

He returned to Cuiabá by train and mule, 1,000 miles as the crow flies, the final 280 miles following his telegraph line because there were mutinies at the outposts: "Construction of the telegraph line required burdensome tasks to which the soldiers did not want to submit." Their attitude, he added, "was one of open indiscipline."

He didn't see his family for two years. Chiquita learned Morse code so they could chat over the telegraph line. She gave birth to daughter Clotilde Teresa, conceived when Rondon had been home for the court martial. She and the children were looked after by Raimundo Teixeira Mendes, who had an aggressive role in the coup and was leader of a broken-away branch called Orthodox Positivism, which embraced the spiritual ("live for others") and rejected the supernatural. Chiquita's Catholicism blended smoothly, as Rondon believed in its "chivalrous" values, if not its missionaries. Teixeira Mendes became Uncle Raimundo.

Rondon wrote him, "I am sorry to find myself far from the surroundings where I have customarily known true happiness, and where I should constantly remain for the sake of educating my dear little children. But this is the only way in which I can make my small contribution to the Holy Crusade of which you are the energetic and wise propagandist and endearing Apostle."[*]

Maybe it was the late-night Morse code communication, primitive texting, that brought them back together. They decided to try again in Cuiabá, so Chiquita and the children again made the long journey on steamers and riverboats—last time down it was a cattle boat from Buenos Aires, because Chiquita didn't want to wait for a passenger ship, exposing her babies to disease in the city. But in Cuiabá, her fears and reservations came true, as she got malaria and worse, yaws, a debilitating disease of

---

[*]   One of Rondon's closest friends at the Military Academy was Euclides da Cunha, who was the same age and size as Rondon and would become one of Brazil's best journalists and authors. A fellow Positivist, da Cunha was expelled from the Academy and jailed for protesting a visit by the war minister. He was released after Rondon and other classmates fought for him. Rondon was godfather to da Cunha's first son. His nonfiction book in 1902, *Rebellion in the Backlands*, describing the military's acts of genocide in a small Brazilian village, has been called a masterpiece of Western prose and was translated into English, published by the University of Chicago Press in 1944, and remains in print. He called the Amazon "an unpublished, contemporary page of the Book of Genesis." He died at 43 in a gunfight with a man who had been having an affair with his wife.

the skin and bones. Benjamin was chronically sick, too, so in 1899 they all returned to Rio.

For a year, Rondon worked on the details of his charts and maps of Mato Grosso, a state the size of Alaska, as the Brazilian economy crumbled, under civilian presidents after a problematic transition from military rule, including a war in the Bahia backlands. Rondon got deeper into Positivism, spending so much time at the Temple of Humanity that the family moved back into the city. He fell further under the spell of Teixeira. "You inspire and constitute in my entire Family, beyond all our sentiments of supreme gratitude, a true, spiritual Father," he wrote him.

First the Monarchy and then the Republic had failed in three attempts to extend the telegraph line south from Cuiabá to Corumbá and Coimbra on the Paraguay River, 300 miles into the Pantanal swampland, the final 50 miles in quicksand. The civilian government, for which Rondon had little respect, assigned him the impossible job, giving him neither the men nor money to do it. He considered quitting the army, but his faith wouldn't allow it. He succeeded by recruiting the Bororo, including warriors that had attacked him: 270 men, not counting their families and pets, who cleared a path through the bush. He persuaded them by speaking their language, signaling his Bororo blood; they trusted him and worked for him out of respect, accepting tools and small goods in payment and living off the land. "The Indians quite easily subjected themselves to the military routine and precise work," he said.

If lack of manpower weren't enough, Rondon was caught between the warlords who ruled Mato Grosso: sugar and mate plantation owners versus cattle ranchers and rubber tappers. In Cuiabá, police on the plantation side slit the throats of 29 men on the rancher side, and fed their bodies to the piranhas. Rondon tried to stay neutral—Chiquita was begging him by telegram to stay out of it—and he once even brokered a cease-fire between the warlords, but his family on his mother's side was in the thick of it—an uncle and three cousins got their throats slit, too. "This grave misfortune disturbed my work plans," he said, as ever not intending to be droll.

Rondon had been pleading with the government in Rio to send troops, to no avail. It came to a head with 2,000 men on one side marching from Cuiabá toward 1,200 men on the other side coming from Corumbá, but a battle was avoided when the anti-Rondon warlord was cornered in a gunpowder factory, killed, and mutilated.

In seven years Rondon had built more than 1,000 miles of telegraph lines south from Cuiabá with spurs, plus 32 bridges and 17 telegraph stations over the parched prairies and festering swamps, leading unruly men through hostile Indian territory and virtual civil war. He was made major, but more important to him than the promotion was his proving to the establishment that, when treated with "patience and good manners," Indians could be productive to the country.

He'd been back and forth to Rio enough times for two more daughters to be conceived and born, Marina Silvia in 1903 and Beatriz Emilia in 1905, followed by Maria de Molina in 1907, born in Corumbá. That's when President Pena called, with a vast ambition that matched Rondon's own: connect the country from Cuiabá 660 miles northwest to the Madeira River, then southwest 280 miles into rubber-rich Acre, and 460 miles northeast through the heart of the jungle to Manaus. More than a mere telegraph line, it was a mandate to map for geography, study for science, survey for minerals, and chart for development. The president officially established the Rondon Commission, to build the telegraph that would drag development by its wires.

For another six years, until the *Expediciao Scientifica Roosevelt–Rondon*, he would survive starvation, malaria with fevers to 105°F, infections, snake bites, vicious insects, poison arrows, wild rapids, piranha attacks, and more to map much of the immense Amazon, including discovery and charting of thousands of miles of rivers, and measuring the width, depth, and flow of tributaries.

He contacted and protected the Paresi, an orderly and once-grand tribe devastated by a century of slavery, who helped him pacify the difficult Nambiquara, tribes with a history of conflict. (The Paresi looked down on the Nambiquara because they slept on the ground.) He carried a gramophone and played operas into the jungle to draw them out. Chiquita wanted him to wear an armored vest (not a chance), and made him buy a more comfortable saddle. He continually preached nonviolence to his men, reminding them that they were the invaders, which drove them to the point of mutiny. His twin burdens of insubordination and lack of support followed him, along with his malarial fever; he would build one telegraph station—just a hut of bamboo and straw—and move on to the next, as the station behind him was deserted on account of hunger by the soldiers left to manage it, a problem he solved by recruiting and training Paresi. He would lose his credit at supply stores, as the government in Rio often didn't pay the bills—it once took six months for the government to pay him.

After the death of his supporter President Pena, the army ordered him to halt the telegraph mission and return to Rio. "Coming back immediately, through the other side," replied the fresh lieutenant colonel, still trying to find a path on the first leg through what is now named Rondônia. Six weeks later he discovered the Duvida.

The first attempt to cross the 700-plus land miles of wilderness from Cuiabá to the Madeira River—over prairie, through jungle, and around mountains—had ended with all but 50 of 660 oxen and mules dead from starvation or disease, and scores of men deserted from hunger or Indian attacks. The second time, Rondon and 41 men with relatively few beasts of burden set out from Utiarity, and after months in the jungle they missed their resupply by more than 70 miles, following a bad map. Before Rondon they were all bad, with geographic hunches turned into vague sketches, sometimes hundreds of years old.

After desertions and three deaths they were down to 14 men including his loyal Lieutenant Lyra, surviving on nuts, honey, grubs, and rats as they cut dugout canoes to keep moving. Six months later they reached the Madeira River near Porto Velho, barely alive. Rondon was jubilant. His charts indicated that he and his crews had traveled 806 miles on land and 707 miles on rivers. The telegraph line now had a path across the Amazon. He'd reached the other side. When he got back to Rio he was met with parades and songs, written about him like Davy Crockett. He was a national hero.

He needed a year in Rio to regain his health, directing telegraph construction by telegram and letters. Chiquita needed a vacation, six months pregnant with their seventh child, and in March he took her to a European spa in the mountains, traveling by train in a private cabin. He worked to establish the Indian Protection Service, a federal agency to protect the Indigenous—the president chose him to be its first director, a position he accepted only after his 17 stipulations were agreed to. At his request, the Brazilian Embassy in Washington began sending him the *Bulletin of Indian Affairs* for his knowledge. In April and May he gave three powerful and brave lectures to full houses in Rio and São Paulo. "The civilized always play the role of the lion," he told his prestigious audience, "and from that conflict, vengeance and carnage result."

He showed his bandeirante blood on the stage, in his response to criticism that the Rondon Commission cost money needed elsewhere. He'd found minerals to make Brazil rich, he said, naming 10 of them, from copper to cobalt to zinc.

He clearly restated his controversial Indigenous position, that they were rightful owners of the land, must be treated with humanity, and introduced to the culture carefully. "Our prideful ignorance has made us write much nonsense and evil with respect to them," he said.

"I have been working among them for 20 years, and have found them everywhere with hearts open to the most noble sentiments of mankind, of a lucid intelligence and quick to learn everything taught to them, indefatigable in the roughest toil, and friends who are constant and faithful to those who treat them with kindness and justice."

Saddened by the actions of seringueiros on Indian land he'd passed through, he said, "Many of the villages had been destroyed by fire; the plantations and barns had been sacked and robbed; the women kidnapped and raped; the children stolen and carried away; sickness hitherto unknown had appeared and was causing a mortality never before seen. In fact, the tribe, which at the moment of entry into relations with the rubber tappers was at 600 in number, could now scarcely muster more than 60."

Rondon had the strength of a position, simple and uncompromising, standing orders to his men: *Die if you must, but kill never.* "This theory contrasted to the bellicose sentiments of our soldiers," he wrote in a report in 1908, "for whom Indians were but ferocious animals that should be attacked."

Rondon's moral rectitude wasn't fully appreciated by army superiors, who argued that building telegraph lines and pacifying natives shouldn't be an army mission in the first place. To staff the Rondon Commission, they dragooned its malcontents and sickest soldiers, some straight off the streets of Rio, spiking Rondon's desertion and death rate. One newspaper editorial took square aim at Rondon, saying, "It is time to insist that the Army recall to the barracks the officers who have abandoned their duties, for they prefer to wander in the middle of the jungle fishing for the souls of savages and country bumpkins."

Historians suggest the telegraph line was a failure from the day it was inaugurated in 1915, after 25 years of impossible labor and prodigious expense. It got lost under the rainforest of radio. But it was the main link to the outside world for 50 years until the telephone. Rondon himself used it maybe the most, for long, lonely telegrams to Chiquita and the children.

Some historians contend that the Rondon Commission was more about development than communication. Rondon seemed to agree from the outset, saying in 1907 that he wanted to "make the Amazon productive by submitting it to our actions, to bring it nearer to us. It is to extend to the farthest ends of this enormous country the civilizing effort of mankind. This is the elevated directive of our great statesman President Pena, for he understands the primordial necessity of the development of our homeland."

Rondon believed his telegraph lines—"poles of attraction," he called them—weren't an invasion, but rather an invitation, a position that was awkward for him to reconcile. "On the question of ownership of lands," he would say, "we in Brazil are not only very backward, but also in a lamentable position—I may even say shameful. The backwoods of Brazil, where no civilized man ever trod, already appear on the books of the public registries as belonging to such and such citizens; sooner or later, according to the convenience of their personal interests, these proprietors will expel the Indians, who by a monstrous inversion of facts, reason, and morality will from then on be considered and treated as intruders, bandits, and robbers."

◆

Francisco de Assis Costa was the FUNAI agent on the Rio Roosevelt expedition. As a farm boy in the south of Brazil, he'd heard stories about fighting among wild Indians. He asked his mother, "Where are these primitive men?" and she answered, "In the Amazon."

"When I was old enough, I came to Rondônia and went looking for them," he said. In 1961 he volunteered for one of the earliest Brazilian expeditions to contact tribes, and was "totally enchanted" living in the jungle for a year. In 1968 when FUNAI was formed he got his dream job as a *sertanista*, as first-contacters are called. "I finally felt fulfilled," he says, "although it was very dangerous."

Before FUNAI, whose mission was to pacify and protect, "Indians were shot on sight," wrote the Brazilian Jesco Von Puttkamer in *National Geographic*. "I know several Cinta Largas with bullet scars, and one who survived a machete slash that almost split his face. Poisoned foods were left temptingly on their trails, and a Cinta Larga village was dynamited from the air."

That was the infamous Massacre at 11th Parallel in 1963. Men hired by a rubber company dropped dynamite from a small plane on an Indian village and then massacred the survivors. Thirty Cinta Larga men, women and children were killed, with two survivors. Horrific details were included in the landmark Figueiredo Report of 1967, which led to the establishment of FUNAI. Rondon's Indian Protection Service of 1910 was intended to stop mass killings and intrusion upon Indian land, but it didn't succeed.

"The Indians also did cruel things," continued Jesco in the magazine. "They killed the young wife of a settler on the Riozinho River. They murdered a rubber tapper with 13 arrows and gruesomely mutilated the corpse. And once a Cinta Larga proudly showed me his prize trophy, a set of false teeth."

The Brazilian government needed to contact and pacify its Amazon Indians because BR-364 was coming through. FUNAI flew over the jungle in small planes and found 22 encampments in Rondônia and Mato Grosso of Indians that would later be called Cinta Larga—Portuguese for "wide belt," describing the 10-inch-wide strip of softened bark the men wore around their waists. FUNAI estimated there were from 3,000 to 5,000 Cinta Larga.

Assis worked on the 30-person FUNAI expedition that first contacted the Cinta Larga in 1970. *National Geographic* sent in their writer Jesco, who interviewed the expedition leader, Chico. "I have had about 30 people camped here for six months," he said. "Has anyone of us seen a Cinta Larga? No, they are ghosts. They take the machetes, scissors, pots, pans, and such things as we set out for them, but they permit us not even a glimpse of themselves. It is most frustrating."

Contact was finally made by Chico's 20-year-old son, who had grown up with the Indigenous—he was named Apoena, for the chief of one tribe. The first contact was a trembling touch of his fingertips with the "magnificent young Cinta Larga warrior we now know as Noara," wrote Jesco.

When a FUNAI outpost was established along the Rio Roosevelt in 1972, Assis was its first director. Over two decades, he watched Cinta Larga culture slip away. "When I started working with them it was delightful. They were real Indians, with no ill will. Their day-to-day life was in their own habitat. But they've lost their way of life. They aren't prepared to live like they're living today."

He quit the job after 10 years, disillusioned. But in 1986, "At the request of Piu and Roberto, I went back to the Rio Roosevelt outpost and worked there for a year and six months. But they were manipulated by White men who told them to sell timber. I wouldn't help them do it, so they asked me to leave. I don't think that's how it should be. I want to be able to do what is right. That's why I went to work with the Nambiquara."

Assis spoke the least but carried the most to the expedition, including a timeless spirit and endurance of a man half his 56 years. He said his good health, good humor, ready smile, and full head of hair came from a lifetime in the forest, embracing its hardships. He now spent two-thirds of his time living with the Nambiquara, and the rest with his family in Vilhena, at their two-bedroom cottage with a jaguar-skin doormat. He invited me in.

His small office was filled with bows and arrows, beads and bones, photos and memories. Dangling over the kitchen table was a big cardboard spaceship, made by one of his 18 children. I wondered aloud how many women it took, and he replied with a sly grin. The spaceship builder was in the living room, watching Annette Funicello sing and dance her way through *The Monkey's Uncle* on television.

"The Cinta Larga have lost their myths," he said. "It's totally different now. For someone who knew them like me, it's very hard to watch them today. They're like caboclos, half Indian and half White man. It makes me very sad to see them like they are today. I try not to get involved any more, I try to ignore it. Although I'm still their friend, I wouldn't work with them again for anything.

"They want to be civilized overnight, and they're just not ready for it."

CHAPTER 7

The Chaos

Either reduce your weight or risk your death.
—Captain Jim Slade

Lighten up or die!
—Tweed Roosevelt

The backsides of five men stuck up from the floor of the Mirage Hotel lobby in Vilhena, on their hands and knees over a spread-out map. Charlie, Fabio, Slade, Boyle, and Oitamina in his orange paisley jams, were planning another attempt on the Road of Doubt. Tatare sat in a chair facing the television in the corner, picking at an elbow and gazing at the screen showing a telenovela. Oitamina tired of the discussion in English, maps meant nothing to him anyhow, so he and Tatare moved to the tiled porch over the sidewalk, leaning over the railing and watching the street as they drank their morning coffee and snickered at the White men. When Kelley had shown them the mountain of gear in the carport, they bulged their eyes and burst out laughing.

Piu had told Charlie there was a dirt road that led to the river about 200 kilometers north of Vilhena, a fairly short distance making it perfect for a resupply, because the rafts could be run light through fairly big whitewater coming early. So a party was dispatched in the red Wrangler to check it out: Oitamina, Slade, Carr Clifton, and Mario Peixoto, who told me all about it when they got back.

Oitamina said the road was rough so it would take two vehicles, and his 4x4 Bronco with off-road tires wouldn't be one of them. The other two Jeeps were occupied on the Road of Doubt.

"I've got a friend with a truck, but he would need two new tires," said Oitamina. So they bought two tires in Vilhena for $240, strapped them to the back of the Wrangler, and drove up BR-364 to Pimenta Bueno where they were to meet the friend with the truck at a gas station. He wasn't there.

Oitamina made a phone call, while a man tried to sell them parrots and macaws trapped and stolen from the jungle. Oitamina came back and said his friend would soon be there. They waited a long time, so Oitamina called again; now they had to drive to Espigão d'Oeste, 30 kilometers east toward the river, where the asphalt ends. No sign of the friend there, either, so they left the new tires at a gas station and drove to the river on the dirt road, which wasn't so bad after all.

It hadn't taken long for Oitamina and Piu to figure out that Charlie was easy for them to manipulate. At their every small con he would tell them how wise they were and express his appreciation. He feared the chiefs' power to end the expedition by bailing out, although that was unlikely with their egos in deep. He didn't want to disappoint anyone, not just the explorers, but also supporters such as the American Museum of Natural History and National Wildlife Federation. So he couldn't afford to upset Oitamina.

The resupply reconnaissance crew reached the river just after dark, and camped next to a bridge built by loggers for their trucks. Most of them enjoyed sleeping under the Amazon stars, but Oitamina wanted to go back out to sleep at a friend's house. He slept in the rear jump seat of the Wrangler and woke up in the morning squeezed on the steel floor over the driveshaft hump.

Meanwhile the headwaters reconnaissance crew was slip-sliding the other two Jeeps through the jungle all day and all night. Charlie, Fabio, Boyle the boatman, and the team's doctor, John Walden, had left the Mirage in the blazing noonday sun. At first it wasn't so bad, as Charlie and Fabio had been over Anselmo's trail before; but it narrowed just as the sun went down. They swung their machetes bathed in the yellow glare of the headlights, and used the Jeeps' winches to get over slimy hills, with the cable looped around a tree and pulling, until it slipped. Fabio nearly got castrated and Boyle nearly got decapitated, to hear them tell it.

Some hills didn't need chopping or pushing if the Jeeps got a good run. They bounced and spun through sloppy ruts, their engines screaming as chunks of mud flew off the tires. At least a dozen times they had to stop to chop stumps left by Anselmo. The jungle's tentacles reached into the Jeeps, slapped the occupants' cheeks, and spit ants down their necks. Fabio drove the Comanche with one hand and smacked his neck with the other, cursing; Boyle switched on the cabin light and ran from the Jeep screaming at the sight of thousands of tiny fire ants, with big black ants dropping from the headliner, onto the floor around a spider the size of his fist.

"All of a sudden there was this skinny guy with stringy hair wearing shredded pants and rubber shower sandals and no shirt, standing in the middle of the trail," said Boyle. "I thought I was hallucinating. Then I saw this green plastic makeshift tent with smoke pouring out of it. There were six or eight other wiry guys there, most of them pretty young, Anselmo's crew, and they said they'd been there about two weeks, cutting the trail to the river.

"We told them we wanted to go to the river, and they said, 'Okay, let's go!' They jumped up, grabbed some machetes and an ax, and the youngest guy, who was barefoot and shirtless, went running off down the trail whooping and dancing in the headlights between these sharp punji stick stumps left when they cut the trail. They walked in front of the Jeeps, chopping at stumps and mounds of dirt with their machetes. There were about eight places where they had to cut trees with Charlie's chainsaw. Their own chainsaw had run out of oil a few days ago. They worked for about three hours and never got tired, never showed signs of weakening or wanting to take a break."

Near the river the jungle got too thick for the Jeeps, so the recon crew strapped on headlamps and walked the final half mile. Boyle hooted and ran down the bank and plunged his arm in the dark water, jubilant beyond fear of losing a finger or three.

Then they turned around and slogged back out. They made it to the Mirage at daybreak after the 18-hour adventure, caked with mud and covered with bites, and with only one Jeep after the Renegade blew two tires when Charlie got airborne at the top of a hill and landed on the front wheels. But they were flushed with success at having reached the river.

◆

When Beth said Charlie discards what he doesn't want to hear, that was only the back half of it; he could hear things that were never said, things he wanted to hear. In Porto Velho, he'd excitedly given me a thick softbound file given to him by a PR man from Varig. Charlie said it was important historical material, a collection of the Brazilian accounts of the Roosevelt-Rondon expedition. It was a tourist guide to Porto Velho, with lists for pizza shops and brothels.

After witnessing firsthand the madness in the jungle at night, Dr. Walden began thinking about his professional responsibility to the expedition: What if Haskell leads them into danger?

"If that's how Charlie led his platoon in Vietnam," I told him, "when he says he doesn't know what happened, what happened was he got fragged by his own men."

Dr. Walden practiced in West Virginia and the magnificent city of Quito, Ecuador, wedged into the middle Andes and only half a day from the Amazon. He knew tropical medicine, and had been on a number of treks and expeditions. I asked him if a dyslexic brain could jumble pieces of information, same as it jumbles words and numbers on a page, so decisions don't add up. He said yes, in extreme cases, the logic isn't linear. "Charlie seriously needs help," he said. "He's highly, if not totally, unable to reason."

"My father is a walking dichotomy," said Chip Haskell. "Half his weak-nesses and limitations he can't or won't recognize, and the other half he tries so hard to overcome that it's a liability and he sort of self-destructs. If he weren't so strong it might be easier for him, but then if he weren't so strong he wouldn't have achieved the tremendous things he has, either.

"I'm only here to protect my dad from himself," he added. "He has a gift for making the wrong decision."

After the recon crew had showered, there was another meeting. The issues were redundant: how to reach the river, and how much to carry down it. Haskell said it might take tractors to finish the job on Anselmo's trail. Someone suggested they use beasts of burden like Rondon and Roosevelt, and it was seconded as a good idea, for historic consistency and environ-mental integrity—the media would love oxen and mules. Haskell said he'd see if he could rent some bullocks from local farmers.

The big Magnavox satellite phone came up and was put down again. A call from Tweed Roosevelt to *Good Morning America* from the headwaters was planned, with the hope that the expedition might catch the world's interest. But was the hassle of the phone worth it? Protecting it from deluge and humidity, charging the batteries, finding a hole in the canopy for a signal. And without the phone, the generator and its can of gas might not be needed.

The four resupply scouts returned in the red Wrangler late in the after-noon. Haskell began the evening meeting with his head in his hands, as if he were trying squeeze solutions out his ears. The phone and generator would go to the headwaters, but not along on the river. There were no farmers with tractors, horses, mules, or oxen to spare. He talked to a Scot-tish missionary who said he fished on Rio Teodoro, and a Turena Indian who grew up on its banks; each knew other routes to the headwaters but finding them sounded too difficult. Carr Clifton volunteered to check into getting tire chains for the three flatbed trucks now parked out back on worn tires, but no one took him up on it.

Joe Kaminsky said that if he had nickel cadmium batteries for his camera, he wouldn't need the generator; but they cost $500 and he couldn't find them, not even in Manaus. He asked Oitamina where he got his. "Paraguay," said the chief.

Jim Slade said the river was running high and fast, it was rainy season, so the danger might not be rapids and rocks, but sheer speed. Weight inhibited maneuverability. He painted a picture of five heavy rafts swept like a runaway train over a waterfall. Either reduce your weight or risk your death, he said. Tweed turned the threat into "Lighten up or die!," his favorite expression when mocking was called for.

Slade suggested they leave their iodine pills behind, since there would be a water filter; ounces add up, he said. Someone said leave the sugar, but Slade said it was needed for morale—that's what TR said when the same issue arose on his expedition. Slade suggested that some might cut their wardrobe in half, without naming names, but possibly thinking about the dozen or more T-shirts neatly rolled up on the bed in Charlie and Beth's room. Beth said dry clothes were as important to morale as sweet coffee.

All opinions about ounces sagged under the weight of the canned food stacked in the carport, topped by the cantaloupe-sized tin canisters of cheese. There were two Sobek cook tables with heavy wood tops and iron pipes for legs. Slade's notion to save weight by cutting iodine pills fell on deaf ears and lips muttering "bullshit." It was resolved that backpacks be limited to 20 kilograms. Weigh-in 10:00 A.M. in the lobby.

The explorers walked down the street to dinner. A torrential rain pounded the sidewalk a few feet from their long table, as a steamy mist floated into the restaurant through the absent wall. Madonna shrieked from a jukebox in the corner.

Assis had joined the group, bringing his friend Iastachio. The Vilhena mayor had recently gotten Iastachio fired from FUNAI, for telling the Nambiquara they were getting screwed in the deal to build a dam and hydroelectric plant on their river. Iastachio said the mayor and his partners from the construction and power companies had offered the Nambiquara a new truck and $85 a month for 30 years; and with the promise of electric lights in their huts and easy fish forever, they'd gotten a Nambiquara chief to agree to the deal, so Iastachio interfered to protect them. He said he was lucky he wasn't killed.

Iastachio had been fired even as the legendary explorer and activist for Indian rights, Sydney Possuelo, was head of FUNAI's *Departamento de Indios Isolados*. Possuelo was passionate about keeping them uncontacted, to spare them from disease and decimation. He began working for FUNAI in the 1970s as a sertanista, someone who contacted tribes, but came to realize that contact with civilization did more harm than good. In 1987 he led a small peaceful revolution within FUNAI that changed their way of thinking. In a petition that led to the establishment of the department of Indios Isolados, he wrote, "We can never forget that in the process of attraction, we are in truth acting as the spearhead for a cold, complex, and determined society, one that has no forgiveness for technologically inferior adversaries. We are invading their lands without their invitation. We are inculcating needs they never had before. We are wreaking havoc with extremely rich social organizations. In many instances, we are taking them to their death."

His successor, the famed sertanista Wellington Figueiredo, agreed, saying well-meaning sertanistas weren't so much agents of contact as they were "agents of tragedy."

"Uncontacted" isn't a literal term. It doesn't mean that a tribe has never seen White men, only that it has chosen not to been seen by them, after experience with them. A few remain to this day. In 2002, Possuelo would lead an expedition to find for demarcation, but not contact, a tribe known as the Arrow People on Javari land in the northwest corner of Brazil, far more remote than Rondônia. He was joined by *National Geographic* writer Scott Wallace, on a 76-day trek that led to Wallace's book, *The Unconquered: In Search of the Amazon's Last Uncontacted Tribes*. The passage from Possuelo's petition comes from that book.

Iastachio had drunk two tall bottles of Antarctica beer, and his eyes were red from stress and alcohol. His T-shirt had a silk screen image of what appeared to be a photo, over the words INDIOS ISOLADOS. With Jose

Cabral interpreting, I asked Iastachio what the picture was, and Beth answered that the image was charred tree stumps. I ignored her and asked Iastachio again, and he said they were spikes, cut from the hard ipe tree and stuck in the ground as a warning for White men to stay away, by the *Indios Isolados*.

Iastachio fairly spit out his opinion of Oitamina and Piu. "You have chosen the worst of Indians to be on your expedition," he said. "They come from Cacoal, which is the center of the illegal cutting of mahogany off Indian lands, which are a biological preserve. Cacoal is also where the cocaine smugglers operate, although it is the Surui who have a weakness for cocaine, not the Cinta Larga."

If Charlie had a gift for making the wrong decision, Beth had one for looking the other way. She interrupted Iastachio and tried to steer the conversation somewhere safe. When I turned it back, asking her to please let me do my job, she got upset and rose from the table, walked to the jukebox in the corner and stood there for a while; then walked out, back to the Mirage Hotel in the rain. Charlie followed, not knowing what was wrong.

They had worked long and hard to get the expedition to this eve of departure. Beth had promised the Brazilian government that the expedition would be nice. She was afraid that some Brazilian official would get wind of journalistic muckraking and stop it all.

She was stressed out. She had been carrying a triple load for 18 months, overcoming bureaucratic barriers and weaving through cultural ones while dealing with Charlie's limitations and dancing around his sensitivities. It had been a monster job to get them there, and she'd done it well. But now her role was unclear, never mind the title coleader. And her authority, as illustrated by the Rio Roosevelt Command Flow Chart she had drawn, was gossamer. It bothered her that no one was listening to her.

She and Charlie worried about each other's hearts, and they did their best to protect them. "I wanted to have three or four women on this expedition, but they just weren't there," Charlie said on the flight to Porto Velho. "You get 18 guys and one woman, and who's she gonna turn to? That's why we have Kelley, who was at my insistence, not Beth's. But I'm very concerned that Beth won't get the respect she deserves. We've got to be careful about that."

Fears were quietly expressed that Beth might lose it on the river. Charlie and Chip had a big argument about it. Dr. Walden recommended she stay behind. But it wasn't easy for her. "I've put my heart and soul into this for a long time," she said.

Charlie and Beth invited me to their room and asked my opinion. I told Beth she was needed to lead the resupply, to direct the logistics. Fabio had a tendency to wander. And someone had to wait for Joe Willie and the fifth raft to be brought to the resupply. Assis would be joining the expedition there as well. "Who better than you to get all this done?"

In the morning there was a final meeting. Beth said she would stay in Vilhena to lead the resupply.

So far Slade had been reserved, but he could take it no longer. He felt he had to take some control. He'd made a list of 37 things that needed to be done in the 24 hours before departure. He began to go down the list but quit on number three since it only brought more talk-talk-talk. He'd made his point.

That afternoon as they loaded the Toyota flatbeds, the mayor of Vilhena took some of the explorers to the Rondon Museum and Zoo. It was Tweed Roosevelt's 50th birthday, making a sweet photo op, a picture to be added to the row of thieves on the mayor's office wall.

The zoo was on the outskirts of town, at the spot where Rondon's telegraph station was built in 1910. Vilhena's oldest living citizen, a quiet gentleman named Marciano, lived there now. He had high cheekbones, leathery feet, a silver flattop, and easy laugh.

He came to Vilhena in 1943 to operate the telegraph. He and his wife raised 10 children there, when it was just jungle—they were the entire population of Vilhena for 20 years. A trip for supplies took six weeks by mule to Mato Grosso and back. It was taken for granted that death came easily. "You got sick, you died," said Marciano.

Two of Marciano's children were buried in unmarked graves out in the jungle beyond the museum, along with another family that came in 1962 when BR-364 was cut. They were killed by Cinta Larga in reprisal for the intrusion of garimpeiros.

Marciano was 79 now. His house was a shack with two happy dogs in the yard and a big poster of a clipper ship on the wall. The garden grew manioc, mango, orange, pineapple, and banana. Young people liked to visit, to be around his spirit. Some of his children and grandchildren sometimes came for a day or two.

His original house is now the museum, a small cement structure featuring rusty relics from the telegraph days. The zoo occupied about an acre, with a few scruffy animals including a pair of jabuti turtles, whose delicate bones are drilled and made into beads on Cinta Larga necklaces; a pair of harpy eagles that swoop out of the sky and fly off with monkeys; two tapirs, good-eating but fast-swimming pigs that the Roosevelt-Rondon expedition could never hit with their rifles.

Heavy gray clouds hung low and moved in a slow semicircle around the zoo. The mayor, trailed by an aide and a photographer, guided the explorers. Tweed presented him with a button from his great-grandfather's expedition, as the photographer clicked away.

Behind them, the king of the jungle watched. The magnificent jaguar, revered as a symbol of freedom and courage, its soul flowing between animal and man. Amazon Indians identify with the jaguar. This one languished in its cage. Its coat, a work of heavenly art, was dirty and dingy. Its hide sagged on its skeleton and its eyes drooped in defeat. It was weak, sickly, and had the hiccups. As the mayor, the man of the future, led the explorers away, the jaguar lay down in its small filthy cage and continued its sad wait to die. Only Tatare took notice.

CHAPTER 8

The Naturalist

But where's the piano?
—Stevedore in Buenos Aires

Theodore Roosevelt's speeches in Brazil, Uruguay, Argentina, and Chile went well. He told the family he was "lionized everywhere." In writing about the tour, he omitted the protests in Santiago, where students met his train shouting, "Down with Yankee Imperialism!" They hadn't forgotten the revolution he didn't discourage when he was president, in order to get the Panama Canal built. He didn't change their minds, but disarmed them by respectfully discussing the issue.

Edith returned to Sagamore Hill on November 26, via Valparaiso and her husband's Panama Canal, and on December 9, TR and Kermit began an 11-week odyssey to the headwaters of Rio da Duvida. In Asuncion, Paraguay, they boarded the *Adolfo Riquielme*, a gunboat yacht sent by the president of Paraguay, and began steaming up the Paraguay River, "a highway of traffic," said Roosevelt.

Father and son shared an appreciation for firearms. They carried the trusty small Springfield rifle that Roosevelt had used so famously in Africa—"great precision and admirable penetration," said Rondon. Kermit brought seven tools: his favorite .405 Winchester double-shot rifle, a .30-40 lever-action Winchester (.30-caliber cartridge, 40 grains of smokeless powder), 12- and 16-gauge shotguns, and three pistols: a Colt six-shooter from the Wild West, a compact and sturdy late-model Smith & Wesson revolver like the one the Rough Rider himself had used in Cuba, and a new German Luger semiautomatic, soon to find its place killing American boys in World War I.

However, said Roosevelt, "Our trip was not intended as a hunting trip but as a scientific expedition." He was dedicated to his museum assignment to bring back specimens of Amazon birds and mammals. In the beginning, it was entirely about speeches and specimens; when he left New York, he'd never heard of Rio da Duvida. Its descent was a change of plans that didn't bump the importance of the museum assignment.

Roosevelt was a dedicated naturalist and could be an eloquent writer, and when the two came together over nature, his passages were beautiful. Like the naturalist writer Peter Matthiessen, who would crisscross 20,000 miles of South America nearly half a century later for his book *The Cloud Forest*, Roosevelt was an especially keen observer of birds—one top ornithologist said TR knew as much about birds as he did. On the Paraguay he was excited to see "crimson flamingos, rosy spoonbills, dark ibis, white storks, and snowy egrets." He loved the prancing of jabiru storks in nests like platforms in the trees, and laughed at the youngsters learning to fly. Rondon too was passionate about birds. He enthralled TR with stories about growing up among the birds on the Mato Grosso.

After three days they reached the Brazilian border, where Roosevelt and his party met the *Nyoac*, a sidewheel steamboat carrying Rondon and his party, chief among them the 35-year-old lieutenant João Salustiano Lyra, who was almost as smart as Rondon. (The IQ total of the four men—TR, Kermit, Rondon, and Lyra—must have been in the 600s.) Lyra was invaluable to Rondon as an engineer, biologist, astronomer, and surveyor; he used the stars to calculate latitude, having studied geodesy in Germany. Others with Rondon included his quartermaster Captain Amilcar de Magalhães, along with a geologist, biologist, doctor, and cinematographer.

Rondon and Roosevelt hit it off from first handshake on the *Riquielme*. They each spoke some French—Rondon could also speak Italian and German—and Kermit translated the Portuguese. They had things in common, starting with big families; Rondon with seven children and Roosevelt six. "Colonel Rondon immediately showed that he was all, and more than all, that could be desired," wrote Roosevelt. "It was evident that he knew his business thoroughly, and it was equally evident that he would be a pleasant companion.

"He is of almost pure Indian blood," Roosevelt added, and not only was he an officer and a gentleman, but also "a good field naturalist and scientific man, a student and a philosopher," and, he would say later, a "pioneering social thinker."

When the full biography of Rondon was finally published 109 years later, author Larry Rohter would write, "He was intensely and genuinely patriotic, adhered to traditional codes of honor, bravery and chivalry, and repeatedly demonstrated a moral rectitude enhanced by a character both ascetic and abstemious. . . . At the same time, Rondon's espousal of tolerance, cultural diversity, and nonviolence, his rationalism, and his recognition of the innate dignity of all human life and respect for the natural world and its ecosystems make him a very contemporary figure."

Eighteen months after the expedition, Rondon gave some nine hours of lectures over three evenings to packed houses, including the president of Brazil and the US ambassador on opening night, in Teatro Phenix, a new and grand Rio de Janeiro theater. If he was sometimes criticized for his mission, he was also adored by the media. "Never has there been among us a more perfect hero than Rondon," said one editorial. Another newspaper declared in a headline: RONDON: THE NEW APOSTLE OF THE JUNGLE. After the final lecture, he went straight from the theater to a steamer bound for the Amazon. A crowd saw him off, waving hats and flags and shouting "Long live Rondon!"

In the lectures he said he wasn't "tormented with nervousness" as he might have been with an ex-president of the United States, because he knew he had to rise to the duty of his job and expectation of his country. He said their meeting was "between a statesman of great intellect and high culture, accustomed to the usages of European diplomacy, and the man who for almost 25 years has lived in the wilderness."

Rondon had been traveling toward their meeting on the Paraguay River while Roosevelt was giving his speeches. On October 4, the same day Roosevelt left New York, he had received a telegram from his boss and old friend the Brazilian minister of foreign affairs, Lauro Müller, telling him to get on the next boat to Rio de Janeiro from his remote telegraph outpost. It would take weeks in a few boats, first by canoe down the Pimenta Bueno River, motorboat down the Gy-Paraná, and steamer to the Madeira and Amazon Rivers at Manaus, where he stayed to make a materials list and recruit the men that would be needed.

At that time there were still four or five possibilities, so Rondon, by telegram, ordered dugout canoes built at each of four rivers. From Manaus he continued east on the Amazon River to the Atlantic Ocean and south to Rio de Janeiro. He arrived on November 11, and got the news from Müller that Roosevelt had chosen the Duvida when he was in Rio on October 21.

Rondon had time in Rio to plan, for "the greatest number of unforeseen difficulties," as he would say in his lectures, suggesting surprise at TR's choice, along with recognition of the kind of man he was. On December 2, he boarded a night train to São Paulo, then four more trains to the end of the line, then horseback for 168 kilometers in Mato Grosso—riding at a trot all night across the prairie—then a special train to Porto Esperanca on the Paraguay River, where he arrived on December 9 and boarded the *Nyoac*, which was waiting with his men and all the equipment he had gathered in Rio; it had steamed to Montevideo, Uruguay, at the mouth of the Paraná River that ascended into the Paraguay. He was now only a couple days upriver from Roosevelt. It had been a two-month journey by boat, train, and horseback for some 4,000 miles.

Rondon lamented missing Roosevelt in Rio. "What a pity it is that they only called me just as Roosevelt was leaving New York," he said, "for I do not own a dirigible with which to fly over the vast territory of our country."

◆

On February 29, 1992, a convoy as odd as the day left the Mirage Hotel in Vilhena heading north on BR-364. It was led by the red Jeep Wrangler and silvery gray Comanche, followed by three faded green Toyota 4x4 trucks whose flatbeds were piled with gear. Chugging along at the rear, blowing diesel smoke, was a tarnished gunmetal gray 1950s bus carrying the new explorers.

At the dirt road that began the slog to Rio Roosevelt, they climbed out of the bus and onto the trucks, finding seats on the ice chests, duffel bags, and two big chrome wheels with repaired tires for the Renegade that had been left in the jungle after Charlie's Evel Knievel moment. They were in high spirits, following the red dirt road as if it were yellow brick, skipping over pastures with thin grass and bony cattle. "The country along this river is a fine natural cattle country, and some day it will surely see a great development," Roosevelt said, half-right depending on his meaning of great.

The country was not fine for cattle or crops. When the trees were slashed and burned, the ash enriched the earth and enabled crops to grow for a couple of years, but after that the soil dried for lack of roots and died for lack of nutrients from leaves, stunting the growth of crops and grass for feed. And without a forest the rainforest doesn't rain, so it doesn't grow back. So the land had to be continually slashed and burned to stay fertile, and the second-growth forest was poor. Thousands of colonists over three decades, erasing rainforest.

The caravan weaved through big charred stumps standing like tombstones. Skeletal remains of trees rose on the horizon, the burned ones blackened and others bleached—those were the Brazil nut trees, spared from slash-and-burn but doomed anyhow, standing alone. Barren branches reached toward the hot blue sky like twisted arms and arthritic fingers, pathetically pleading too late to be saved. Still there was elegance in their stance. It took a stretch to see it.

Already some of the explorers wanted to slow the whole thing down. The pace suddenly seemed breathtaking, with Kaminsky jumping from truck to truck with his video camera trying to get everyone in the movie, unable to slow the train for a passing shot. We were rushing off into a conundrum: by design, we weren't a cohesive team, we were a dozen professionals with disparate assignments having incompatible demands.

Carr Clifton could have spent hours hiking and waiting for a sunrise or sunset in the best light for his coffee-table book. The scientists could have spent days catching fish and chasing rainforest remedies. I could have spent weeks hanging out with Indigenous people (and later did). But Slade's assignment was to get the explorers safely down the river to Manaus, and his boats and boatmen back home as quickly as possible. Time was money to Mountain Travel Sobek. "We were doomed from the start," Haskell would say, too late.

We found the knee-capped Renegade under a tree and mounted the front wheels. We stopped at a stream to wash off dust and fill jugs, and Haskell casually mentioned that he had left the Magnavox satellite phone behind.

What? What about the call to *Good Morning America*, such a big deal. Why?

"How am I supposed to know something unless someone tells me!" Charlie responded, as if the call had never been discussed. Tweed Roosevelt, booked on the show, was outraged, and outspoken in his measure of our leader's thought process.

The dirt road turned into a thin, slick trail, cut by Anselmo. As it climbed in steep spurts, the worn tires on the Toyota Bandeirante* trucks

---

* Bandeirante dates to the 1500s, the name later given to the early Brazilian and Portuguese slavers of Indigenous people. Their expeditions to capture Indians, sometimes armies to capture thousands of Indians, were called *bandeiras*. Indigenous slaves were cheap to acquire, African slaves were expensive. But Indians wouldn't work, even knowing they would be killed for it, so the bandeirantes eventually gave up. Today the bandeirante is mostly seen as a soldier of fortune, the word suggesting bold, rugged, brave, adventurous. Good name for a truck.

looked up at the explorers and laughed. The tires spun into the earth until the tailpipes blew mud bubbles. We needed mules.

Darcio, one of the Bandeirante drivers, said the trail had been a road decades ago, and now that it was again, it would be used by Anselmo and other farmers. Anselmo was happy, getting paid to clear the road he needed! The Rio Roosevelt expedition was opening up the rainforest for development, as the Rondon Commission had with its telegraph lines.

The convoy came to a long steep hill, lined by hooting explorers as the trucks began blasting to the top, one by one. Driving the black Renegade, Charlie was flagged off, and the Jeep roared away in an explosion of mud-balls, leaping over humps and lurching in ruts. Charlie kept it floored as it flew over the peak and toward the jungle; when it landed he locked the brakes and skidded to a stop a few feet from a fat tree, to wild cheers. He jumped out like a NASCAR driver after a celebratory burnout, whipped off his black ballcap, and whooped.

"The throttle was stuck!" he shouted with a huge grin. The impact from the landing had released it. It was the most fun he'd had in weeks.

◆

The *Nyoac* and the *Adolfo Riquielme* steamed together until afternoon, when Roosevelt boarded the *Nyoac* to discuss the expedition with Rondon. They talked about a number of things, including Indigenous assimilation, and afterward they had tea and told piranha stories. Rondon eyed his boot to dismiss the toe that a piranha had taken in one chomp. He told about the fellow who was bitten on the buttocks and survived by grabbing a branch and pulling himself out of the water with the fish clinging by their teeth to his butt. And the story about the lieutenant whose mule came back without him. They went to the river and found a skeleton wearing his uniform, "every particle of his flesh stripped from his bones," as Roosevelt described it. Rondon didn't reveal to Roosevelt that he had broken down in tears. Just three weeks earlier on this river, Roosevelt reported, a 12-year-old boy had been "literally devoured alive."

Roosevelt wrote about piranhas almost as much as he wrote about birds. "The razor-edged teeth are wedge-shaped like a shark's, and the jaw muscles possess great power. The rabid, furious snaps drive the teeth through flesh and bone. The head with its short muzzle, staring malignant eyes, and gaping cruelly armed jaws, is the embodiment of evil ferocity. The only redeeming feature about them is that they are themselves fairly good to eat, although with too many bones."

Their stories moved to anacondas, which had snatched two of Rondon's dogs, and jaguars, which Rondon found nearly as lurid as Roosevelt found piranhas. At the Rio theater, he would tell his rapt audience that a jaguar hunter could never miss the first shot, because the jaguar would pounce. "Standing erect on its hind legs, it subjugates the hunter by the shoulders with powerful claws, and with formidable teeth crushes his skull." (TR would confirm this technique in his book, retelling a story with "the jaguar driving his fangs through the man's skull into the brain.")

Behind Rondon on the stage, a screen projected still and moving images from the expedition, including the two jaguars that Roosevelt and Kermit shot. Rondon was at the vanguard of filmmaking, eager to experiment with the latest technology—his commission had a cinematography sector. He used films for edification and propaganda, for example Indians raising and saluting the Brazilian flag.

The steamers continued north for two more days, with Paraguay on the west bank and Brazil on the east, as they neared Corumbá, a small frontier town on a steep hillside. Boats came from both banks to greet them, with bands playing and passengers cheering, as Brazilian gauchos on horseback waved from shore, and women washing clothes on the rocks waved and smiled and wondered. TR said it was like being on the Hudson River coming into New York.

The next day there was a state dinner (lunch) at their small hotel, while *camaradas* moved Roosevelt's expedition gear onto the *Nyoac*. The American Museum of Natural History didn't pull the plug after he changed the plan, so it was all the food and equipment for the cast-aside Roosevelt South American Scientific expedition. It had traveled from New York to

Rio de Janeiro and on to Buenos Aires on the *Vandyck* (the bill of lading showed five tons), where it was transferred to a smaller steamer (prompting one stevedore to ask, "But where's the piano?"), and sent up the Paraná and Paraguay Rivers to Corumbá.

Roosevelt asked Rondon to go over the gear he had brought, and carefully writes that "Colonel Rondon at the end of his inspection said that he had nothing whatever to suggest," adding that Rondon described the gear as "the things most necessary, with the minimum of bulk and maximum of usefulness."

Rondon was too proper to be revealing about edgy issues in his statements, and his language was often vague, stiff, and cumbersome, with losses in translation. In his lectures, he made a cryptic reference to "verifying the baggage of the American commission, and examining the convenient propriety of certain articles which they had intended to be used in the wild."

Rondon's quartermaster, Captain Amilcar, was aghast at the Americans' 99 crates—most of them food, he noted—compared to the Brazilians' 38 boxes for many more men, containing tents, equipment, tools, and food. Along with Lieutenant Lyra, the 34-year-old Captain Amilcar was Rondon's most trusted officer, having perfect Positivist pedigree, nephew of Benjamin Constant, son of a general, and Academy graduate military engineer. Rondon received Amilcar's report, yet told Roosevelt his gear was perfect.

Rondon made it more clear that his duty was to "render homage to our guest." And if Rondon did anything to a fault, besides play the Brazilian national anthem on the gramophone at daybreak, it was to be dutiful. He didn't want to offend the ex-president by telling him he had brought too much stuff. Which was now piled on the *Nyoac* on top of Rondon's gear. The small steamer's waterline was submerged.

The *Nyoac* waited for seven days while they went jaguar hunting. Roosevelt shot his jaguar out of a tree from a distance of 70 yards, with the same trusty Springfield he'd used to shoot lions in Africa, a remarkable shot for a man who was mostly blind in one eye. Kermit got his cat the next day, a huge male cattle-killer—big as an African lion, said TR—after they chased it all day through swamps on horseback. Local hunters, who had been unable to kill it, were grateful.

It might also be said that they went jaguar hunting for seven days while Rondon chased money to keep the expedition alive. As revealed in documents from the national archives, and reported in *Into the Amazon*, Rondon got a cable on December 17 at Corumbá from his old friend Müller—best of friends in fact, from their time together at the military academy—yanking funding that Rondon was expecting in Corumbá. "Insisting necessity shorten expedition in view current financial difficulties," cabled Müller.

The timeline presents a puzzle with pieces having an odd fit. On December 17 they left Corumbá "on a shallow river steamer for the ranch of Señor de Barros," wrote Roosevelt. Müller had suggested to Rondon that he ask the State of Amazonas for money, so maybe Señor de Barros was like one of the elusive tycoons that Haskell had chased for funding. Roosevelt writes of their week at the fazenda, "In the evening after dinner we sat in the bare ranch dining-room, or out under the trees in the hot darkness, and talked of many things." With Rondon, he said, "the conversation ranged from jaguar-hunting and the perils of exploration in the 'matto grosso,' the great wilderness, to Indian anthropology, to the dangers of a purely materialistic industrial civilization, and to Positivist morality."

Rondon wanted to know everything about the Bureau of Indian Affairs, how it all worked. Roosevelt would write that he was enlightened and changed by Rondon, and his view that Indians' tribal identity must be maintained. Surely they discussed the naturalists Darwin, Wallace, and Rondon's hero von Humboldt, a man much like Roosevelt. They might have talked about their wives, strong intelligent women whom both men were proud of, and who bore them 12 children. If they talked about the night Rondon helped overthrow the Brazilian Empire, they never mentioned it.

Nor the money. Would Rondon have admitted the expedition's financial crisis to Roosevelt, under the trees in the hot darkness? Probably not. The embarrassment would have been severe. If he did, neither man ever revealed it. They might have agreed never to do so.

Meanwhile Rondon's loyal and longtime lieutenant Lyra was back in Corumbá desperately trying to buy supplies on credit. Rondon ended up borrowing from the budget of the Telegraph Commission to keep the expedition alive, and "it took years for the federal government to reimburse Rondon for most of the money he advanced," writes Rohter in *Into the Amazon*.

The party got back to Corumbá on Christmas Eve at 5:00 P.M. Roosevelt wanted to be back on the river by 7:00, so he told everyone to hurry up and get the *Nyoac* loaded, but Kermit had photographs from the jaguar hunt to develop, which needed to go out with Roosevelt's first dollar-a-word dispatch to *Scribner's*, so they didn't get away until 10:00 P.M. It was a melancholy Christmas Eve for the naturalist George Cherrie, who missed a white Christmas around the fire with his Vermont farm family.

Cherrie had come from New York on the *Vandyck* with the Roosevelt party, and during TR's speaking tour had collected some 800 specimens of birds and mammals in Uruguay and around Corumbá for the American Museum of Natural History. Everywhere he went, he packed animal skins and skulls, scores of them in a couple of trunks—or dead animals when he didn't have time to skin them—sending them back when he could.

The 48-year-old Cherrie was the Rough Rider's kind of guy, "unusually efficient and fearless." A Vermont farmer and family man with six children, rugged naturalist and ornithologist, head of his local school board, nearly faced a firing squad when he was running guns for the good guys in a South American revolution. He'd never been to Brazil but this was his 18th expedition to South America, according to hashmarks in his diary, whose account was often the most perceptive and blunt. Cherrie observed early, "The more I see of Mrs. Roosevelt the more I admire her."

On Christmas they ate canned turkey and plum pudding on the boat decorated with palm leaves, sleeping on the decks of the *Nyoac* at night because it was 118°F in the cabins. On December 26 they ascended the swirling brown Rio San Lorenzo, on December 27 they moved onto the yellow Rio Cuiabá, and on December 28 they anchored near the big house at Fazenda San Juan, where they were welcomed by the governor of Mato Grosso.

Neither Roosevelt nor Rondon mentioned the governor in their writings and lectures. Cherrie's diary got to the crux when he later described a campsite: "This is the site of a former Indian village that was burned and the inhabitants massacred by a brother of the present governor of Mato Grosso." Rondon had communicated with the governor prior to that incident, knowing that gunmen had been hired, but he got nowhere. Imagine Rondon's discomfort at dinner.

They went hunting from the fazenda in a "motley cavalcade" with a dozen dogs who cornered a sharp-tusked peccary; Roosevelt grabbed a spear from a guide and stabbed the "truculent pig" to death the way locals do. Cherrie said he was once treed by a herd of 300 peccaries.

They steamed back down the Cuiabá and farther up the San Lorenzo, looking for more jaguars. The New Year's Day hunt was fruitless but epic: they chased a phantom jaguar—"a very sly beast" said Rondon—for 11 hours with no food, hacking through the jungle, slogging through swamps, trekking in the sun, torn by thorns, and bitten by mosquitoes "which we barely noticed when the fire ants were found," said Roosevelt. He added, "All dread of the latter vanished when we were menaced by the big red wasps."

Twice they had to swim through swamps inhabited by crocodiles, their rifles held high with one arm. Roosevelt grumbled that his wristwatch, "a veteran of Cuba and Africa, came to an indignant halt."

Anthony Fiala, the team's quartermaster, entertained readers of the *New York Times* with his version of the story:

"One of Colonel Roosevelt's most stirring adventures occurred on New Year's Day, when he went away from the camp at daylight with Kermit and two Brazilian officers and three Indians to shoot tiger cats. We did not hear from the party until late in the afternoon, when a big Indian came running into camp, shouting 'Burroo-Gurra-Harru,' which meant 'Plenty work. Tired.' He fell down in a corner and went to sleep. Twenty minutes later another Indian ran in, apparently all used up. He said 'Gurra-Harru,' and he went to sleep.

"The third Indian arrived then and said, 'Harru,' as he threw up his arms and went off into a trance.

"This caused me to become anxious about the safety of the Colonel and his son, and we started to look for them, as it was getting toward sundown. After walking through the forest for a short distance we came to a small open space, where we found one of the Brazilian officers lying on the ground, so dead tired that he could go no further. His clothes were torn, and his face and neck were covered with dust and blood.

"Leaving him in the care of three of the natives to carry him back to the camp, I pushed on further and in another clearing I saw Colonel Roosevelt and Kermit dragging the other Brazilian officer after them through the jungle. I shall never forget the awesome appearance of the intrepid Colonel as the falling rays of the sun streamed through the trees and lit up his dusty and begrimed features. His clothes were torn to tatters and Kermit was in the same condition, but had not his father's warlike look.

"I called out to him: 'Are you all right, Colonel?' and he replied, 'I'm bully,' and then we went to camp with the used-up officer. Next day the Colonel and Kermit were about the camp as if nothing had happened out of the ordinary, but the Brazilians were laid up for two days. The Indians regarded the Colonel with awe after that trip."

CHAPTER 9

Angel of Adventure

We were now in the land of bloodsucking bats.
—Theodore Roosevelt

The Rio Roosevelt explorers literally pushed on, against trucks bogged in the mud, as the forest began climbing. Daylight waned and the sky softened, stacks of puffy pink resting on the green rim of the rainforest. Frogs began to chirp. Bloodsucking bats darted in the dusk.

Night was fraught with risk. With the trucks stuck on a hill, a snakebite or broken ankle was one step away. Bodies stumbled in the dark, slipping near spinning wheels and falling in front of lurching vehicles, tripping over logs and walking into swinging machetes. Sandals and sneakers were buried beneath bug-bitten ankles. Headlights sprayed the forest with dancing beams of unnatural light.

Reaching a plateau, the convoy continued through a long dark tunnel. Boyle was riding shotgun with Charlie when leaves slapped through the window and delivered a hundred bites to his face and neck. He switched on his headlamp to see a million red ants on the floor. He ran screaming from the Jeep, for a second time.

◆

For four days and two nights, the overloaded *Nyoac* struggled against the current of the narrowing Paraguay. They bought wood when they could and burned it in the boiler fast as they could; twice at night they ran aground on sandbars. Roosevelt wrote, "The shallow little steamer was jammed with men, dogs, rifles, partially cured skins, boxes of provisions, ammunition, tools, photographic supplies, bags containing tents, cots, bedding, and clothes, saddles, hammocks' and other necessaries for a trip through the 'great wilderness,' the 'matto grosso' of western Brazil."

When the *Nyoac* reached São Luiz de Cáceres, last stop in Mato Grosso before crossing into Amazonas, Roosevelt "was received with the exploding of many bombs and a brass band," said George Cherrie in his diary. The gearhead Anthony Fiala broke out the Evinrude motor he'd brought, clamped it to a local dugout canoe, and gave rides on the Sepotuba River, which Rondon had mapped and named ("tapir river") in 1908.

For two days they pushed up the Sepotuba, narrow, twisty, and swift as it rushed down from the Highlands. At 3:00 A.M. on January 7 they reached Porto Campo, where they cleared trees to expand the camp. It was as far as the *Nyoac* could go without continually running aground.

They hired a flat-bottomed launch beautifully named the *Anjo d'Aventura*, the Angel of Adventure. She towed two small *pranchas*, barges with a hut, for the gear. But the *Anjo*'s small kerosene engine couldn't pull the weight, so she left one of the pranchas there and chugged with the other to Tapirapoa, where the overland trek would begin. Cherrie went with the *Anjo*, as its engine "throbbed and trembled," towing the prancha that he called a "heavy houseboat."

For six days, they waited for the *Anjo* to return, living in two rows of big tents. It was a large party—Roosevelt with 6 men and Rondon with 11, including a taxidermist and cinematographer. Roosevelt went tapir and peccary hunting for the Museum and had a wonderful time, except when he was "badly stung on the face, neck and hands" by big red wasps, and when the bugle blew at sunrise and sunset every day as they raised and lowered the flags with everyone standing at attention. Roosevelt successfully pleaded with the disciplined patriot Rondon to push back the wake-up call by an hour.

Rondon stayed with Roosevelt instead of going on the *Anjo* to Tapirapoa, where he had a ton or five of work to do. In 1908 he'd built a warehouse there to store food, tools, and telegraph equipment. He needed to be there now, to get his massive pack train ready to cross the Brazilian Highlands. He had no interest in hunting tapirs. But his duty was to "render homage to our guest."

When the *Anjo* came back they loaded on 30 men, five dogs, some big tents, guns and ammunition, a few slabs of meat from four tapirs and five peccaries, and a huge turtle named Lizzie tethered on deck, on her way to the Bronx Zoo where she would live a long and happy life—she had been intended for soup, but they all fell for her. They made about two kilometers per hour as the small engine "strained and sobbed," said Roosevelt, with the attached prancha being poled by camaradas to keep up.

They reached Tapirapoa at noon on January 16. With a telegraph station there, TR sent a cable home to let the family know where he was and that all was well. His daughter Alice was worried about her father and little brother Kermit, as they all were, and might have replied with the news that her grandmother, Caroline Haskell Lee, had just died at 79. Alice was very close to Grandma Haskell Lee, as was TR, to his first mother-in-law.

Theodore Roosevelt's first child Alice was named after her great-grandmother Alice Haskell, wife of auctioneer Elisha Haskell, descended from militia Captain William Haskell, who sailed from England in 1635 and settled to farm in the Massachusetts Bay Colony—the Haskell homestead near Salem still stands. When her mother, also Alice, died at age 22 just hours after giving birth, Roosevelt was overcome and couldn't embrace his infant daughter. He called her "Baby Lee,"" for her grandmother Caroline Haskell Lee, because he couldn't speak the word *Alice*, so deep was his grief.

Within days, he buried himself in his work as a New York State assemblyman in Albany, and within weeks was off to North Dakota. He left Alice with his older sister Anna to raise. "She would be just as well off without me," he wrote a friend from the Badlands. He didn't return to get her until she was four years old, after he had married Edith, who insisted. Separating Alice from Anna—Auntie Bye—broke both of their hearts.

As a far-reaching consequence, Alice grew up feeling less loved by her father than her five younger stepsiblings, borne by Edith. "Father doesn't care for me . . . one-eighth as much as he does for the other children," she wrote in her diary. Alice was "a virtual orphan in a clannish family," writes author Stacy A. Cordery in her biography, *Alice*, the primary source for this sidebar.

TR never mentioned Alice's mother to her; the only things she knew about her, she learned from Auntie Bye and Aunt Gracie, a Haskell. "My father never told me anything about this [his love for her mother], which was absolutely wrong," she wrote in her autobiography, *Crowded Hours*, published in 1933. "The whole thing was handled very badly. It was awfully bad psychologically."

Young Alice had a mind of her own, like her father, along with his brains and perception—she might have been the smartest of his six smart children, smarter even than Kermit. TR half-joked that he had to be nice to her because she had more money than him. She had Haskell money as well as blood, enhanced by grandfather George Cabot Lee, whose Boston investment banking firm, founded by his father, financed the beginning of General Motors.

As a teenager in the White House, Alice was spoiled by her allowance from her grandparents, $2,000 per year, more than four times the average annual family income in 1902. She spent much of it on clothes, including gowns for the many balls she attended. Before her own debutante ball in the White House, she got a bit "sniffy," as she put it, because her parents could only afford punch on their presidential salary, already stretched to pay for the 2,000 flowers Alice wanted. Alice offered to pay for champagne out of her own money for the 600 guests, but Edith wouldn't allow it.

The relationship between Edith and Alice wasn't easy. Edith called Alice's mother "dull," as in not very bright. There was history. Edith was in love with TR when "Sunshine" Haskell stole his heart. At that time he didn't love Edith back; he told a cousin that it was love at first sight with Sunshine. After their third time together he vowed to win her heart, he wrote in his diary.

Overnight after that debutante ball in the White House, a month before her 18th birthday, Alice became the first female celebrity of the 20th century and she ran with it. The media called her "Princess Alice." The *New York Times* covered the ball on the front page, "one of the most charming social events Washington has ever seen." The *New York Tribune* said Alice "was as attractive in her dignified simplicity and natural grace as she was beautiful. Tall, with a striking figure, blue eyes, and a fine fair complexion, she is certainly one of the prettiest girls in Washington." She looked like her mother Sunshine Haskell.

But Princess Alice, the Princess Diana of her time, was burdened by self-doubt because of her place in the family, and she didn't buy her press. In an interview at age 90, she would call herself "a rather pathetic creature, terribly homely, and they were just saying I was pretty because I was the president's daughter." But the striking old woman sells her teenage self short. Photographs—chosen by Edith after they had hired the first-ever White House press photographer to deal with the public demand for photos of Alice—show a confident young woman with steely eyes that engendered a color known as "Alice Blue," and were said to change shades with her moods.

Soon the First Daughter was filling in for the First Lady, who had miscarried and recovered slowly. She made her public service debut before a crowd of 5,000 to christen Germany's American-made imperial yacht, the *Meteor*, invited to do so by Kaiser Wilhelm II. The French and Russians were envious, worried about political influence on the American public. Alice was nervous but didn't show it; the *New York Times* said "Miss Roosevelt was the most self-possessed person on the stand," adding, "It is only a few weeks since she left the schoolroom and in a day she has become one of the most regarded women in the world."

That regard scarcely wavered even after she became the White House wild child, if not the First Feminist. A "mistress of the occult and black arts," according to the *Washington Times*, she smoked cigarettes, played poker, let her lacy white slip show, or worse wore pants, bet on the horses, chewed gum with gusto, carried a pet snake in her purse, danced the hoochie-koochie, sneaked whiskey into teetotal events hidden in her elbow-length gloves, shot the pistol TR gave her for Christmas off the back of a train, and gathered speeding tickets, again making the front page of the *Times* after one shocking unchaperoned road trip with a girlfriend to Boston to see Grandma Haskell Lee. Later she bought her own car, a long and sleek 1904 model she called the "Red Devil." She opened the driver's door for women.

Everywhere Alice went she was followed by throngs of female fans and photographers—paparazzi, 60 years before they had a name. It didn't go over well with TR and Edith. He told her there would be "no smoking under my roof," so she climbed up on the roof of the White House to smoke. "I wasn't going to let him get the better of me," she would write. She added injury to insult by corrupting her little brother Kermit with a corncob pipe.

But Alice could be the perfect First Daughter when she wanted to be, charming and decorous, obedient to protocol, an asset to the presidency. At first she did it just to prove to TR and Edith that she could, but as the positive press improved her self-esteem, she continued to rise to the occasion. Still . . . "Got a talking to this evening at having no interests in life from Mother and Father," she wrote in her diary. The next day she was off to the yacht races in Newport with her superrich friends that her parents vehemently didn't approve of. "No hope for Alice," she added in the diary, a wry comment that became a refrain that could have been the title of her autobiography. "I am bored to extinction by everything," the teenager wrote in her diary about Sagamore Hill, where the family spent their time away from the White House. "I care for nothing except to amuse myself in a charmingly expensive way."

She wanted to be in New York City with her fast friends—tribal friends, she called them—or in Boston at the house on Beacon Street of Grandma Haskell and Grandpa Lee, as well as Uncle Georgie and Aunt Hattie Haskell who sometimes lived there. "I was treated there as belonging," she wrote of the Haskell Lee home on Chestnut Hill. Same as TR, when he was dating her mother. "I really feel almost as if I were at home when I am over there," he said.

"There never were such kind, affectionate, indulgent grandparents—four aunts and an uncle as well—who let me have my way until I ought to have been spanked," she wrote. Some afternoons Grandma Haskell took her out in the two-seat carriage driven by a coachman and pulled by two "reliable, rather than dashing" horses. "When the time came to go home I used to dissolve in woe at leaving my grandmother, partly because she was dear to me and I loved her, but I fear also because I missed having the world swing about my small selfish self."

As she matured, she grew into First Daughter. At ages 23 and 24 during TR's final two years in the White House, says author Cordery, "He increasingly sought her advice and discussed political situations with her." She shared his ideals and goals, and passionately supported his politics. She wrote in her diary, "His fight is the fight for all that is great and advanced and human."

When Grandma Haskell Lee died on January 14, 1914, with TR two days from Tapirapoa, Alice was just shy of 30 years old, and already, as the subtitle of Cordery's book calls her, a Washington Power Broker. She died at 96, propelled to that age by her Haskell genes.

In the Sunday *New York Times* of January 23, 1927, there was a dispatch from Commander Dyott, who with his handful of men had poled their prancha up the Sepotuba for 11 days to reach Tapirapoa. They carried three tons of food and equipment, including the movie cameras, a wireless radio transmitter, and two canvas canoes for the descent of Rio Roosevelt. Dyott had read Roosevelt's book and Kermit's diary, telling him to stay out of dugout canoes.

◆

Whenever Charlie was asked if the caravan would be stopping for the night, he would look around for Fabio for help with the answer, but Fabio was always up front dealing with the next obstacle. Fabio never considered it. Driving into the jungle in trucks with smooth tires during rainy season at night was already taunting Mother Nature, and every extra second there was like asking for Her slap in the form of a downpour. When things bogged to a quiet pause, we looked up through the canopy for assurance from stars in a clear sky. "Look, I think that's the constellation Orion," said Dr. Walden, full of wonder.

At midnight a Bandeirante slid off the path on a hill, stuck with its left rear wheel over the edge and its left front perilously close. The right wheels were sunk to the hubs, axles submerged. A dozen shadowy bodies floated around the truck, pushing in both directions, rocking, grunting, shouting. The engine revved and tires whirred; in reverse, mudballs from the spinning front wheels flew straight up in front of the headlights and blasted like little brown rockets through the canopy.

Now there was a cable attached to the truck. It crawled out from between the headlights and up the slimy hill, stretching to a winch over the steel front bumper of the Wrangler, which was pointed down the slope with its rear end cabled to a tree. With all wheels driving, 10 or 12 people pushing and a winch pulling, the truck got nowhere, as the Jeep slid sideways and the winch bound.

There was a long quiet interval from Fabio's end of the cable. Soft voices discussed the stars. A flash of heat lightning gave a glimpse of ghostly shapes under Brazil nut trees billowing over the canopy. Bugs and frogs played basketball, a thousand players to a team, running up and down court in squeaky little sneakers.

Suddenly, like scruffy angels, two woodsmen appeared. Fabio had raced the Comanche ahead to the camp of Anselmo's crew and brought them back. They borrowed headlamps, checked the corners of the truck, and said, "We'll have you out in five minutes." They told half the explorers to push down on one side of the chassis, and half push up on the other side. The Bandeirante was out in five minutes. "Our logging trucks get stuck all the time," they said.

◆

It was 280 kilometers from Tapirapoa to Utiarity Falls, nine days by mule train over the Highlands (today it's a four-hour drive along BR-364). Rondon spent five frantic days of "incessant toil" organizing and loading in Tapirapoa, with "some confusion" if you believe Roosevelt, or complete chaos if you believe Kermit, who wrote to Belle that he wanted to kill them all, starting with his own nasty mule, then the unbroken oxen that bucked off their loads, then the people. He didn't tell her about the malarial fever that kept him in his hammock for three days, and lingered. "He still looks sick," said Cherrie.

Rondon was desperately and belatedly buying oxen, hiring men, packing, and loading the huge carts with their wooden wheels seven feet tall. He had already hired 110 mules and 70 oxen to carry the expedition more than 600 kilometers from Tapirapoa to Vilhena, but after seeing the 5 tons of stuff that Roosevelt had brought from New York, packed in the 99 large wooden crates and many smaller boxes crammed on the *Nyoac* and now stacked in the warehouse at Tapirapoa, he rounded up another 50 or so oxen that arrived straight and wild off the *planalto*. More were appropriated from his biologist, on assignment to collect specimens for the National Museum of Brazil, who got mad and quit.

Rondon's position (like Haskell's) was compromised. It was Rondon's idea to take Roosevelt down the Duvida; when Müller asked him to take the ex-president of the US on an expedition, his mind surely went to the numbers, led there by the pragmatism of Positivism. Charting the Duvida had been on his list of projects for five years, and this expedition would pay for it.

Rondon (like Haskell) was under pressure to bring back a pretty picture. It was important, all the way up to President da Fonseca, the man who helped Rondon get into the academy, that Roosevelt tell the world that Brazil was ripe and ready for development. It mattered to the Brazilian economy. The Brazilian ambassador to the US had cabled Müller from Washington to say that Roosevelt should "be offered all the facilities for his voyage and the most ample and gracious hospitality among us." So they gave him a silver saddle, to ride on his worn-out mule, and the portly old man must have looked and felt ridiculous. But he was as polite as Rondon was dutiful, so he was stuck on it. Maybe he didn't ride it all the way—nobody talked about it. He called it "exquisitely unfit" for the mission, in a confidential letter to John Keltie, secretary of the Royal Geographical Society, a year after the expedition. "I would have given deep offense to very good and kind people if I had not used it," he said.

Cherrie usually stayed out of it, but he saw trouble coming long before Tapirapoa, when he wrote in his diary, and underlined it, ". . . a greater lack of organization seems hardly possible!"

Rondon hired 148 more camaradas from among the local cowboys, river men, and soldiers based there. The gauchos wore fringed leather aprons with wicked knives squeezed inside their belts, and cursed in two or three languages as they lassoed, blindfolded, and loaded the oxen. Wrote Leo Miller, Cherrie's young partner from the Museum of Natural History, "When the covering was removed from the animals' eyes they frequently gave a few sharp snorts, and then started through the corral in a series of rabbit-like leaps, eventually sending the packs, saddles, and all flying in every direction. After freeing themselves of their burden, they gave a few extra high kicks of exultation, and then ran into the huddled mass of their fellows for concealment."

It wasn't easy to recruit more men despite Rondon's "doubled wage." His expeditions were notorious for being back-breakers and killers. Muleteers and drovers were needed to keep the animals moving, with little grass or water to sustain them. Dropped-dead bullocks would feed the camaradas, roast or dried meat; the weak animals would become martyrs, sacrificed to piranhas as decoys to keep Roosevelt's "ferocious little monsters" occupied, while the rest of the animals and people swam across upriver. There would be five or six rivers to cross, as the rivers ran longitudinally and the expedition moved northwest.

Commander Dyott used six mules to carry his men, and 28 oxen to carry and pull his three tons in two carts. "I figure on each animal being dead at the end of the trip," he said.

"One man can travel easily over this trail to the River of Doubt," Dyott told readers of the Sunday *New York Times*. "Two men increase the difficulties fourfold; three men is increasingly difficult, but four men is infinitely worse. When you come to ten men, as in our case, then the work becomes colossal unless backed by big resources." Rondon had nearly 200 men.

In Tapirapoa, the two tense issues between Rondon and Roosevelt arose: weight and time. The weight issue began in Corumbá, when Rondon told Roosevelt that his five tons of gear was perfect. Rondon apparently believed the 99 crates contained creature comforts the ex-president needed and, out of respect, should have. The boxes weren't labeled, Rondon didn't ask what was in them, and Roosevelt wouldn't have known. All Rondon knew was that it took too many days to load on the backs of too many mules and unhappy long-horned oxen, one of which would creep into TR and Kermit's tent and eat their clothes while they somehow slept through it.

Ironically, Roosevelt was feeling unexpressed frustration over the things that Rondon carried. "Enormously heavy tents were provided with the greatest pride by the Brazilian government and Colonel Rondon, although they were utterly unsuited for the work," he told Keltie in the letter. "Our companions cared immensely for what they regarded as splendor." He accepted with a sigh the carpet that was provided for the floor of his tent. Because he didn't want to hurt Rondon's feelings, he left only half of the tents behind in Tapirapoa, which took a great deal of tact, he said.

The other big issue was time, not yet life-threatening. Rondon wanted to send his Captain Amilcar ahead to repair bridges if necessary, but Roosevelt didn't want to wait. His drive to keep moving made life difficult for Rondon, who accepted it as the need of a great man to get back to leading the world. So, "according to the expressed wish of Mr. Roosevelt," Rondon gave up on his plan to maintain the infrastructure of his supply route. "In this way Mr. Roosevelt would not undergo the disappointment of having his voyage hampered by some drawback on the road," he said.

By the time of his lectures, Rondon might have read a translated version of Roosevelt's book, enabling him to avoid contradiction. The book was fulsome in its praise of Rondon, who never would have betrayed the tribute. In fact, Roosevelt dedicated the book to Lauro Müller and Colonel Rondon: GALLANT OFFICER, HIGH-MINDED GENTLEMAN, AND INTREPID EXPLORER.

Roosevelt suggested dividing the expedition into two pack trains, one led by Captain Amilcar with the oxen and heavier equipment, and the other with the mules for the crates and personnel. So the mule train was "under the head of the ex-president of the United States, assisted by myself," said Rondon.

"We were now in the land of bloodsucking bats," Roosevelt said as they departed Tapirapoa.

CHAPTER 10

Mule Train

In Utiarity we abandoned all hope of finishing our work.
—Colonel Rondon

Captain Amilcar Bothelo de Magalhaes's pack train of 150 mostly oxen left Tapirapoa on January 19, with some camaradas riding the oxen, guiding them by a thin rope through their nostrils and lip, alert for the tossing of a very long and sharp curving horn that could poke out a rider's eye with one sneeze. Two days later Roosevelt's train of 98 mules, some oxen, and 9 horses followed toward the planalto, the Brazilian Highlands, twice the size of Texas. Roosevelt said it looked like Oklahoma.

They got a late start, and rode at a trot for more than four hours—a hard ride, said Cherrie. At camp, a few thatched huts along the Sepotuba, they had to wait four hours for the carts with the tents and food. It was Roosevelt's pace. As Rondon said, "under the head of the ex-president of the United States, assisted by myself."

On the second day Rondon reduced the Brazilians' rations. No time to stop for lunch. He told his Dr. José Antonio Cajazeira, who worried about the health of the two dozen men in Rondon's party, that he had to cut their food so the Americans could keep eating in the manner to which they were accustomed.

The Americans ate canned salmon and fruit from New York (Roosevelt loved the peaches), from 100 tin boxes each containing one day's rations for six men—and venison when Kermit shot two deer. TR also had a stash of chocolate. The camaradas ate rice, beans, and meat when another ox bit the dust. Or boiled vulture, which even Rondon said was nauseating. When Rondon cut the Brazilians' rations, Roosevelt cut the Americans'. Edith had suggested to her 230-pound husband that he might skip lunch anyhow.

The next day they crossed the Sepotuba on a crude pontoon ferry made by planks placed over three dugout canoes, and rode in dense tropical forest without eating until 10:00 P.M. They made 14 miles. Cherrie's diary was terse on account of exhaustion. Roosevelt was upbeat and enjoyed the birds.

On the third day they climbed 2,000 feet to the Paresi Plateau, where Roosevelt stood on the Brazilian Highlands and looked down on the Amazon Lowlands, "back over the vast Paraguayan marshes, shimmering in the long morning lights."

"Day after day we rode forward across endless flats of grass and of low open scrubby forest," he wrote. Kermit sometimes rode by his father's side as they recited poetry, a family thing. Kipling was a favorite. Other days, Kermit the loner would take his dog Trigueiro and one old camarada and go off on a horse hunting all day, return to the empty camp in late afternoon to grab his things, then ride all night to catch up. When he described those days to Belle, it sounded like relative rapture. Trigueiro had been given to him in Corumbá—"biggish, nondescript, obviously a good fighter," said TR of the loving yellow mongrel.

Kermit said TR was a "born raconteur," fondly recalling the ghost stories his father told around the campfire when he and his siblings were small. The Highlands campfires were more like bonfires, with many people and abundant firewood; TR and Kermit both told stories from their African safari, and they had a lot of them, having shot 17 lions, 7 cheetahs, 3 leopards, 11 elephants, 11 black rhinos, and 9 white rhinos. Cherrie told about the time he was fighting with Venezuelan insurgents and faced 20 charging lancers on horseback; he and five rebels shot and killed 10 of them, as the rest ran.

Rondon told of his first contact with the Nambiquara, in 1907 when he discovered the source of the Juruena River. While riding a mule on a trail with Lieutenant Lyra and two Paresi scouts, a long arrow whizzed past his ear, another whacked his pith helmet, and a third stuck in the leather bandolier over his heart. As he calmly turned and trotted away, the Nambiquara retreated into the jungle, believing he was an immortal. He returned and left gifts for them. He later made contact and wary friendship, drawing them to his camp by playing an Italian opera on the gramophone.

It was about here, just past the Paresi plateau and onto Nambiquara land, where Rondon hugely impressed Roosevelt by his skill with Indians. Some Nambiquara had raided a Paresi village to steal women, and one of them was shot and killed by a telegraph soldier. Somehow, through conversation and negotiation—sitting on a hammock with a child on his lap—Rondon satisfied both tribes to solve the crisis that could have escalated to end the expedition. "It has been his mixture of firmness, good nature, and good judgment that has enabled him to control these bold warlike savages," wrote Roosevelt. "The Paresi received me as a friend and chieftain, to be loved and obeyed," wrote Rondon.

The mule train began passing dead beasts from Amilcar's oxen train, and other oxen left for dead with broken-down legs. Imagine Roosevelt's dismay when he saw crates in the mud along the trail with his name on them, stamped ROOSEVELT SOUTH AMERICAN EXPEDITION. The wild oxen were still bucking off the loosening crates, and the drovers weren't likely to stop and strap them back on. Or maybe, Captain Amilcar, shocked by the Americans' opulence the first time he saw them—(!) he wrote after "99 boxes"—was casting them off. To save weight for them, he had left behind a crate of his own, with hard candy.

On January 30 they reached spectacular Utiarity Falls, where the Papagaio River quietly rolls 280 feet over a cliff, taller—by 100 feet—than Niagara Falls, as Roosevelt pointed out. The wide river is swallowed by a black hole in the rainforest floor, like a tunnel to another world. The Paresi say they named the water for their descendants, the Utia, who live in the future beyond the falls.

It rained for most of the three days they stayed at Utiarity, which was ridden with malaria from mosquitoes breeding in the many pools. All seven of the telegraph station workers there had fevers. Kermit's fever had relented, but now he had saddle sores.

One long evening they watched a ceremonial dance by Paresi men, who circled, chanted, and stomped for hours, wearing only a string of beads around their waists and a rattle on one ankle. One cloudy afternoon they watched the same men play a game that TR called headball, where they dove headlong toward the dirt and used their noggins to whack an eight-inch ball made from latex. "Why they do not grind off their noses I cannot imagine," he wrote.

Rondon had never done a survey of Utiarity, and wanted to do it now, but Roosevelt wanted to keep moving so they did. Rondon had just spent a week hunting with Roosevelt, precisely what he'd told Müller he wouldn't do, and the pack train was a mess because of it. Then he had to give up maintenance of the supply road to Utiarity. Now, no survey.

There were breathtaking waterfalls for Roosevelt to enjoy; he'd spent an afternoon there, gushing with awe and appreciation. There were entertaining Indians. He was staying in his own stone house while the others camped in the rain; and there was writing to keep him busy. He could have given Rondon time for the survey. But the world was moving on without him, and he was restless. President Wilson had been leaning toward sending troops into Mexico when he left, and there was no telling what Wilson was doing now.

"In Utiarity we abandoned all hope of finishing our work," lamented Rondon.

◆

At about 3:00 A.M., the Rio Roosevelt explorers reached the camp where the road crew had been living under a plastic sheet for 18 days, and were greeted by a *churrascaria*. The woodsmen had spit-roasted a huge chunk of beef over the fire, sliced off thin succulent pieces, and served them up all-you-can-eat. After the feast we pitched tents or sacked out in the truck beds, snatching a few hours sleep.

The camp was made where the chainsaw ran out of oil. The trail to the river was cut by machete, down to sharp stumps about four inches in diameter and eight inches high. The morning passed at a walking pace, as they were trimmed.

A couple miles from the river, the truckers went on strike. Fabio had told them they would only have to take the expedition to the camp, not all the way to the headwaters; but that morning he said the Jeeps alone couldn't take the gear, and they wouldn't be paid their $700 each unless they went all the way to the headwaters. The Bandeirantes stopped in their tracks; the drivers turned off their engines and refused to go further without more money.

There was 30-minute negotiation. The truckers said there were too many spikes on the trail. Haskell said if they squeezed more money out of him he'd slash their tires at the headwaters. A compromise: no money, but the explorers had to walk ahead and cut the sharp stumps flat.

Hoots, yelps, and splashes came from the headwaters, followed by a blood-curdling yelp, as the scientist Cabral grabbed a log and two fingers touched an electric caterpillar, whose hairy black antennae inject a poison that hits like a shock, followed by hours of throbbing pain and days of swelling and numbness. Dr. Walden gave Cabral a painkiller and offered a shot of Demerol, but Cabral was tough. His fingers would have hard lumps for weeks.

Dr. Walden told the explorers that for the entire time they were in the jungle, it would be unwise to touch anything. Not a living thing, not a branch, not a leaf. Don't brush or slap at your body without looking. Never sit on a log or the ground. Do not go in the water. Cover 100 percent of your skin at all times.

Words. Cabral's pain was in living, vivid, screaming color. It kept us all safer. Remember Cabral, I would think before grabbing a branch for balance. Don't be like Cabral.

CHAPTER 11

Headwaters

Hope is a luxury no one can afford in the Amazon.
—Some dame in a B movie

It was clear from their rocky crossing of the Highlands that the Roosevelt-Rondon expedition carried impossible weight. Just past Utiariy, bodies as well as baggage had to be cut. First to go was the 63-year-old priest with a PhD that nobody but Roosevelt liked: the Reverend John Augustine Zahm, a former physics professor at Notre Dame and author of a treatise titled *Evolution and Dogma*, the introduction of which attacked Positivism; as well as two South American travel books. He'd requested and been granted an audience with Roosevelt in the final year of his presidency, hoping to draw him to the Amazon. "If Mr. Roosevelt could be induced to penetrate the little-known territory of Matto Grosso and Amazonas . . . I felt that he, with his boundless energy and prestige, could do a certain much-needed missionary work there," he would write in the chapter titled "Origin and Organization of Our Expedition," in his subsequent third South American travel book. He had his own big picture: the ex-president of the United States helping spread the word of God to the natives.

Rondon's Positivism hated missionaries. "The supreme aspiration of the pseudo-policy of Christianization of the jungle is to exploit Indigenous labor on the missions," Rondon once told a Rio newspaper.

But Zahm pitched science to Roosevelt, not religion. Christianization of the Indigenous was his "stronger reason" for wanting him, he admitted in writing; but he also knew that a visit by Roosevelt the naturalist would spur scientific exploration of the Amazon, and "Nowhere is there a richer field for the botanist, the zoologist, the geologist, the ethnologist."

Zahm and Roosevelt stayed in touch after their White House meeting. Zahm supported TR during the losing Progressive campaign when other friends had not. When Roosevelt got the invitation for the South American speeches, he met with Zahm at the American Museum of Natural History, which brought in George Cherrie, and the Roosevelt South American Scientific expedition was born, to travel up the Paraguay River and down the Tapajos.

That summer Roosevelt took his sons Archie, 19, Quentin, 15, and nephew Nicholas, 20, cougar hunting on the rugged north rim of the Grand Canyon, "the borderland between savagery and civilization," as he described it. He was awed by Pueblo cliff dwellings and intrigued by Navajo mythology, which he wrote about. In TR's absence, said Zahm, "the task of making all the necessary preparation for the long and arduous journey before us devolved on me." He fired off a letter to the Brazilian ambassador in Washington, asking for a yacht to "contribute materially to the comfort and pleasure of our journey," he said in the letter.

Zahm hired Anthony Fiala, 44, to be quartermaster, "a man of persistence and persuasive charm," said the American Alpine Club in 1950 upon his death. He sold sporting goods in a New York department store, where Zahm had met him while shopping for expedition gear and been impressed. Fiala had been a correspondent for the *Brooklyn Daily Eagle* during the Spanish-American War, and in 1901 he'd been the photographer on a failed North Pole expedition. He led a follow-up expedition in 1903, charting frozen islands in Franz Josef Land until his ship was crushed in the ice, stranding 38 men for two years. They lived in a provisions camp that had been established in advance, until a rescue party came from Norway, "who for six weeks persistently forced their way through solid floes of ice and finally reached us," Fiala told the *New York Times*.

Fiala was drawn by adventure, while being more artist than explorer. "During his two Arctic journeys, he exposed what are said to be the first motion pictures taken in the polar regions, and his artistic talent gave expression to valuable and beautiful interpretations of the aurora borealis," said the American Alpine Club.

Roosevelt supported Zahm and Fiala without paying much attention to what they were doing. The others were irritated by Zahm—baptizing Indians at every turn—and amused by Fiala, called "Thermos" by George Cherrie for his love of new technology. Unlike Zahm, Fiala did his best to be helpful. He fancied he could speak the native tongue. He asked the Nambiquara what Rio Duvida was like, and they told him, "Burrrooo-bom, burrrooo-bom."

Kermit and Cherrie were either in Roosevelt's ear or biting their tongues. They could see that Zahm and Fiala were in over their heads—anyone could, said Cherrie. Kermit called Zahm "completely incompetent and selfish," a "commonplace little fool," and an "incessant annoyance" in his diary and letters to Belle. But Zahm could quote famous poets in foreign languages and had studied the conquistadors and settlement of Brazil. He and Roosevelt could talk.

What did it take to give Zahm the boot? He'd already ridden much of the way in a truck,* offended because he had to sit beside the driver who was Black. Now he wanted to be carried Cleopatra-like in a litter on

---

* At camp on the fifth evening, a trio of trucks with their Indigenous mechanic showed up in a 30-mph cloud of dust on the red horizon, carrying more gear. They were French vehicles the Brazilian government had bought for the Telegraph Commission; like those soon to see action in WWI, they had tank-like treads attached to their wheels and could carry two tons. But they were of limited use because of the difficulty of getting them across the rivers.

the shoulders of four Paresi Indians. Rondon could see that Zahm was using TR to spread Catholicism into the Amazon, and now the insult of expecting Indians to carry him. When Rondon said no, Zahm appealed to Roosevelt. "Indians are meant to carry priests," he said, knowing full well that Rondon was "of almost pure Indian blood" as Roosevelt said, and that Roosevelt's favorite camarada, Antonio, was Paresi.

His white supremacy was over the line. Roosevelt sent his "cronie" the racist priest packing, and with him the Swiss assistant he'd brought, a former US Army nurse who cooked and repaired things, at least. Wrote Cherrie, "Dr. Zahm had gotten much on TR's nerves!"

Fiala was another story—or as Cherrie called him, the utterly incompetent Fiala. Some of the food he'd brought came from another world, such as the malted milk and marmalade. It appears that Fiala did the shopping with Zahm over his shoulder, although the Rhine wine and stuffed olives were likely Zahm's. Fiala spent a fortune on movie cameras and photography equipment, as well as a steel motorboat (Zahm's idea), with gas for the outboard engine, all intended for the original expedition.

But Fiala, having traveled more than 4,000 miles by boat and sledge in the Arctic, had some experience with cargo. When he'd been told they'd be descending the Duvida, first thing he asked was how were they going get all the gear to this extremely remote river, and what if it's full of rapids? But he goes missing in the tense discussions between Rondon and Roosevelt about baggage. For all his colorful descriptions in interviews, and creativity, he never wrote about the expedition. He never mentioned or explained how cases of olive oil and mustard were carried all the way from New York nearly to the Duvida. Rondon either missed or ignored them. Imagine Captain Amilcar's fury when he saw that for more than 500 miles he had carried a case of mustard instead of his own hard candy.

Fiala had brought two wood-framed, canvas-wrapped Canadian canoes like the North American Indians' birchbarks. Roosevelt had taken one of them tapir hunting on the Sepotuba, and pronounced it "a beauty: light, safe, roomy, made of thin slats of wood and cement-covered canvas." A canoe could carry four men and "a fair burden" of cargo, said the manufacturer, as much as half a ton; and it weighed 160 pounds, one-sixth as much as a four-man dugout. Rondon rode in it, too, but apparently dismissed the idea of taking the lightweight Canadian canoes down the Duvida—he never mentioned them.

Rondon had already ordered dugouts to be built at the headwaters by the Nambiquara, who were not known for craftsmanship. The Canadian wood-and-canvas canoes would have to be carried another three weeks. So Fiala's brainchildren were left behind to be used at the telegraph station by the Paresi.

Roosevelt let Fiala down gently (he was "almost in tears," said Cherrie), by offering him a trip down the 500-mile-long Papagaio River (named by Rondon for the parrots there) to compensate. Fiala took Leo Miller, Cherrie's young partner from the museum, two Brazilian officers, and six Paresi paddlers in three dugout canoes. On the first day, he said, "We were shooting the Diablo Rapids when suddenly our native canoes went out from under us." They lost two canoes with all their gear, and he nearly drowned. But "Augustino, a tall Indian, grabbed me by the hair and lifted me out of the water just when I was all in. He saved my life." The persistent and persuasive Fiala went back to Utiarity, got his Canadian canoes, and descended the Papagaio, Juruena, and Tapajos Rivers, running 39 rapids, he told the *New York Times*. Being a Jersey City and Brooklyn boy, a home-town explorer, and great storyteller, he was treated well by the *Times*. They called him Captain Fiala, and said it was a first descent of the Papagaio.

He didn't tell the *Times* that every member of his party contracted malaria, as Dr. Cajazeira reported, suggesting that Fiala had "imagined that we were exaggerating the damages emanating from malaria," and "abandoned the prophylaxis followed as far as Utiarity just as soon as he began to navigate the Papagaio."

In his first lecture at the Rio theater, Rondon added to the story of Fiala's near-drowning in vivid if second-hand detail. What comes through in his telling, of how a panicked Fiala pulled down the man who was trying to save him, is a powerful resentment of the discrimination against caboclos like Augustino and himself. He called Augustino a savior willing to defy death to save the White man who could barely swim, and "an inhabitant of the wilderness, an obscure hero as fearless and devoted a camarada as generally are the representatives of our strong race of caboclos, so incessantly abused by national and foreign writers, who exceed one another in criticizing all that is Brazilian, and in destroying in the minds of all the confidence in the future of our nationality, underrating the value of its men, their honor, and their character."

Whew. No wonder he wouldn't let his Paresi brothers carry Father Zahm.

Last thing before the pack train left Utiariy, Roosevelt managed to unload three more of the heavy Brazilian tents. He said it took a second round of tact with Rondon.

◆

As soon as the Bandeirante flatbeds were unloaded at the headwaters, Fabio started to return to Vilhena with the vehicles and drivers. It was a shock to the media crew, since Haskell had said at meetings that the Jeeps would stay at the headwaters until the rafts departed. The call to *Good Morning America* was out, because there was no phone; but *GMA* still expected footage of the departure, to be shown with the upcoming call from Tweed at the resupply.

And there was a dispatch that had to be written and sent with Fabio, who would FedEx it to *New York Newsday*, to be published by newspapers around the country by the *Los Angeles Times-Washington Post* news service. Fabio couldn't leave; the Jeeps were the whole plan!

Haskell said that if Fabio wanted to leave he couldn't stop him. But Charlie, you're paying him to do exactly this. "If Fabio wants to leave I can't stop him," he repeated. But he was persuaded to go to Fabio and explain the dilemma, so Fabio assigned Telmo to stay until morning with the Wrangler.

Telmo cooked another churrascaria for dinner, and afterward Oitamina asked Charlie if he might have a few words with the team. The fire threw an orange glow onto the chief's puffy face, his dark eyes like black holes. He spoke softly, as bugs and frogs sang backup.

Oitamina had been eyeing the rafts, tethered to the riverbank. He was concerned about the safety of the explorers, he said, descending the angry river in rubber boats filled with air. But he said Rio Teodoro—that's what the locals called it, a name Roosevelt himself preferred—was the river of his people, and he was well respected by them, so he would protect the team. He took out his *taboca*, a bamboo flute that he said was the voice of the Cinta Larga, and played a tune that sounded like "Mary Had a Little Lamb."

Then he retired to his tent and switched on his boombox. For the next hour Michael Jackson hooted from the forest and moonwalked around camp. Finally he fell silent as Oitamina went to sleep, snoring like a peccary.

I went to sleep in my hammock early, and awoke after midnight to write by candlelight at the camp table until daybreak, thrilled by the sounds of the jungle. As Rondon said, "It was as if all the fauna around us were conferring among themselves." The first dispatch made it to New York and ran as scheduled.

February 26, Vilhena, Rondônia, Brazil. The Amazon jungle holds many dark secrets, not least of which are the stories of explorers who have vanished into it. Over the last 450 years, countless expeditions have skipped off into the rainforest wilderness full of faith and optimism, or floated blithely away on a murky river leading into the unknown, and their horror stories remain untold for want of tellers. The Amazon jungle is known for eating its victims alive and swallowing the bones.

The Rio Roosevelt expedition hopes to descend this river formerly known as the River of Doubt, still unknown to white men, and come out alive. But as Amazon settlers will tell you, there are no guarantees in this place. As a dame once said in a dark B movie, "I didn't have the heart to tell him that hope is a luxury no one can afford in the Amazon."

It was 300 kilometers from Utiarity to Vilhena. The Roosevelt-Rondon expedition departed in the blazing sun and soon torrential rain, in sand or mud that sucked the heavily loaded oxen in place. They passed small piles of stones with a cross and a name, "desolate little mounds," said Roosevelt of those traces from Rondon's previous path. The parched bones of bullocks were scattered along the telegraph trail, along with fresh carcasses from Amilcar's train up ahead.

"There were many swollen rivers to cross," wrote Roosevelt. "Some we waded at fords. Some we crossed by rude bridges. The larger ones we crossed by ferry."

It was a wobbly platform ferry, planks strapped onto a trimaran of dugout canoes, held against the current by a cable stretching between the banks. Crossing the Buriti River, narrow, deep and fast, a mule fell overboard and a load of supplies was flushed down the river. The oxen swam. "Half a dozen of our men—whites, Indians, and negroes, all stark naked and uttering wild cries, drove the oxen into the river and then, with powerful overhand strokes, swam behind and alongside them as they crossed . . . utterly at ease in the rushing water," wrote Roosevelt.

Rondon once swam across a river pulling a raft he'd made of branches and hide, with his teeth. It's doubtful he bragged about it to TR.

By the fourth day 10 mules had dropped, leaving 42 of the beginning 98, and another 10 were teetering. One of the two oxcarts was left on the trail, as Rondon culled more crates, "always taking care that these reductions did not include in any fashion our respected guests." But they did include food for his own men. Rondon said they could live off the land, pick Brazil nuts off the ground and eat them with grubs and honey, like he had.

Roosevelt and Kermit had a talk with Rondon, and this time Roosevelt was firm. "I cross-examined Colonel Rondon, just as far as I could without having an actual break," he said. Rondon assured him that they had all the provisions they would need to get down the river. Roosevelt told Rondon that if there were any doubt, the men should continue on foot so the remaining mules could carry all the food. But Rondon would never have allowed his expedition make an ex-president walk.

Roosevelt, Kermit, and Cherrie cut their gear in half; Kermit lost photo equipment and Cherrie his taxidermy tools. TR got rid of his *The History of the Decline and Fall of the Roman Empire* but kept others. Books were as important as food to TR. "Reading with me is a disease," he once said. Rondon put it in a positive light, saying that TR "let no opportunity to acquire knowledge pass."

In that three-page confidential letter to John Keltie of the Royal Geographic Society, Roosevelt made it clear that he believed Rondon's organization was wholly misguided, and that he and Kermit could have done better; but he would never say so publicly because there was no point in doing so after the fact, and the Brazilians were such "very fine fellows."

He began the letter to Keltie, "I have given, and shall continue to give, every possible credit to my Brazilian associates for what they did in the exploration of the river. But, strictly for yourself, I must add that there would not have been any exploration if I had not taken hold of the thing."

"Their shortcomings in preparation were astonishing," he added, a judgment he skipped in *Through the Brazilian Wilderness*, also sparing his own lapse by allowing Zahm and Fiala to initially take hold of the thing. In a follow-up letter he blamed it on the "Latin mind." It wasn't just the heavy tents in pursuit of splendor. "They had all kinds of other stuff," he wrote by hand in the space between lines of the second typed letter, again mentioning that "exquisitely unfit" silver saddle.

On the sixth day they marched 20 miles "under the burning tropical sun" to reach the Juruena River and telegraph station. The wife of one of the camaradas suffered a miscarriage. It was not uncommon for wives of Rondon's men to accompany them on the telegraph line, enduring the hardships, rising at reveille at 4:00 A.M. (although not taking a swim first thing, as he always did, followed by a cup of hot mate, never coffee), washing in a river, and marching as much as two hours to the work site. Dr. Cajazeira mentions this woman in his report. She was already carrying her two-year-old, and after the miscarriage, "she continued walking 20 miles a day as if it were nothing," he wrote.

They were met at Juruena by 25 Nambiquara, "who manifested great rejoicing and surrounded us before we could get off our horses," said

Rondon, who always brought them gifts. Roosevelt called them "light-hearted robbers and murderers," who crowded, stared, and touched. They spent the night "feasting, dancing, and singing until the early hours of the morning." And drinking the native chicha, which the Nambiquara wouldn't let them refuse. Cherrie called them "real savages," whose naked dancing was vulgar and they knew it. They devoured the beef Rondon fed them, better than snakes and ants. The children spilled honey in the sand and scooped it up and ate it.

Kermit's fever was back, and his saddle sores had become boils, including one on his butt making him ride his ornery white mule standing in the stirrups. In a letter to Belle it was clear he just wanted it to be over. Rondon might have understood, remembering what it was like to be 24 and in love and separated by wilderness. Roosevelt certainly did, having been separated by worse than wilderness from Sunshine Haskell. He knew his son's heart was with his fiancée. He suggested twice to Kermit that he just skip the Duvida and go home from Vilhena. But Kermit couldn't. "I have hated this trip," he wrote Belle, "and have felt miserable enough at being so far from you." But to turn back, he added, "would be far worse than never to have come at all."

After partying with the Nambiquara all night, they rested and washed clothes for a day before crossing the river. The clear Juruena was 100 meters wide, with sandy beaches at the bottom of a deep valley. Across the river they could see Captain Amilcar's pack train in the distance, climbing the green slopes.

As they got closer to Vilhena, Rondon limited the marches to 20 kilometers per day, and gave them back lunch. They reached the Campos Novos telegraph station, with good pasture for the skeletal animals, and got 10 fresh oxen. Rondon's Uncle Miguel on his mother's side managed the farm there, which had pigs, chickens, turkeys, and goats, spit-roasted and washed down with milk ("even watermelon," said TR). Kermit shot a pheasant-like curassow with the Luger, and the cook used it to make *canja*, a Brazilian soup with fowl and rice that Roosevelt loved. Rondon teased that all TR could say in Portuguese was "mais canja."

"Our serious difficulties were over," said Roosevelt.

PART II

DESCENDING THE RIVER

CHAPTER 12

Doubt

Now I know is there, is all I can do.
—Pharmacologist Jose Cabral

Kelley Kalafatich rose first, restoring the fire's embers with twigs to make coffee. Her blond hair fell toward the fire and was turned to gold by the light of the flames. Beyond her shoulder the river lay waiting, in light ripples visible in the gray dawn, with four rafts parked against the bank and pointed downriver like racing cars at Le Mans, their fat tubes bearing big Varig and Banco Económico stickers. A green wall 100 feet high loomed across the river. The gentle notes of Oitamina's bamboo flute wafted from his tent as the others shuffled toward the fire for tin cups of Kelley's strong coffee.

Seventy-eight years and two days after Roosevelt and Rondon, the Rio Roosevelt expedition rowed off down the River of Doubt. Joe Kaminsky filmed from the bank as Tweed Roosevelt made a few remarks for *Good Morning America* from his raft in the pondlike headwaters. As the four rafts drifted around the first green bend and Kaminsky readied his kayak, he couldn't find the tape. Telmo was waiting in the Wrangler, and the rafts were getting away, so Joe gave up looking and let the Jeep go. When he caught up to the rafts he didn't say anything about losing the tape.

Birds barked at the explorers from the forest, and bugs buzzed in hot circles around their heads. A male white bellbird, loudest bird in the world and Roosevelt's favorite, hooted like a chainsaw in a tunnel. A metallic blue Morpho butterfly, big as a salad plate, floated past. A cayman, *jacare*, sunning on a bank at a switchback, stood and stared back, stretching its leathery neck to stand five feet tall. TR called them "dull-nerved, cold-blooded creatures," adding, "They are often dangerous to domestic animals, and are always destructive to fish, and it is good to shoot them." He and Kermit picked them off from their boat for target practice.

We reached the remains of the telegraph bridge where Rondon and Roosevelt began. Two empty beer bottles and a small pile of fish bones lay in the grass at the base of the bridge.

The river flowed slowly, winding tight into the jungle. "The course wound hither and thither, sometimes in sigmoid curves," Roosevelt said, noting that for every kilometer of northward progress there were two kilometers traveled. The boatmen cranked casually on the long wooden oars, deftly maneuvering the rafts forward, backward, and sideways, following currents and eddies. A green arch closed over us. Vines coiled up trees and along branches, dangling back down to the water. Wooded liana vines crawled along the earth and reached for sunlight. Climbers and creepers filled every gap.

Strands of boritana palm grew to the surface, goosed by the current into a samba-like sway. The water rippled over branches, and stems stuck up like spikes around *Indios Isolados*. The raft bottoms were sneaker-sole rubber; over a rock, a bulge moved along the bilge like a rat under a rug. But the tubes on the sides were vulnerable. Mike Boyle hit a branch that poked a small hole in one tube, easily patched. "Good thing it didn't happen to me," Kelley told him, "or I would have been the dumb girl."

The pharmacologist Cabral hoped to research the medicinal uses of rainforest plants by gathering specimens and interviewing Indigenous people. He spotted something he wanted, a *catasetum* of the orchid family, growing like a pod of cigars on a branch over the river. It was an aphrodisiac popular with Brazilian men; just mash it up, mix it with a drink, and stand back, he said. He asked Boyle to move in so he could snatch some, and Boyle cheerfully did so, but it took a few minutes and put them behind the others. Cabral saw how it was going to be. "It's very frustrate for me," he said. "I can see, but I can't bring with me. Now I know is there, is all I can do."

As we were making camp, a distant buzz turned into a scary whine, like an avalanche of insects zooming in; as we looked at each other with widening eyes, it turned away, replaced by the roar of Charlie's chainsaw, cutting small trees that a machete could hack. Charlie didn't see the same chainsaw the others did, a big, loud, bright yellow symbol of what the expedition was trying to avoid.

In the evening, the explorers were treated to gentle New Age music from the Walkman of photojournalist Greenberg, which he had placed in a bucket to reach a wider audience. With popular support, the next day Captain Slade made a new rule: Any electronic device playing music will be fed to the piranhas, maybe along with its owner, and that includes Chief Oitamina.

◆

The Roosevelt-Rondon expedition reached the Duvida on the evening of February 25. The Nambiquara dugout canoes were disappointing. "One was small, one was cranky, and two were old, waterlogged, and leaky. The other three were good," said Roosevelt. Rondon could have built two or three new ones, but didn't. That night two canoes sank in the rain while roped to the bank. Kermit helped the camaradas drag them out of the water, as they were all stung by wasps. They spent the day sealing seams with sap on all seven boats.

All of Rondon's previous expeditions into the region had been in the dry season, for good reason. This one was in rainy season because that's

when Roosevelt was there. But it was Rondon who took them in deep
to the Duvida, knowing that the difficulties and dangers, including to
health, would be greater; and that food, both animal and vegetable, would
be much harder to find. "Everything became moldy except what became
rusty," said Roosevelt.

They knew there would be rapids, because the elevation of the telegraph
station at Vilhena was 832 feet, making a long drop to sea level. Roosevelt
said "no one knew whither" the Duvida flowed, but Rondon was pretty
sure it met the Aripuaña. He had sketched every curve of every river in
the Amazon that he was sure of, most of which he'd discovered himself.
He said the Duvida was "wedged in the interior of great wilderness by
rivers," and couldn't get out without running into one of them; but the few
cartographers and South American explorers couldn't agree which one,
after corresponding for a couple of years. Rondon argued that his evidence
pointing to the Aripuaña was "valid and decisive," but recognized that it
could only be proved by exploration. "It would have to be decided by the
Roosevelt-Rondon expedition," he said.

Roosevelt, Kermit, and Rondon went over the food a final time. There
were 50 tins of rations, each with food for 6 men for a day, giving them 50
days to descend the river. Enough for the six of them, including Cherrie,
Lyra, and Dr. Cajazeira, but none for the 16 camaradas—13 caboclos, one
White, one Black, and one Indian, whom TR said were "lithe as panthers
and brawny as bears," adding that they "looked like pirates" but were
"hard-working, willing, and cheerful." And two dogs, Rondon's Lobo and
Kermit's Trigueiro.

Roosevelt would write Keltie of the Royal Geographic Society, "When
we got on the Unknown River I found that despite his explicit assurances
to the contrary, he [Rondon] had left behind several muleloads of provisions
for our boatmen, including the sugar,* which is necessary for an exhausting

---

*   There were things that Roosevelt didn't know, for example that sugar wasn't needed
     because honey hung from trees, and sap could be boiled into sweet syrup; and that
     cassava root was better than the heavy sacks of wheat flour that came down from
     New York.

trip. Of course there was no remedy for this; and I simply cut down our own rations one-half at the outset, giving the rest to the paddlers. We therefore began with half rations.

"I was well aware that there was a chance of disaster because of this rather absurd lack of forethought, but I was not going to give up on the trip. Of course, it would have been mere folly for me to have quarreled with my companions about what was then too late to remedy. I simply took charge of things from that time on, exercising through Kermit a close supervision over everything that was done but being more than courteous and polite and friendly with my Brazilian companions."

Strapped to oxen, the last three tents made it as far as the headwaters. "I had to insist on throwing away those that were left," said Roosevelt. "It almost broke the heart of good Colonel Rondon." In fact, as Rondon would write, he was glad to be rid of them.

That night they wrote letters to be carried to Manaus by Leo Miller from the Museum of Natural History. Cherrie was wistful, hoping he would make it home to his Vermont farm in time to plant potatoes in spring. Kermit wrote his mother, with no small wit. "Here we are ready to start down the Duvida, all well and cheerful. No one has an idea, or at least everybody has half a dozen—which come to the same thing—as to where the Duvida goes."

Roosevelt sent a short cable to the *New York Times* that became a one-paragraph front-page story on February 28, with the headline ROOSEVELT FINDS A RIVER. He finished his seventh dispatch/chapter for *Scribner's*, and bundled it with 45 of Kermit's and Cherrie's photos.

"If the river proved very long and difficult, if we lost our boats over falls or in rapids, or had to make too many and too long portages, or were brought to a halt by impassable swamps, then we would have to reckon with starvation as a possibility," he wrote. "Anything might happen."

"On February 27, 1914, shortly after midday, we started down the River of Doubt into the unknown."

CHAPTER 13

Oitamina

Nobody comes to the forest to see the truth.
—Chief Oitamina, aka Roberto Carlos

C hief Oitamina perched on the tube in the back of Mike Boyle's raft with his short legs dangling overboard and broad leathery feet skimming the water. He wore paisley jams, a Banco Económico T-shirt, and a dark blue JEEP cap that he kept taking off and putting back on, as if the cap gave him status but not comfort and he couldn't decide which was more important. With pharmacologist Cabral translating, he answered my questions with thoughtful replies, speaking softly and simply in Portuguese, rhythmic responses that all began with "*nanh-nanh-nanh iee*," and were described by delicate gestures, even as he tugged the bottom of his shirt where it exposed his big brown belly.

He said he was 34, but as they say in Brazil about Indians and numbers, that might be plus or minus 500 percent. He was about five-foot-four with a Buddha belly and short legs, arms, and fingers. He had a ruddy face with puffy cheeks, a high wide nose, rectangular ears, thick black hair, a shiny gold bicuspid, and sparse chin whiskers like electric-caterpillar bristles.

"I am the George Bush of the Cinta Larga nation," he boasts, flashing his best gold-toothed grin. "There are six Cinta Larga villages in Rondônia and Mato Grosso"—he counts the villages on stubby fingers—"and I am the chief of all the Indians in both States. Piu obeys me. Tatare is third in line. In my language, the name Oitamina means *I am a man*."

But mostly he goes by Roberto: I am a rock star.

I ask him what he sees in the future for the Cinta Larga. He raises his dark eyes to the white sky, as his hands beseech the gods. He turns to the forest and scans the treetops for answers, and goes off on a tangent.

"In the last two or three years the Cinta Larga have gotten a lot of bad press," he replies. "People say we are destroying the forest; we try to sell all the trees. People from the other nations, like France and Europe, think that the Cinta Larga only want money and big cars, and don't care for the forest. But this is not true.

"Nobody comes to the forest to see the truth. That is why we have allowed the Rio Roosevelt expedition onto our land, to show that we still have all the good things, like the mahogany and fish in the river. We want you to see that we are good, and to tell the world that we take care of our forest."

When BR-364 was cut through the Amazon, Brazil's military government took 2.5 million acres of Indigenous land, much of it on what is now the Roosevelt Indigenous Area. It was given away to ranchers and farmers in parcels with vague property lines, so there were disputes and sometimes violence; but the road created growth as intended, while decimating the Indigenous population in the road's path and beyond, which was unintended but predictable.

Oitamina was born near Rio Roosevelt in about 1958. When he was six, as the road came through, his father and uncle, both chiefs, were killed by seringueiros. His mother, one of his father's four wives, continued to raise him. Five of his eight siblings died in one epidemic of mumps that swept through after they'd been contacted.

"Thousands of people died, everywhere in Rondônia," Chief Piu would say later, taking over the story. "My father died, my mother died, my uncle died, my aunt died, they all died of diseases. There were four of us kids, and we were left alone, abandoned. We didn't know what to do; we felt quite lost. Then my brother died. I buried him. I was one of the only people who didn't get sick. I was seven years old.

"One of the adults took us away from the dying, to the village where Roberto lived. She didn't know that the same thing was happening there. At that time I was inexperienced. I wasn't strong. Roberto was three years older than me. He took care of me, he saved me. Nobody would believe what we went through at that time. We ate mice and rats to survive."

Oitamina's contact came on the banks of the Rio Roosevelt, about a year before *National Geographic* contacted the Cinta Larga in 1970. Attracted by the sound of an outboard motor, he and others found two garimpeiros, gold prospectors, and threatened them with arrows, spears, and scary faces. The garimpeiros offered them food. An opening lesson in *esperto*, or craftiness: scare the White men and they'll give you things. "The garimpeiros were afraid of Indians, so they let us take anything we wanted," says Oitamina.

I snapped open my watertight briefcase and took out a child's drawing to show Oitamina. At May Street Elementary School in my hometown of Hood River, Oregon, I'd dazzled the kids with visions of pink dolphins, snails big as apples, butterflies quick as hummingbirds. Vampire bats sucking big toes, spiders crawling like octopuses, bees like basketballs, anacondas able to swallow a fat man, and giant catfish that leaped out of the river to snatch monkeys from trees. And fierce Indians tamed by kazoos.

The kids drew pictures, and I'd brought my favorite one along. Titled *Sam's in Trouble*, I was staring down the shaft of an arrow in the drawn bow held by a red-skinned savage. I had a kazoo between my lips and was frantically blowing notes, as a laughing chief stood nearby saying, "Stop, don't shoot, this guy is funny!"

I passed the picture to Oitamina and tried to explain it all, including the anthropologist who told us a kazoo was the best defense against wild

Indians. When Cabral finished interpreting, Oitamina tilted his head, squinted, and imagined it; then he howled with laughter, his gold tooth glowing from his happy mouth. He loved the reputation his tribe had on the other side of the world.

◆

Colonel Rondon made it clear that his mission was to chart the River of Doubt, not merely descend it. He could not have been luckier, to have Kermit Roosevelt along. An engineer straight from two years building bridges in the Xingu, a daring canoeist, and a young man with inexhaustible energy, Kermit stepped up and said, I can help with that.

They stopped 114 times on the first day, moving from eddy to eddy in performing a fixed-station survey. Kermit, leading in the smallest of the three good canoes with two paddlers, would stick a sighting rod into the ground, while Rondon and Lyra followed in the midsize canoe with three paddlers, taking readings using a compass, barometer, and theodolite, a surveying instrument with a rotating telescope that could measure horizontal and vertical angles, to determine distance.

But the Bull Moose needed to keep moving. There wasn't much action in his dugout watching a survey, so he went ahead to look for a camp, in the big canoe with George Cherrie.

Time was the issue. Rondon's job wasn't part of Roosevelt's plan. He had agreed to chart the river with Rondon, apparently without realizing how slow and tedious it would be. Charting the river reduced the esteemed guest to tagging along. And, he could see that it exposed his son to the first arrow from an Indian attack.

They made 80 kilometers in the first four days. Kermit shot a monkey for dinner and TR said it was good eating, like piranhas and jaguars. Then came *burrrooo-bom, burrrooo-bom*, whitewater that stopped the canoes. They hacked through the jungle at the riverbank for nearly a mile, along continuous rapids that tapered into a very narrow torrent between walls, before crashing over two six-foot waterfalls. They named them Navaite Falls, for a subgroup of Nambiquara that lived in the forest there, according to TR.

The campfire conversation grew serious. "We were still wholly unable to tell where we were going or what lay ahead of us," said Roosevelt. "We had no idea how much time the trip would take. We had entered a land of unknown possibilities."

◆

Oitamina moved to the bow of Boyle's raft and straddled the fat tube as if it were a rocking horse. He took off his T-shirt and let his belly hang over his jams. Around his neck were six strands of what looked like black leather, hundreds of tiny beads from palm nutshells, chipped, rounded, drilled, and threaded onto a string of vine to make the necklace. A rotating halo of red and yellow butterflies spun around the chief's head. He continued to scan the treetops for things only he could see. His soft voice carried over the buzz of a bumblebee big as a golf ball, as he continued his story.

Drawn by free food, young Oitamina started hanging around the garimpeiros' camp—the food was salty but you didn't have to go hunting all day to get it, he says with a chuckle. At 12 he left his tribe to live with them. They liked him, and gave him clothes and a machete. They called him Roberto Carlos because of his big hair like the Brazilian pop singer up there in popularity with Elvis. Oitamina liked the name and kept it; today he introduces himself as Roberto, and his fellow Cinta Larga rarely refer to him by his Indian name.

Oitamina and Piu made their way to Espigao d'Oeste, skyscraper of the west, 30 miles into the jungle from the dirt road that was BR-364. From coffee plantation to boomtown and beyond, overnight. First tractors, then bridges, trucks, machinery, and a big chugging generator for lights. A sawmill cut logs into planks to build tin-roofed houses. In Espigao there was coffee, sugar, raincoats, tools, tobacco, and rum! Oitamina shoots his arm into the air in excitement.

Cinta Larga and Surui were drawn there, and in time there were gentle, sad Indians in the muddy streets of Espigao begging for food and money, which they didn't understand. FUNAI doctors found young Indian girls with venereal diseases, dropped off by truck drivers along BR-364. Oitamina's hand drops over his heart.

CHAPTER 14

Diamonds

Sweetest 25 bucks I ever made.
—Kelley Kalafatich

The Roosevelt-Rondon expedition needed two-and-one-half days of "severe and incessant labor" to get around Navaite rapids and falls, working in a drizzle under branches shedding fire ants. For more than a mile in rapids, they guided the empty dugout canoes by ropes, as they struggled to stay on their feet, sometimes dragging them through the jungle along the riverbank.

Roosevelt's big dugout was split when it bashed against the rocks, and another canoe sank and was dragged back. They had swollen hands and faces, "bitten by huge horse-flies, the size of bumblebees," said Roosevelt. Kermit was bitten by a big black ant, probably a bullet ant, named for its bite that feels like a hot bullet. The pain almost made him forget about the boils on his thighs.

Roosevelt's description of the portage is a vision of Hell. "A road was chopped through the forest and a couple of hundred stout six-foot poles,

or small logs, were cut as rollers and placed about two yards apart. With
block and tackle the seven dugouts were hoisted out of the river and up the
steep banks, and up the rise of ground until the level was reached. Then
the men harnessed themselves two by two on the drag-rope, while one of
their number pried behind with a lever, and the canoe, bumping and sliding,
was twitched through the woods."

◆

When it was time to camp, Chief Oitamina told Captain Slade to park
the rafts against an overgrown bank. Oitamina walked off into the jungle,
as Tatare mumbled that he was nuts. He stayed gone while the dubious
explorers swatted insects, and came back saying it was a good place to camp.
He said "follow me," and floated back into the jungle.

The explorers pulled out their machetes and hacked away. At the front,
Dr. Walden called, "Hey! Look over here!" He found scorched posts with
M.I. FUNAI carved on them, for Ministerio do Interior; they'd been stilts
for a shelter. In 1986, a team of FUNAI surveyors descended some 200
kilometers of the Rio Roosevelt, mapping the land and marking boundaries
prior to demarcation of the huge Aripuaña Park, seven times bigger than the
900-square-mile Roosevelt Indigenous Area on the west side of the river.

If Oitamina knew the old FUNAI camp was there, he didn't let on. The
explorers marveled at his sixth sense, and he accepted their awe. He used a
Cinta Larga expression: *Giana-kanapo*, meaning "I told you so."

As dinner was being cooked by a rotating four-person crew, Oitamina
visited Tweed's tent for a chief-to-chief chat—Tweed was a chief by birth-
right, he said. He wanted to talk about the legacy of Theodore Roosevelt.
Tweed was hanging a white sheet with a gas lamp behind it, a big bug
magnet. He wore a khaki safari suit and green shrimper boots, and a camp
table held a butterfly net and insect guidebook.

Oitamina wanted Tweed's opinion on an environmental matter. He
brought the INPA forest biologist, Joao Ferraz—"Joba" to his friends—to
interpret. He said there were diamonds in the river, as well as gold, and

because of this, and because the river was beautiful, many people wanted
to see it. "They come to Porto Velho and ask permission from FUNAI,
and FUNAI asks the Cinta Larga if it's okay," he said, "but we set a price
that's very high so they don't come." After the expedition many people from
Tweed's world would want to come and enjoy the river. What did Tweed
see in the future for Rio Teodoro?

It was a sophisticated question requiring a speculative answer, which
Tweed wasn't prepared for. So he gave a diplomatic one, saying he hoped
the Rio Roosevelt expedition and Theodore Roosevelt's history would be
used to gain respect for the river, which would help the Cinta Larga protect
it. Oitamina considered this for a moment, then told Tweed a story. Tatare
stood nearby, staring at the dark ripples on the river, appearing uninterested.

"It has been handed down for three generations among the Cinta Larga,
the history of the expedition by Roosevelt and Rondon," said Oitamina.
"Roosevelt and Rondon collected gold and diamonds from the river and
made a figurine from them. They buried this treasure along the river with
its head facing downriver, so its spirit can travel down the river and roam
without resistance. It's a monument to the land.

"We know that Rondon and Roosevelt preached that the Indians
and the forest must never be molested. This statue is their spirit, and it
protects the Cinta Larga and their forest. The statue is sacred, and that's
why we take such good care of the land, and oppose all people cutting trees
in the forest. Because you are the great-grandson of Theodore Roosevelt,
and the statue is his soul, we want the Rio Roosevelt expedition to see that
we have preserved the forest."

There was another thing Oitamina wanted to discuss with Tweed.
"When I go to meetings in Brasilia to represent my people with officials
from FUNAI and IBAMA, people don't believe an Indian can speak
so well. When I explain all the problems of my people in detail and in
an articulate manner, they are surprised. Many people there have much
schooling, but I was born in the jungle, my education is not on paper. What
is important is what people speak from the mind and heart, not on paper.
Don't you agree?"

"Yes, I do," replied Tweed. "You are very wise."

"Un-huh. But sometimes I have trouble, because sometimes I meet people and they say, 'You are a chief, but my God, you are so small!'"

"Many great men were small. Napoleon was very short, and he was a great warrior," Tweed replied, forgetting Rondon, who was five-three. He missed the opportunity to tell Chief Oitamina he was like Colonel Rondon.

Assured that his height didn't stand in the way of his leadership, Oitamina ended the conversation. "Only the gods know what the future is," he said with a wise sigh.

As I fell asleep in my hammock that night, I heard a siren screaming in the distance on Manhattan's West Side Highway. I awoke a few hours later to the thump-thump of a drumstick beating on a Tupperware bowl, increasing in tempo to announce the deluge before dawn.

◆

Garimpeiros and Indigenous people knew that the narrow rapids trapped diamonds on the river bottom below the falls. Oitamina said Piu had scored at Navaite a couple years ago, dredging diamonds and selling them in Cuiabá. There were fewer garimpeiros now, he said. "People don't come to catch diamonds because they are afraid FUNAI will arrest them, or the Cinta Larga will kill them."

One of the earliest garimpeiros on the Rio Roosevelt was a man named Augusto, who dug for diamonds in the river in the late 1940s. "It was hard, but diamond seekers are not afraid," he told me. "They are courageous, and they confront death.

"I lived in the forest along the Duvida. I have traveled the full length of the river many times, and I know it well. Life was very hard in those days, and the Cinta Larga were very hostile. The chances of being pierced by the arrow of an Indian or the fang of a cobra were great. And it was accepted that you would be bitten by the mosquito that carries malaria; I have had the disease six times, myself."

When Augusto was digging for diamonds he wore a primitive deep-sea diver suit with its 30-pound helmet on his shoulders, as a partner manually pumped air down from the riverbank. At depths up to 45 feet he says, he groped around on his hands and knees in total darkness, filling a burlap sack with rocks and pebbles for his partner to haul up. There were many ways to die: caymans, piranhas, anacondas, stingrays, and electric eels in the water, but more likely mechanical failure of the pump. Or the pumper might be shot by another garimpeiro, who could get two men with one bullet and take over the operation. Or the partner might find diamonds in the sack and cut the hose to the diver.

"I was attacked several times by Indians, but not by Cinta Larga. When I was a diamond seeker on the Duvida, the problems were with other garimpeiros who were envious. The Cinta Larga would sometimes attack diamond seekers, but only when you wandered from camp. They are smart. When you stay together they don't attack."

Twice in his three years at the bottom of Rio Roosevelt, Augusto found huge diamonds, which he sold to travel around Brazil, and to South America, Europe, and the US—New York, Philadelphia, and Washington, DC. He says he will forever remember the view from the top of the Empire State Building.

Augusto was now a charismatic old man living in Porto Velho, the leader of a cult of believers in the power of a hallucinogenic brew he called *vegetal*. His late garimpeiro partner Gabriel had founded the cult, after dreaming he was in the forest and picked two plants, *chacrona* and *mariri*, boiled them in water from Navaite Falls, drank the bitter tea, closed his eyes, and saw the future.

Augusto said that vegetal means "plant," although a tighter translation says "vegetable." That's all he's ever called it—the plant. He says the high state of spirituality that comes from drinking it is called *borracheira*, the word for "tire-changer" or maybe "flat-fixer." Things have been lost in translation, or not. The plant enables you to fix the journey.

When Augusto describes the path to borracheira, it sounds like a jungle echo of Colonel Rondon's orthodox Positivism: "sympathy for all beings, toward whom one feels brotherhood," and "everything converges toward Love and the Common Good." He showed the positive effects of four decades of drinking the plant. He was strong, mellow, bright, cheerful, alert, lean, and fit, with a sharp sense of humor and distinguished gray hair.

One of his followers was a woman named Silvia, who cooked tropical-fruit chocolates in her kitchen and sold them out of wicker baskets, delivering around Porto Velho in a beat-up Volkswagen Thing. She sold her rainforest bonbons to the Rondon Palace hotel where the Rio Roosevelt expedition stayed two nights; in the lobby she met Mario Peixoto and invited him to try vegetal at Augusto's house. Mario wanted a companion for the trip, and invited me.

Silvia wore a cotton granny dress, clogs, straw hat, and Indian charm necklace. She had a soft voice, easy smile, gentle dark eyes, and a tell-tale streak of gray that fell to the side of her forehead. As we bounced over the bumpy streets to Augusto's house in her Thing, she said the two plants represented the paths of force and light, and when merged they lead to harmony with nature through clarity of vision offered in vivid scenes of the future.

Augusto's modest cinder block house was surrounded by cement walls with sharp pieces of broken bottles embedded at the top. Inside it was tranquil, a living room surrounded by rainforest murals painted on smooth stucco walls. In the biggest painting, vegetal vines writhed up a thick tree, as snakes and parrots filled branches, and two golden-bellied macaws flew between puffy clouds in the blue sky. A Santa Claus hung from a long branch, saying "Feliz Natal" to all.

A white rabbit, tripping on the plant, poked around on the cement floor. A small archway led to a garden, where a shaky six-foot television antenna stood between chacrona and mariri plants growing in the corners against the chipped whitewashed walls.

Among six others there was a seringueiro named Antonio, a teenage girl with long black hair, a girl about seven, and a four-year-old boy named Solsano, with dark curly hair and Milk-Dud eyes. Solsano's mother said he was beautiful because he'd been nourished by the plant when he was in her womb—and, she added, he was high at that moment, wildly steering a dump truck on the floor and crashing it into a three-legged plastic giraffe. A normal four-year-old, with mesmerizing spooky gorgeous wide eyes.

Mario interpreted as I interviewed Augusto about his days diving for diamonds on the Duvida. A small red hen sat chirping on the arm of his vinyl easy chair. His wife came out of the kitchen carrying a pink plastic pitcher and poured half-glasses of chilled vegetal like thick cloudy tea, brewed by boiling chacrona and mariri in a tub all day. Augusto recommended chugging it, since it was too bitter to sip.

We moved to a chapel-like room to wait for the vision, as awful Brazilian pop music blasted from a cheap stereo wired to two four-foot-high speakers that bounced the sound off the tile and stucco. Blaring horns and brutal percussion played a disco/samba/mariachi. A chorus screamed along. Silvia said they were singing messages of peace, love, and harmony.

Twenty patio chairs faced a podium with a poster of Gabriel holding a glass of vegetal as a beam of divine light touched his hands. Nearby was a big photo in a green metalflake frame of Augusto, 30 years younger, a black mustache under his dark eyes, looking like a dictator in a blue shirt with epaulets and gold stars. Between them was a chest-high picture of scales, symbolizing balance, and a big pyramid with plastic letters saying UNION DO VEGETAL.

We trippers were told to close our eyes and empty our minds but the music made it impossible; and the ceiling lights were so bright when you closed your eyes you saw orange. The bulbs were barely shaded by blue paper-mache falling like fringe from the ceiling.

The seringueiro Antonio sat in a chair in the corner, one ear inches from a speaker. He muted the sound and began to sing and chant, and it was like heaven for a few moments until he turned the blaring music back up, two or three times between agony and ecstasy.

Except for making Antonio's patio rocker look like a praying mantis, the plant hadn't much effect on me. Mario saw no visions but was lightly freaking out. He checked his anxiety by going back in the living room and talking to Silvia. She was eager to turn on if not convert her new friends, so she offered another four-ounce glass, which I accepted.

Things started to kick in then. I closed and covered my eyes to block out the ceiling lights. I felt my pulse in my tonsils, beating time to the samba music. My hands were like an infrared lens, as I watched a grass hut turn into a two-car garage with open doors. Carr Clifton's face, horizontal and grinning goofily, jumped in like a photo bomb, filling the frame, making me laugh out loud. An intricate orange cobweb flashed like a thin neon light against a dark empty background.

That was all. Silvia took Mario and me back to the Rondon Palace where I wrote for a while and then threw up, as Mario was doing in his room. I got in bed and closed my eyes and the trip began.

I sat up with a start. I'd seen the face of a demon, with glowing yellow eyes and a comic-book expression of evil, looking into my face as it floated upward out of sight.

I lay back down, closed my eyes, and waited. A second demon, with menacing red eyes, popped up as if out of a toaster, and glided through the top of a black box; followed by a third, with fangs and a grimace.

I closed my eyes again. Two more demons with less angry eyes passed upward, like gliding bears in an arcade shooting game, and after a while another dropped by, and then they stopped.

I tried to bring them back by closing my eyes and imagining one. When that didn't work I focused on the spot where they had appeared, making beams of light from my eyeballs like Superman with his X-ray vision, and a new demon popped up. After two more I lost the power and fell asleep, twice startled awake by vivid flash dreams I can't remember.

Silvia said that after the trip the force would be with us. Mario never felt much, but for me it was energy. I was awake, alert, and productive for 80 of the next 88 hours, and then slipped into a normal sleep pattern without crashing. And I felt a certain calm, confidence, and clarity for the next week or so, my toe lingering in the waters of borracheira.

I had seen the future. Two days later Carr Clifton sneaked up behind me and, wearing a goofy grin, suddenly poked his face inches in front of mine. And months later the demons returned, lolling on blankets spread on the sidewalk at Copacabana Beach, replicas down to the angry red eyes. They were molded clay marijuana pipes, shaped by Argentinian artisans and sold on the street.

The next day pharmacologist Jose Cabral laughed when I told him about the evening. "Yes, it's like a movie!" he said, adding that he had taken a few trips himself. His son was follower of a similar cult in Manaus. "My son, the first time he take it, he see things with his eyes open! Me, I have open eyes is normal. I close my eyes it begin. But my son! He can be talking to you, and he see things now."

Then he told me of his own vision. On one of his vegetal trips he had been flying, and looked down on a city. Years later he got an invitation to speak at a seminar in Memphis, and when the plane approached the airport prior to landing, he recognized the city he'd never seen.

Navaite rapids began as a distant deep hiss from around a bend, growing to a faint roar, as Kaminsky beached his kayak and the rafts followed. The boatmen and a couple followers got out and walked along the bank to get a close look at the long rapids.

"This is nothing!" said Tweed. "You see people on TV going down stuff like this all the time."

Captain Slade admonished him. "This is *serious*," he said. "Make a mistake, you die." Added boatman Boyle, "There's no reason anybody should be going down this rapid for fun. There are big consequences down there."

Rapids are graded by size, speed, and drop. Class I is a bit bumpy, Class VI is a run of big drops. Classes III, IV, and V include factors such as technical difficulty or consequence: a Class III technical rapid might be bumped up to IV or V if it's a two-day hike to get out after a crash.

Slade was basically saying that in the Amazon, where everything is deadly, it's all Class V. Slade and Boyle were responsible for the safety of a bunch of whitewater greenhorns, and the first lesson was respect for the water.

After some discussion, Slade decided that each raft should carry just one passenger, positioned forward to balance the weight of the gear in back. The rest would walk. This raised the issue of who should ride . . . because why? Each boatman could have chosen his or her passenger, based on their weight and confidence, but there was more than efficiency at play. There was a big picture, literally: the video.

As expedition leader, Haskell could have chosen the four riders. But he'd stepped away from that role when the rafts hit the water, and seemed relieved that Slade was boss now. He was ready to enjoy the expedition like everybody else.

Slade allowed a discussion to choose the riders, which couldn't escape the question of why the expedition was there. Was it about adventure, science, education, or media? When the choices were made, it appeared that entertainment ruled. It made little difference. Tweed was right. The rapids were nothing. It seemed to surprise Slade that we ran them so easily, but if he felt silly crying wolf he didn't show it.

A star emerged in Navaite rapids, as Kelley Kalafatich nailed the technical line. At five-foot-five and 120 pounds, lacking brute force, she rowed with her head, finding clean lines in gnarly sections. For half of her 31 years, her life had been whitewater. Her first boyfriend was a guide on the American River in Northern California, and when they rafted together he turned over the oars. In time she had it down. One Saturday a guide missed his boat and she stepped in. "Sweetest 25 bucks I ever made," she said.

She turned pro the next year at 17 when she graduated high school, and worked her way through most of American River College by guiding on the Stanislaus and Tuolumne Rivers. When she got a job offer with a pioneering rafting outfit on the Zambezi River in Zimbabwe, she never looked back. For four years she lived at the top of Victoria Falls, called the smoke that thunders. "Every day I felt fully alive," she said, even dealing with land mines from the Rhodesian Bush War.

After a stint on the Boh River in Borneo, Indonesia, she now worked in winter for Sobek on the wicked Bio Bio in Chile, and summer guiding with Joe Willie Jones in Alaska. She figured she had more experience in big rapids than any of the other guides, including Slade. She was hired for the job because she was a woman—Mountain Travel Sobek told her that, she says—as Mario Peixoto was chosen because he was Brazilian.

Sometimes she was the only woman on a raft trip, and being the guide and leader made it easier. She learned how to get along with guys, how to deal with them and put up with them, and she put up with a lot before she proved herself. Now she did it with ease, but still had to let some things slide. She called herself a boatman, laughing at the notion of "boatperson." She could pull her shorts aside and pee off the back of the boat and no one even knew it.

Kelley's attitude toward hard work and discomfort was the best; she was first to help and last to complain. She strove for diplomacy and generosity when others lacked patience, self-discipline, or self-control. Without her uplifting spirit and beauty, the expedition would have been double-doomed.

CHAPTER 15

Mahogany

I doubt if I would still be alive if I
had stayed in the forest.
—Chief Piu

The Rio Roosevelt expedition rafts were beached about 50 yards above Navaite Falls, two six-foot waterfalls that looked like gushing root beer, tumbling into a small rocky gorge that drove the river through a skinny gap in the sandstone walls. A photo in *Through the Brazilian Wilderness* shows Roosevelt reaching all the way across the river with his rifle. Tweed would reenact the picture on its 78th anniversary, using a butterfly net. He had a healthy dose of the stuff that fired his superhuman great-grandfather: intelligence, education, vision, good cheer, spirit for adventure, and a fierce sense of self-interest.

A log spanned the skinny gorge over the sluicing water, leading to broad flat rocks littered with two tin cans, a few chunks of an old blanket, and a soggy two-month-old copy of *Manchete*, a weekly magazine of everything sensational, mostly celebrity and skin. Who recently sat there, eating beans and thinking who-knows-what? Possibly a garimpeiro, digging for diamonds in the pools below the falls. Maybe it was "JRS," who painted his initials on the rock at the entrance to the heart of the jungle.

When Rondon and Roosevelt camped in the same grass, they were ravaged by sand flies, pium, and invisible boroshuda—they were the worst, said Roosevelt: "They brought the blood at once, and left marks that lasted for weeks." He tried something called Fly Dope, and wrote a brief review of the product that could describe insect lotion today: lasts about half an hour, effective until sweat slides it off.

There were nine charred posts, remnants of a garimpeiro camp the Cinta Larga had burned, and termite nests growing like tumors high on the trunks of trees. The termites there ate Roosevelt's skivvies, and Cherrie found his poncho "literally alive" with them, but they left us modern explorers alone, having no taste for rubber and Gore-Tex.

That night, a sweet breeze from the river carried the clickety-clacks of cicadas over the whoosh of the waterfall. A giant in high-top sneakers skipped along the waxed hardwood floor under my hammock.

Chip Haskell radioed the Brazilian Air Force in Manaus, and was relayed a message from Beth McKnight saying she would be a day late to the resupply, because Joe Willie was having trouble getting the fifth raft through customs in São Paulo. So it was a day off at Navaite Falls. The waterfall over a small slab of sandstone got continuous use as a lovely shower. Pharmacologist Cabral grabbed Chief Oitamina for a hike to gather medicinal plants, although the chief told him that no secrets would be revealed. Carr Clifton and Tweed went looking for butterflies, armed with camera and net. Tatare found a dark *tuari* tree, made slits in the bark with his machete, and stripped off about four vertical feet to take home and make a broad belt, a *cinta larga*.

Slade studied his research material and Boyle smoked cigars, watching the smoke drift through his cowboy mustache as he read a Louis L'Amour paperback. He fished from the bank for piranha and caught four that were good eating like TR said. The ichthyologist Mendes caught no fish, his net thwarted by current.

We all were covered with bites and racked with itching, except the Indians and Dr. Walden; I awoke every night and scratched for 30 minutes from knees to feet. Dr. Walden said preventing bites was simple, stupid: just stay covered from head to toe at all times, and seal the cracks with insect repellent. Even so, the bugs could stick their evil little needle-noses through T-shirts and inject their itching venom; Tweed and Joba had bites and welts on their backs and shoulders. The bites could last for weeks or months, said Walden, especially from the chiggers now living under the skin of the shins and ankles of those who wore shorts on the push to the river. The doctor practiced the medicine he preached, and slept comfortably at night.

Oitamina and Tatare swatted mosquitoes same as the White people, but no bites appeared on their brown bodies wearing only jams—Tatare's were lime green. But Oitamina said he was sometimes taken down by malaria, brought in on BR-364.

That evening Oitamina wanted to talk to me, so we met in the scientists' tent. He was curious about the Native Americans—not unlike Rondon, who researched documents from the US Bureau of Indian Affairs before establishing his Indian Protection Service in 1910. Oitamina remembered seeing television reports in 1987, when the Sioux chief Red Crow visited the Kayapo chief Raoni at his village in the Amazon. The two activists shared stories over a peace pipe; Red Crow told Raoni about his ancestors Cochise and Sitting Bull, and Raoni told Red Crow about Indians lured by landholders with gifts, then gunned down by *pistoleiros* and buried in an unmarked mass grave, near the Bolivian border.

Oitamina knew that Native Americans were years ahead of his people, and he wondered what happened to them, what might be his future. I wanted to give him some cause for optimism, but all I could tell him was a story he already knew. Settlers take native land with superior numbers and firepower, as governments make promises and sign treaties soon broken. So goes America. Doesn't look much different in Brazil. He nodded knowingly.

The next morning we pulled the plugs on our 110-pound rafts, rolled them up and carried them on our shoulders over the sandstone flats to the far end of the falls.

◆

Theodore Roosevelt never quite said so in his book, but he wasn't happy with Rondon's choice to use only dugout canoes, let alone secondhand canoes bought from Nambiquara at the headwaters. The boats could barely be steered, and had to be dragged around rapids. "They would not have lived half a minute in the wild water," he said.

"How I longed for a big Maine birch-bark. It would have slipped down these rapids as a girl trips through a country dance." Bark canoes were used in Brazil at the time, by Indians of other tribes, and Roosevelt wished Rondon had acquired a slim canoe or two. Or that he hadn't left the Canadian canoes behind at Utiarity Falls.

Roosevelt made it sound inevitable, necessary to save weight. More likely, as Todd Diacon writes in *Stringing Together a Nation*, "Rondon insisted that the Americans abandon the canvas canoes they had brought with them."

After Roosevelt's return to the States, in the confidential correspondence to the secretary of the Royal Geographical Society, which published his account in its journal, he said that if he'd been in charge he would have taken four bark canoes, which would have enabled them to "make the journey with fewer accidents, with more comfort, and in two weeks less time."

There was a lot more that Roosevelt didn't say in *Through The Brazilian Wilderness*, issues ignored or danced around, painting the picture he wanted for posterity. He explained that his content choices were about diplomacy and courtesy, and he was writing as a naturalist, not a journalist. "It would have been more than ungrateful to let any of these things be public," he said. "It would accomplish absolutely no good."[*]

---

[*]   Among all US presidents, Richard Nixon did the most to support Native Americans, respecting and addressing their grievances. He fought hard for their rights.

◆

Back on the river, Oitamina continued telling his story. He and Piu learned enough Portuguese to understand most of what was going on around them. They were the only Cinta Larga boys making that kind of progress, surviving by their backs and wits. "We did whatever had to be done to feed ourselves," said Oitamina. "We were handymen. When we had lived in the forest we planted gardens—beans, rice, manioc—so we knew how to do that. We knew how to put up fences, because we had to do that to keep the White men from burning our land. And we built a road and an airstrip for the garimpeiros, so we knew about construction and earth-moving."

A black bumblebee was drawn to his rockstar hair, joined by a crimson butterfly, and together they carved diving turns around the chief's head. He knelt in the bow of the raft, his elbows on the tube and hands clasped as if in prayer, silent save the buzz of the bumblebee and soft splash of oars. Oitamina's eyes stayed fixed on the forest. He spotted a monkey and pointed, as it moved through the treetops.

Chief Piu continues the story from his white wicker rocking chair on the porch of his home in Riozinho, interpreted by the Brazilian boatman Mario. "I thought everything was amazing in the White man's world. What impressed me most was vehicles. The first time I saw a car, I thought it ran on its own. I didn't know it needed a driver."

The two hard-working Indian boys were abused and exploited because there was so much they didn't know or couldn't control. Scaring White men into giving you stuff only worked when you outnumbered them in the forest.

"We had no concept of money," Piu says. "When they started paying me money for my work, I thought, 'What good is this stuff?' I asked what I should do with it. I didn't want this paper. I was going to throw it out. Sometimes now I wish I had."

His eyes stayed fixed on the rainforest as he finished his story. "When FUNAI established its post, we met Assis, their first agent. Roberto and I were lucky to have him as our friend. He sent us to school in Cacoal, where his wife was a teacher. She taught us Portuguese and some arithmetic.

"At that time I didn't want to go back to the forest, but today I realize there are problems living in town. Now I think this world is doing us more harm than good. When we lived in the forest we didn't have to worry about anything, like bills. Now we have to pay to be born, and pay to die. But the good part is that I'm here and I'm alive and talking. I don't know if I would still be alive if I had stayed in the forest."

Oitamina, Piu, and Tatare became chiefs after demarcation. Between 1989 and 1991, 10,425 square miles were delineated by the government and given back to the Cinta Larga, in four contiguous indigenous territories: Roosevelt (230,826 hectares), Serra Morena (147,836 hectares), Aripuaña (750,649 hectares), and Aripuaña Park (1,603,250 hectares). The boundary was a stretch of nearly 200 kilometers along the eastern bank of the Rio Roosevelt.

The legal transfer of land back to the Cinta Larga meant that the loggers had to leave or start paying the Cinta Larga for the mahogany they'd been taking for years. The garimpeiros were harder to pin down, here and gone, leaving a forest riddled with landing strips and littered with crashed planes.

Oitamina and Piu were already de facto chiefs, but demarcation made it official with the Brazilian government. They chose Tatare to be a third chief, because his father was a chief.

Oitamina says the mahogany trouble began a few years earlier, near the Serra Morena outpost in Mato Grosso. About 25 men were caught cutting mahogany, and 700 logs were found. Some Cinta Larga tied them to trees for three days, debating whether or not to kill them with arrows, while they waited for the arrival of FUNAI agents and Chief Oitamina. He says his brothers wanted to kill the woodsmen—he wrings his neck, sticks out his tongue, and bulges his eyeballs—but he ordered their lives spared because the men were mere workers, not bosses. FUNAI confiscated the wood and helped Oitamina sell it, but FUNAI couldn't control the distribution of the money.

Assis, the fair FUNAI agent, shrugs and smiles when he hears Oitamina's stories. He recalls that in 1984 FUNAI confiscated 400 cut logs in that area, and they sometimes still have to intervene to keep the Cinta

Larga from killing settlers and mahogany cutters on their land, or scold them when they do. With demarcation, Indian law rules: FUNAI might mediate an issue, but the government in Brasilia stays out of it.

The biggest deterrent for Indians against killing intruders is bad press. That's why Oitamina brought it up when I asked him about the future.

The chief continues, "Then we started fighting with FUNAI over the issue of timber sales. They said we couldn't do it. The environmentalists are hassling us now, too; they say we shouldn't cut our trees. But there seems to be no other way for us to get money for our community, so we do it anyhow. If they could at least give us some money then we would agree to stop; but if they don't, what are we supposed to do? It's not because we want to cut down the trees in our forest, it's just because there is no other way. Selling timber is quite lucrative if you know how to do it. It brings in good money."

Says Assis the faithful FUNAI agent, "The Cinta Larga have been influenced by people who don't know the value of an indigenous culture, don't appreciate its worth. They've had contact with lumber dealers who say, 'Sell us your wood and you'll be able to get this, you'll be able to get that, you'll be able to buy a car, you'll be able to buy a video camera, you'll be able to buy a television.' And it's not just the lumber dealers. There have been FUNAI outpost supervisors fired over this issue, because they were cooperating with the lumber-selling venture."

Assis's hands carve gestures as if choreographed, as he speaks. Sitting next to Cabral, he gently grabs the scientist by the shirtfront to plead a point. He turns his palms upward, elegant hands holding a half-century of hard labor. He points to his temple, swings his arms, slaps his heart, waves at the rain, and salutes the sky.

He continues, "That's why I asked to get out of the Rio Roosevelt area, because when the whole lumber business started up, Piu and Oitamina proposed to me, 'Let's sell lumber,' and I said 'No,' and they just ignored me and went ahead and did it, so I asked to be transferred. It's no use FUNAI telling the Indians that they can't log on their land any more, it's just no use. The Federal Police are responsible for enforcing it, but when they're called they say, 'No, we're not coming,' because some of them were tied up the last time they tried it. So they won't come any more.

"I'm their friend, but I don't want to be involved with this type of problem. What makes me the saddest is first of all that they're cutting trees, but especially it's the way they're doing it. They started selling it all of a sudden, they didn't have any patience. I wish they had more patience to try and do it well, if they're going to do it. I used to tell them to hold on a bit, wait until you know more about civilization before you get into a business like this, but they didn't want to wait. So they got taken advantage of by the White man, a lot. It doesn't happen as much any more, but it still happens.

"Oitamina, Piu, and Tatare are different from the other Cinta Larga in that they've had more exposure to White man's society. They know how to deal with money. But there's so much money changing hands under the table, they have to give some of it to the other Indians, too, and then those others spend it and waste it. The others get a pocketful of money, they have no idea of its worth and they get ripped off.

"But nobody can tell them what to do any more, nobody can give them advice. They do what they want to do. Now I just keep quiet, I wouldn't dare try to tell them what to do. I was better friends with them before. I'm still friends with Piu and Roberto and Tatare, I can't hide what I feel for the three of them, but it's really hard with their logging money now. I just don't agree with the way they're behaving."

Back on the river, a downpour came and went with a cloud. A garbage bag and cigar box floated past.

ABOVE: Theodore Roosevelt never saw the River of Doubt from an airplane, but he got it right when he said it "wound hither and thither, sometimes in sigmoid curves." *Credit: Mark Greenberg.* BELOW: Charles Haskell and Elizabeth McKnight carried heavy loads on their backs, and worried about each other's hearts. *Credit: Mark Greenberg.*

ABOVE: Tweed Roosevelt, following in his great-grandfather's wake, lamented missed opportunities to "carve his notch on the Roosevelt measuring stick," as TR put it. *Credit: Mark Greenberg.* BELOW: Best boatman among the five, Kelley Kalafatich had been a whitewater rafting guide for fifteen of her thirty-one years. Without her grace and spirit, the Rio Roosevelt Expedition would have been double-doomed. *Credit: © Carr Clifton.*

ABOVE: The primadonna Polish pianist scored ten grand from New Century Conservation Trust to play to an empty house at the kickoff event in the magnificent Teatro Amazonas in Manaus. *Credit: Mark Greenberg.* LEFT: Hallucinogenic peek into the future, brought to you by the plant. *Credit: Makani Kai Moses.*

ABOVE: Wherever cameraman and kayak scout Joe Kaminsky filmed, Chief Oitamina was sure to follow. Later the chief showed the author his video. He got it all. *Credit: Mario Peixoto.* RIGHT: Assis, the faithful Indigenous agent, had been with the *National Geographic*-supported expedition that first contacted the Cinta Larga in 1970. He didn't like where they were now, misguided by mahogany money. *Credit: Mario Peixoto.*

ABOVE: The worn-out tires on the Toyota trucks looked up at the explorers and laughed. *Credit: Mark Greenberg.* LEFT: With just enough clearance for the Jeeps, Charlie didn't get to use his chainsaw. *Credit: Mark Greenberg.*

ABOVE: The pharmacologist Jose Cabral was tough, and declined the doctor's Demerol injection after being stung by an electric caterpillar at the headwaters. The searing pain lasted for hours and hard lumps on his fingers lasted for weeks. *Credit: Mark Greenberg.* BELOW: The biologist Joao Ferraz had a high position at INPA, the National Science Institute. Joe Willie Jones, strapping backwoods Georgia boy and paddleboat leader, comes along the trail. *Credit: © Carr Clifton.*

ABOVE: The happiest raft: the popular Dr. John Walden, RIP; the young, hooked-on-whitewater Chief Tatare (left); multi-talented Brazilian boatman Mario Peixoto at the oars; and filmmaker, rock star, and mahogany Chief Oitamina (right). *Credit: Mark Greenberg.* BELOW: Because they were freelancers, Mario got stuck with the heaviest raft and Kelley, the girl with the strong arms and charm, was assigned the non-self-bailing "bucket boat." She piloted the worst raft to the smoothest runs. (See the grin on Tatare's face, up front.) *Credit: Mark Greenberg.*

ABOVE: Between rapids, Chief Tatare told the story of the decimation of the Cinta Larga. Later he would travel to Rio de Janeiro for the Earth Summit and represent his tribe in a meeting with Ted Turner and Jane Fonda. *Credit: Mark Greenberg.* BELOW: Women and children bear the legacy of the Cinta Larga as ancestors of the survivors of decades of epidemics brought by development. *Credit: © Carr Clifton.*

ABOVE: The cocky paddleboat crew with Joe Willie in the back shouting commands and using his paddle like a rudder. They called themselves the Candirus, for the tiny fish with barbed fins that slither into the penis. *Credit: Mark Greenberg.* BELOW: Chief Oitamina, dreaming about diamonds on the soles of his feet. *Credit: Mark Greenberg.*

LEFT: Home alone in their remote house on the riverbank, the girl with chestnut curls sifted beans before bonking her little brother when he snatched the gemstone that photographer Clifton gave her. Meanwhile, baby sister was the deadpan queen of comedy. *Credit: © Carr Clifton.* BELOW: Dr. Walden told the boy he would die from the snake bite if he didn't get to a hospital. The boy said he would try to find a ride for the 10-hour trip out of the jungle. *Credit: Mark Greenberg.*

ABOVE: The author Sam Moses and star boatman Kelley Kalafatich watched for snakes with every step as they portaged the paddleboat past the remains of a murdered mahogany tree. *Credit: Mark Greenberg.* BELOW: Cowboy boatman Mike Boyle, master of worst-case scenario, with passengers Tweed Roosevelt and Dr. Walden. *Credit: Mark Greenberg.*

LEFT: After these bothersome bites, Charlie began wearing a mosquito net around his head, hung from the brim of a bush hat. He carried pantyhose to deter the terrifying candirus, but kept them in his duffel because of the teasing. *Credit: © Carr Clifton.*
BELOW: His insect net wouldn't have deterred this large but friendly fellow. *Credit: Mark Greenberg.*

ABOVE: Mario Peixoto struggled with the heaviest raft. He avoided the Class IV line here, but got turned sideways in a Class III hole. The scientist Geraldo Mendes and Chief Oitamina went under, but popped up whooping. *Credit: © Carr Clifton.* BELOW: If the modern explorers were exhausted portaging around two waterfalls, imagine Rondon and Roosevelt's *camaradas* pushing and pulling their one-ton dugout canoes for 48 days around endless rapids their boats couldn't run. *Credit: Mark Greenberg.*

ABOVE: Co-leader Beth McKnight brought the satellite phone to the resupply, along with an ice chest of beer that was enjoyed and packages of 85-octane noodles and rice that were not. *Credit: © Carr Clifton.* BELOW: Hey Chip Haskell! Don't pull the EPIRB! Don't pull the EPIRB! *Credit: Mark Greenberg.*

ABOVE: The deluge had been building for twenty-four hours. Fierce splashing on calm water made the river smoke. *Credit: © Carr Clifton.* BELOW: Jim Slade with his passengers McKnight and the timid ichthyologist Mendes. A split-second later he dropped his oars, the left oar whizzing inches over Beth's head, as Slade sprawled on the duffel bags to prevent a highside. *Credit: © Carr Clifton.*

ABOVE: Painting a pretty picture of deforestation. Not much of it looks as sweet as Fazenda Muira-quita. *Credit: © Carr Clifton.* BELOW: The author Moses and Brazilian Mario left the expedition after the biggest rapids were run, to follow the mahogany raiders. On their way out, they met logging trucks moving back in. *Credit: Mario Peixoto.*

CHAPTER 16

Resupply

I never saw a man who talked so much.
—Colonel Rondon

After Navaite Falls, the Roosevelt-Rondon expedition had two good days with easy water, making 12 and 19 kilometers; George Cherrie shot a jacu, a bird like a turkey but better looking, and Luis, helmsman in Roosevelt's boat, "a powerful negro," climbed a tree to raid a nest of stingless bees and came back with honey that was "delicious, sweet, and yet with a tart flavor."

In the lead canoe, Roosevelt heard the roar. Rapids stretched for half a mile, over three steps. Cherrie called them the 6th of March Rapids for the date, but they could have been the 7th, 8th, and 9th. The dugouts were dragged around the first set of rapids, 16 camaradas pulling the one-ton boats over rolling logs; floated empty through the second, guided by ropes, led by Kermit struggling with footing on the rocky bottom, stung and bitten by ants from trees; and the third set was run in the three smallest dugouts with paddlers, *canoeiros*. "Seeing the men run the third rapids in the empty canoes was quite exciting," said Cherrie.

Roosevelt went hunting (never successfully, as Rondon pointed out, blaming it on TR's eyesight), or read from his stack of books that still included *Utopia*, as well as plays by Sophocles, Marcus Aurelius (an emperor and military man, like himself), and Epictetus (a stoic philosopher, like himself). With the canoes sinking under the weight of their loads, it's clear how important reading was to him. It was shocking to Rondon, but for Roosevelt it was a given, food for the brain. He took a "library" along on every expedition, and because he read so fast, it had to be big.

Kermit, too. "I had brought along a selection of Portuguese classics and a number of French novels." He also carried *The Iliad* and *The Odyssey* (in Greek), and other books. "Perhaps I would have found the day tedious if Kermit had not lent me *The Oxford Book of French Verse*," said TR at the 6th of March Rapids. Kermit threatened to take it away from his father, "if he didn't stop assailing my favorites."

Rondon, who had cut back on food for his men to save weight for the books, said he'd never seen a man who read as much as Roosevelt. "An essential part of his baggage was made up of many cases containing a large number of books. A volume of one of these works he always had with him. He scarcely arrived at a resting place or a momentary halt, when he wouldn't cover the ground with a hide and throw himself onto it and reconvene his studies as if no other thing in the world preoccupied him."

Rondon added that he also never saw a man who talked so much. "He would talk all of the time he was swimming, all of the time during meals, traveling in the canoe, and at night around the campfire. He talked endlessly and on all conceivable subjects.

"But in spite of all this, he did not change, even in the slightest measure, his habit of writing down every day, the notes on his impressions of each moment, and a few more pages of the book in which he intended to divulge the things which he saw and the facts that were occurring during his travel across the Brazilian wilderness."

Cherrie's diary describes another Roosevelt. "There was no camp duty that the Colonel shirked. He stood ready and willing to do his share. And in the evenings, after all was ship-shape for the night, when we gathered about the camp-fire to discuss the day's happenings, someone would always ask for a story from the Colonel's seemingly endless store."

After the 6th of March there were more rapids. The river rose that night and swallowed one canoe moored to Roosevelt's big one, and when the men woke in the morning they found flotsam from both canoes downstream in an eddy. They named it Broken Canoe Rapids. They would have to build another canoe, big enough to carry as much as the two that sank and smashed.

◆

It was only 16 kilometers from Navaite Falls to the resupply at the mahogany-raiders' bridge. In the morning Captain Slade scolded Charlie, Tweed, Dr. Walden, and photojournalist Greenberg for taking the time to shoot a photo of Charlie and Tweed standing on the rock where Rondon and Roosevelt had posed for a photo that appears on the first page of *Through the Brazilian Wilderness*. At first Charlie hadn't been invited to the photo shoot, but he went looking for the other three, and when he found them, insisted that Greenberg take the photo of him with Tweed, instead of Dr. Walden.

Since no one but Slade minded leaving at 7:45 instead of 7:00 A.M., the brief public lecture only stirred resentment over Slade's authoritarian attitude. Later Haskell suggested to Slade that he air his issues in private. Slade had managed to make use of the time anyhow, by removing the Varig and Banco Económico stickers that Beth had applied over the Sobek logo.

Slade's push for speed reduced the expedition to a rafting trip, making its leader a rich guy on vacation, thus ensuring Mountain Travel Sobek's own snide description. Slade argued that wasted time was dangerous, because much was unknown about the river—TR's argument to Rondon. He carried charts he said were from Rondon, but was coy about what they revealed. Haskell didn't want to pull rank; if Slade said the boats had to be on the river by 7:00, then they did.

Two yellow-bellied macaws chased us down the river. Bleating raspy croaks from 100 feet, they circled the parade on the water. They landed ahead on a palm tree and watched the rafts float toward them. They made a second pass overhead, flew out of sight over the canopy, and a minute later came back from the rear and dived at the rafts. They banked up and flew off squawking, exposing broad wingspans and long forked tails, having said what they had to say.

Bumblebees bombed the boats like cannonballs, as brilliant butter-flies darted, flitted, and weaved. The boatmen maneuvered around logs and fallen trees, and when one blocked the way Oitamina did a belly flop off the tube of his raft, surfaced at the fallen tree, climbed up and bounced on it in his bare feet and jams, until it broke with a muffled crack to open a line for the rafts. That was the closest we would come to needing Charlie's chainsaw.

There was a small shipwreck at the riverbank, a semisunken canoe. Downriver, a bearded brown specter in shorts and sandals walked along the bank carrying a shotgun. Startled, he froze. Joba the biologist called out a greeting, introduced himself, and tried to explain the expedition as 15 more people in three more rafts arrived. The man warily said he was a tenant farmer who lived nearby, raised a few crops, tended some pigs and chickens, and never took anything from the forest. We passed his decrepit farmhouse, a wire-fenced pasture with slash-and-burn scars, eight pigs, and one horse tramping around inside a neglected thatched shelter surrounded by tall termite mounds.

The expedition reached its resupply point, flat and dry. The landowner drove up in an old truck. He was about 50—Italian, he said—emaciated, graying blond hair, sharp blue eyes, and long sideburns with a neatly trimmed mustache crawling around the corners of his lips, dangling a long damp cigarette rolled with notebook paper. His clothes were ragged and ripped, and rubber flip-flops dangled from his earthy feet. He acted as if large expeditions in rubber rafts passed this way all the time.

Joba, a forest conservationist and soil specialist, interviewed him and got a familiar story. A 170-hectare plot of jungle was given to him in 1972 by INCRA, the National Institute for Colonization and Agrarian Reform, a government agency "to bring men without land to land without men." He was required to clear and plant the land, which he did, but soon learned that rainforest soil died when the leaves were gone.

Right on time, the three Jeeps rolled out of the jungle. The crew included McKnight, Joe Willie Jones, Assis, Fabio, Darcio, and one handsome Indigenous helper. They carried the fifth raft, satellite telephone, generator, more food, and a giant cooler bulging with Brazilian beer. Within minutes the place was jumping; the generator was chugging and beer cans were popping and being thrown with a satisfying clank onto a pile, while pharmacologist Cabral began cooking a rice stew. The satellite dish was unfolded and aimed skyward, and people crowded around as Chip Haskell tapped buttons to talk to the world.

The first call was to Peter Riva's farm in upstate New York. He listened to versions of events from Haskell and me, and asked what happened to *Good Morning America*'s tape of Tweed at the headwaters, a question that had to be referred to Joe Kaminsky since only he knew it hadn't been delivered. Next Haskell checked in with his mother, the matriarch Antoinette Marsh, then turned the phone over to others to make calls to loved ones. The next morning Tweed finally talked to *Good Morning America*, although they had to record the conversation for a future show because they had no film to go with it.

It had been a challenging week for Beth and Joe Willie. The raft got stuck in customs in São Paulo, which was out to Carnaval. Beth said she must have spent $800 in phone calls from the Mirage Hotel, trying to free the boat. Officials demanded a document from Joe Willie to prove that he was a member of the Rio Roosevelt expedition, which she was reluctant to provide because the permit didn't name him. A meeting was arranged with a man from the office of the minister of economics, and Joe Willie sweet-talked his way to freedom for himself and his boat. They got on the next plane to Cuiabá and bus to Vilhena.

McKnight was being tested on her "expertise in problem solving," as her résumé stated. She was down to $150 and still needed to buy food and beer, but no banks were open. The Bandeirantes were demanding the money they'd been denied at the headwaters. Mountain Travel Sobek was calling the office of New Century Conservation Trust in Maine, wanting their 11 grand for Joe Willie and the raft.

McKnight had the opportunity to "easily adapt to variable and complex situations with relative ease," as that night a tropical storm howled around the Mirage, blowing rain in the room through the cracks as trees crashed around the walls. The next night she used her "human relations experience" and ability to "interface with a cross-section of people," when the police came and searched her room. They were quite cordial, but confiscated her cans of Mace—for snakes, she told them.

It was Friday night at the resupply camp. There was a big meal that left a bad taste in our mouths, literally. Much of the food had been packed in the bed of the Jeep Comanche against the gasoline, and fumes had permeated the grub. The cereal, crackers, rice, and noodles got the worst of it, but as the days would go by, more would be spit and thrown out. Slade and Boyle blamed it on Beth, who said she "told them" not to put the gas against the food.

As Carnaval rocked throughout Brazil, the explorers partied in the jungle. Some stayed up late and washed down the gasoline with beer and vodka. Tweed carried the Roosevelt zest for life and figured a buzz in the jungle at night was an experience that shouldn't be missed, while Boyle was less cheery about it. As most of the others drifted off to sleep, the sounds of the jungle included his loud release of opinions critical of how the expedition was being led, and he didn't mean by Slade.

Finally, a jungle critter picked up a rock and clanged it against a steel pipe, as if telling Boyle to shut up. Or maybe he or she was calling the others to their own party, birds and bugs and frogs singing until 4:00 A.M., before quitting like a bar at closing time. The day broke with sweet songbirds. The sun rose on the emerald curtain of trees across the river, turning the mist on the pasture to soft orange smoke.

CHAPTER 17

Tatare

They died and we let them lay on the ground.
—Chief Tatare

Tatare (tataray) said he was 29, fumbling as he counts the years and kids on his fingers. There's a girl, 12, a toddler that Tatare said was three or four, and a baby daughter. He and his wife had a fourth child, a daughter who died of hepatitis at three. They were living on the FUNAI post at the time, and there was no doctor, nurse, vehicle, nor working radio.

Assis the FUNAI agent believed Tatare was 23, which was about how old he looked. He had a smooth boyish face, full lips, excellent teeth, and innocent eyes, at least compared to Piu with his esperto eyes. His voice was soft like his features. He neither talked nor smiled much, unlike Oitamina, but he laughed easily at slapstick. Ask about the past, and he'll say it's not easy to forget.

Tatare rode in the back of the raft guided by Mario Peixoto, who interpreted as he rowed. Wearing a T-shirt with an image of a '58 Oldsmobile convertible, he hung over the stern, scooped water in his hand, sucked it in and spit it out in a long, far squirt. He stared off, searching the forest. He talked about his life in a matter-of-fact manner, and the words came out sketchy, not easily. "Our story is very simple," he said. "We live in nature."

As far back as he can remember, there was dying. His brother and two others were killed by Surui, who attacked a Cinta Larga hunting party near Broken Canoe Rapids. His father, the chief, was shot by arrows in three places, the wounds healed with a paste by the *paje*.

"I know very little from my grandfather and grandmother," says Tatare. "They both died when I was very young. I remember a lot of people lying dead in their hammocks, and in the dirt in their huts. I think 10,000 people died in two weeks. Many people died, in such great numbers that we couldn't bury them all. They died and we let them lay on the ground. Only God knows how the rest lived. My mother died. I was very very sad because I lost a lot of relatives. I felt very alone."

Cinta Larga ceremony buries the dead on the banks of the Rio Roosevelt, headed downriver so their spirits can flow. Bodies are wrapped in hammocks, the men with hunting and fishing tools for the next life. There are three days of mourning. But epidemics killed them faster than they could be buried.

According to Oitamina, 20 years ago there were 20,000 Cinta Larga. His numbers loosely reflect FUNAI statistics, influenced by politics. In 1969, *National Geographic* estimated 5,000, based on aerial observation of clearings in the canopy. Today there are about 1,000.

"My grandfather was a great chief," continues Tatare. "He warned that White men would change our way of life. He said that many of us would die. Now I remember what he and my grandmother said, and they were right.

"The sickness came after the first contact with White men. It began with colds and spread to pneumonia. Then there were other epidemics, like yellow fever. My sister died of mumps. People just kept on dying; they would get sick and sicker and then they would die. Every day more people died.

"I remember the second wave of dying better because I was older. I was a young man and I knew a lot because I was told what would happen by my grandfather. He was very wise, and he told the tribe that they had to split up and move away and live in small groups, so the sickness would not spread among us so fast and kill every one of us. I walked more than 200 kilometers and saw many people dead in their hammocks and malocas. I was alone with 10 people and my father was very far away and I grew up very isolated. Mostly it was only old people who moved away. The young people preferred to stay and take the place of the old."

Tatare often visits his father the retired chief, whose cluster of huts, *aldeia*, is 20 miles back into the jungle from the FUNAI post on the river. He keeps his distance. Life is simpler.

Dark clouds appear, and Tatare tries to ward off the thunder with a deep whistle, a subtle smile suggesting his own skepticism. As the rain falls, the story turns to genocide.

"At that time there was no FUNAI, and White men were taking advantage of the situation. Killing, killing. I was 12 years old. Two men came and they wanted to take gold and diamonds from the river but they feared the Indians. They wanted us gone so they killed us. Their names were Manelao and Justino. They mixed poison with sugar and manioc flour and gave it to the villages. People got sick, and a few days later they died. My brother and my uncle were poisoned.

"Manelao died in a plane crash. Justino lives in Cacoal. He's an old man now, and soon he will die. When I see him I don't get upset. I have more important things to think about than revenge. Back then I would have killed him if he ever came to the jungle, but he never left town. I was 14 then.

"At the time, I felt hate for the people who did the killing, but not all White men. Each time I go to the forest I remember."

The rain gone, Tatare hangs over the side of the raft looking for his reflection. He rises to his knees and points to the treetops. Nothing, until a branch shakes and a spindly shadow swings across the sky to a tall thin tree, making it sway. Wild screeching, as five or six spider monkeys burst from the leaves at 100 feet, shaking the rainforest canopy.

Later I asked Assis about Tatare's poisoning story. "The Cinta Larga talk a lot about poisonings," he said, "but with so many deaths from diseases, it's easy to confuse the two. I wouldn't be so sure it really happened. I've never heard of this Justino, and I knew a lot of garimpeiros. Although this happened before FUNAI, so I wasn't there at that time.

"But Tatare's story sounds similar to one I know about. This man was killed by the Cinta Larga near the Cardoso River. He was called Sapecado. He was really a wild man, and he got blamed for poisoning them. He started living with a Cinta Larga woman and he ran away with her, and this caused a lot of trouble. He treated her badly so she left him and came back to live with her relatives. He found diamonds and gold in the river near here, and went away and had a good time with the money, but when he came back, the Indians killed him. He was always heavily armed with a revolver and a rifle, but they followed him and when he put his guns down they clubbed him on the head and shot him with an arrow, and left the body there. They came back to town and told the head of the FUNAI post what they'd done, and the police came and investigated but they left the body there. The skeleton is probably there today. They say that Sapecado was one of the people who poisoned the Indians, so he died like a snake."

The Indians were unpredictable. A few Cinta Larga killed the FUNAI agent at the post, along with a journalist because they didn't like his taking pictures. "It was Oitamina's brother who killed them," says Tatare. "He didn't plan to kill the journalist, it's just that he was there at the time. We knew that FUNAI was trying to help us, but people were disgusted just the same. They were unhappy that everything was changing."

Tatare started hanging around the post, where the new agent liked his intelligence and willingness to learn, and gave him food and clothes and taught him how to grow crops and build things; he explained money, the good and bad, and paid him for labor. "He was a really good person. He was honest and he cared about Indians. He taught me everything. There just aren't people like that anymore. Well, Assis is a good man, too."

He was asked to help contact other tribes, some hostile. "We would go into the forest and build a shelter where we left gifts for them, pots and machetes. They would come at night and take them. After many times they would come and stay and we would contact them. It was difficult because

I couldn't speak their language. They knew I wasn't a White man but they had suspicions about me."

When Tatare was 17, his mentor agent was killed in a plane crash with four others from FUNAI. Tatare married Piu's sister and they had a baby. A Cinta Larga chief was killed in a car crash, and Tatare was the natural choice to replace him—Oitamina, Piu, and Assis wanted him, and his father was a chief.

"I've known these three for a long time," said Assis. "I've known Piu and Roberto since they were little boys, and Tatare since he was 12. I would say the one who could get annoyed most quickly would be Roberto. Piu is the most good-natured. Piu is very intelligent, he got to grade four; in fact, my second wife was his teacher for two years. Roberto got as far as grade two and then quit. Roberto and Tatare know how to write, but Piu went further in school.

"Tatare is quite calm. He's a good person, he's good with his people. We talk a lot. He tells me about his ideas. Sometimes he gives other Indians money, and they spend it on drinking, and he doesn't like that."

Recently Tatare had been thinking about resigning as chief, unsure if he wanted the responsibility. But his mind was clear now, he said; he would dedicate himself to improving life for his people by representing them in their dealings with White men. His people need him.

"Today Roberto and I are the chiefs," he says. "We have meetings, we help our people who aren't able to understand, we explain politics, we prepare them for the struggle. Roberto takes good care of the community. He takes care of problems when they need something. I'm the person that deals with FUNAI, I ask for things from them. Our people aren't able to take care of themselves, so we can't be away from them for very long. But we get tired. We have so many things on our mind.

"I'm waiting for my turn to be number one, for my time to come. I want to take measures to help my people. I hope to make communication better with FUNAI in the future. But only God knows what will happen."

CHAPTER 18

Candirus

Maybe you'll come up a mile downriver,
or maybe you won't come up at all.
—Joe Willie Jones

Joseph Willis "Joe Willie" Jones began canoeing when he was a strapping 12-year-old in backwoods north Georgia. By age 18, standing six-foot-three, he had canoed and kayaked thousands of miles on the long and beautiful Chattooga, Oconee, and Chattahoochee Rivers, in Cherokee country.

He became a firefighter, but traded fires for rivers when he was able to make a living as a river guide. He got jobs on rivers in North Carolina, West Virginia, Tennessee, Texas, and Maine. He had a rafting business for five years on the Rogue River in Oregon. In Northern California on the Stanislaus, he met and fell for a blue-eyed blond guide, Kelley Kalafatich.

The 15-foot raft he carried from Miami lacked an aluminum frame for an oarsman. Like the canoeiros in their dugouts, its occupants would paddle from the sides as Joe Willie, captain and helmsman, shouted commands from the rear, his paddle the rudder.

On Cherokee land in 1828, a hunter literally tripped over a rock of gold, triggering the Georgia Gold Rush. The expression, "There's gold in them thar hills!" led prospectors into the Cherokee hills, beginning the decimation and displacement of the tribe.

The state of Georgia held lotteries to give Cherokee land to gold prospectors. In 1830 President Andrew Jackson passed the Indian Removal Act that led to the federal government taking all their land east of the Mississippi in an 1835 treaty; the $5 million negotiated price was never paid. In 1838 President Martin Van Buren evicted them to the Oklahoma Territory. More than 16,000 Cherokee were rounded up by 7,000 soldiers, who looted their empty homes. The Cherokee were moved west during the winter of 1838–39, by rail, boat, wagon, and foot. One-fourth of them died. The Cherokee call it the "Trail of Tears."

In 1903 President Theodore Roosevelt approved Senate Bill 25 that in effect ended the Cherokee Nation. In 1906 their tribal government was dissolved, and in 1907, still during his presidency, Oklahoma became a state and Cherokee land was opened to settlers.

"The conquest and settlement by the Whites on the Indian lands was necessary to the greatness of the race and to the well-being of civilized mankind. It was as ultimately beneficial as it was inevitable," wrote Roosevelt in his book *The Winning of the West*, published in four volumes beginning in 1889. "All men of sane and wholesome thought must dismiss with impatient contempt the plea that these continents should be reserved for the use of scattered savage tribes."

Slade said the river would get serious now, but selection of the paddleboat crew got lost in the shuffle. As the explorers began to leave the resupply, most of them climbed back in the raft they came in. Hurried by Slade, four rafts stroked away.

Joe Willie was left standing on the bank in the rain with the leftover explorers: two Americans, two Brazilians, and one Indian chief. Chip was there for the workout, I was there for the story, and Cabral, Assis, and Oitamina were there because they were lost.

Facing deadly whitewater, requiring precision control that depended on immediate response to shouted commands, the crew spoke three languages, almost four counting backwoods Georgian. Cabral's English held lapses despite his doctorate from Ole Miss; Assis spoke no English at all; and Oitamina's Portuguese was simple.

Joe Willie positioned his crew in the raft, told them to strap on their helmets and life jackets, and gave a quick laconic crash course in whitewater paddling. As Cabral translated, Assis grinned and nodded enthusiastically while Oitamina tried to look cool, clutching his video camera like a security blanket. The Nambiquara have an expression, "The water has no hair"—nothing to grab, when you're in you're in.

There were a few life-or-death commands and maneuvers. All Forward, All Back, and Full Stop were easy. But left-side paddles for right turns and right-side paddles for left turns took some thinking. If we miss a turn and crash sideways into a rock and get wedged by the current . . . "just don't get yourself body-stuffed," said Joe Willie, meaning pitched out of the raft and trapped under it. "Maybe you'll come up a mile downriver, or maybe you won't come up at all."

Cabral said we should call ourselves something, and suggested Candirus, for the tiny fish with barbed fins that wiggles into the orifices of mammals, which to this crew meant up the penis (shudder the thought, penis amputation the cure). The candiru (kan-ja-ROO) was taken seriously, no peeing in the water while bathing, the little monsters follow the urine home. Better safe than sorry, Charlie carried pantyhose to wear while bathing, but the snickering was worse than the risk, so he left them in his duffel. Too late, the vision was planted.

We Candirus stroked off filled with spirit, a capsize rushing to happen. Chip and I were in front, translating words into action: we did what Joe Willie said and the others copied. Joe Willie shouted "All forward!" "All back!" and "Full stop!" which we nailed. When he shouted "Right turn!" we went at it as if possessed, and kept thrashing as the boat spun in a perfect pirouette. As we were high-fiving ourselves, Joe Willie yelled "Left turn!" and we grabbed our paddles and spun another perfect circle in the opposite direction, whooping and cheering.

Oitamina was asked to lead the Candirus in a Cinta Larga battle cry, and he came up with a diaphragm-deep, "Ooh! Ooh! Ooh! Ooh!" We paddled downriver playing warriors, growling "Ooh! Ooh! Ooh! Ooh!" We passed a house, waved, and *ooh-oohed* the kids on the porch, stunned and agape.

Soon we heard the 6th of March Rapids. The boatmen jumped out to scout, Joe Willie leading in long weaving strides over big sandstone rocks and through tall grass. He peered through the trees to see a lush island splitting the river about 200 yards ahead, revealing the tops of white rapids on the sloping left branch and concealing the channel on the right.

The rainforest had been pushed back, slashed and burned for a few hundred yards over steep and hilly terrain. The boatmen split up and studied from different positions, as Joe Willie hiked nearly a mile, curving back down to the river until he found himself standing on a tiny sandy beach, where the rapids ended. (Roosevelt called the spot "charming and picturesque.") He picked his way back upriver, on shore and wading in rocky water, and found the other boatmen studying the whitewater and shaking their heads.

The channel was full of whirlpools and holes, swirling horizontal vortexes made by current rushing over a boulder and getting sucked back over itself; down, forward, and back up, maybe 10 feet deep, around again and again until the next drought or flood. It's like an underwater cyclone on its side.[*] "The thing about a hole is you can never tell what it might do to you," said Joe Willie, translating the black-art physics of fluid dynamics.

We pitched our tents and hung hammocks in a weedy pasture under the munching gaze of nine curious short-haired horses with donkey ears. Across the river to the east, the jungle was a green fortress with walls

---

[*] The inspiration behind this loose explanation of holes comes from David Quammen's wonderful book *Wild Thoughts from Wild Places*. He went to the World Whitewater Rodeo on Tennessee's Ocoee River, and watched kayakers perform spins, pirouettes, cartwheels, barrel rolls, and enders (nose stands) on the lips of Hell's Hole.

200 feet high. To the west, a half-dome of light rose at dusk over the pushed-back rainforest. A solitary charred Brazil nut tree, bursting with barren branches, stood in silhouette against the sky inside an amphitheater of lingering light. Fireflies filled the evening, dancing and flickering as if the sky had fallen and stars were blinking their dying farewells.

The expedition was now 20 percent bigger and 1,000 pounds heavier than it had been at the start, having added a boat, three people, 10 gallons of gas, a generator, and three times more food. After sleeping on those numbers and considering the anticipated difficulty of the 6th of March Rapids, in order to salvage some maneuverability for the rafts, Slade cut them to one passenger in front to balance the load.

He chose four people. Beth wasn't one of them. She'd looked forward to the moment for more than a year. She'd worked hard to get 20 people there. She skipped the early whitewater to do the resupply. If there was any time Haskell should have pulled rank, this was it. "I didn't work 18 months planning this expedition to be told I have to walk around the whitewater," she grumbled as she trudged toward the beach. She was pissed. Slade's decision was stupid.

Slade had told his boatmen he assigned the boats based on seniority. So he and Boyle got the two new Avon Pro Grey self-bailing rafts, Mario got the blue Hysider, and the girl got the old Avon non-self-bailing boat, destined and doomed to take on water in rapids, so one or more people have to bail like mad. "Rowing a bucket-boat means rowing a slug," said Kelley. "Everyone's feet are in bilgewater all day."

Slade and Boyle went first, hugging the bank where the current was slower, working their rafts carefully, turning them this way and that, picking and weaving away from the worst spots, sometimes rowing in reverse to slow down. Mario negotiated the narrow run next, giving the spectators a scare when his raft was spun in a whirlpool, but he reached the eddy with a smile. Kelley came fourth, standing to row, her tank top exposing strong shoulders and muscular arms as she levered the long oars. Her run was smoothest, technically spot-on. Her bailer was photographer Carr Clifton, who had rafting experience. "Kelley's a brilliant boater," he said. "On the dime every time."

Joe Willie told his paddlers that there were two lines: fairly challenging or real challenging. The line close to the bank was fairly challenging. The real challenging line, farther out in the river, probably Class IV, had three standing waves in a row, which would have to be met head-on at full speed. Which route did the Candirus want to take? Did he have to ask?

"Be prepared for the boat to stand straight up when it hits the waves," he told us. "On impact, lean way forward or else the boat might flip over backward."

The Candirus had lost Oitamina, filming from a boulder at the bank over the first big wave, where he sat like the Buddha chanting to the Cinta Larga spirits for his teammates' safe passage, while dreaming of getting footage of a raft flipping over backward in the rapids of Rio Teodoro.

We shoved off with our war cry and skipped over and through the waves like surfers paddling through the break, squeezing into the eddy with the other rafts. We raised our paddles over our heads and *ooh-oohed* each other. Joe Willie told his boys he'd take them anywhere.

The rapids that came five kilometers downriver were steeper. Here, Kermit had used block-and-tackle to drag the dugouts up the small cliffs to the bank, for the camaradas to push and pull on rollers over the land.

The boatmen scouted and reported that there was one big boulder that had to be dodged, followed by another just beneath the surface that created a three-foot-high standing wave, a spout that shot upward like a geyser and splayed out like a fan. The line ran to the left of the boulder and to the right of the wave, forcing an S-turn; and just past the wave there was a long fallen tree stretching from the bank to the middle of the narrow channel, so a third sharp turn was necessary to avoid getting speared. "The problem is if you hit the boulder or the wave you're screwed, and if you miss the boulder and the wave you're screwed," said Boyle.

When the cocky Candirus got there we blew it. We got around the big boulder, but when Joe Willie commanded "Right turn!" somebody paddled left. "I said right turn!" shouted Joe Willie, which panicked and confused the side that had been doing it correctly, and some reversed to the wrong way. "Your other right, dammit!" yelled Joe Willie.

He could see we were going to be carried into the wave, so he commanded "Full forward! Hard! HARDER!" and the Candirus bared their teeth like piranhas and paddled furiously, headlong into the wall of water. We felt the whump of the boulder that created the wave as it passed under our feet and bounced our butts off the tubes, and the big spout lifted the raft, which submerged when it came down. It popped back up and into the air again, before sticking the landing and surfing down the backside.

Soaked and pumped with adrenaline, the Candirus kept paddling at full speed all the way to the eddy. We pulled in whooping and yelling, as the other explorers, walkers and rafters alike, watched in envy. Oitamina got it all.

There was a symphony that night, a sonata with each living instrument section taking its turn. The frogs began with deep barumping, fading to a chorus of cicadas chirping, ratcheting, clicking, and clacking at 100 decibels, until the music suddenly stopped as if by a conductor. An eerie buzz floated in before daybreak, bringing the hooting monkeys and perfect chaos of the parrots.

CHAPTER 19

Simplicio

He keeps my heart in my throat.
—Theodore Roosevelt

A t Broken Canoe Rapids, Rondon's men spent another three days cutting a new dugout, working in the heat, rain, by torchlight, and under a full moon: "the foaming river gleamed like silver." They christened the new boat the *Aripuaña*, after the river Rondon had mapped, and it was a beauty, a giant made from a tatajuba tree five feet in diameter. Replacing two canoes, it was 24 feet long and weighed as much as an ox. Roosevelt rode in the *Aripuaña*, 220 melting pounds of him, along with Cherrie and Dr. Cajazeira, all bailing as three canoeiros paddled.

Kermit was out front in the smallest canoe, together with his yellow mongrel Trigueiro. Kermit and Trig were balanced between the bowsman, a boy (as Cherrie called him) named Simplicio, and the helmsman Joao. They paddled hard until dark that day, gaining 16 kilometers.

For all their reading of literature, TR and Kermit might have heeded Shakespeare's soothsayer to "Beware the Ides of March." On that day, said

Rondon, "The waters commenced once again to flow impetuously, and rushed through a dangerous channel of a new waterfall into which they emerged in furious bubblings." He tied his canoe to a tree and told Kermit to wait, as he and Lyra looked for a path around the rapids.

Roosevelt was seeing new things in his son. Kermit had been a timid child, but by age 19, on safari in Africa, he'd become a "cool and daring fellow," said TR. "He keeps my heart in my throat." From safari he wrote his sister Corinne, "Since we've been here twelve men have been killed or mauled by lions. When Kermit shows a reckless indifference to consequences when hunting them, I feel like beating him."

On what he called their "point-to-point" hikes in Oyster Bay, he had taught his sons, "Over, under and through—but never around." Kermit took it to heart. He didn't listen when Rondon told him to wait at the top of the rapids. He told Simplicio and Joao to paddle across the river to an island so he could view the far channel.

Said Roosevelt, watching with his heart in his throat from the *Aripuaña*, "Before they had gone a dozen yards, the paddlers digging their paddles with all their strength into the swift current, one of the shifting whirlpools whirled them around." They went sideways over the falls. "Poor Simplicio must have been pulled under at once and his life beaten out on the boulders beneath the racing torrent."

Joao swam to shore as Kermit was washed into more rapids, riding the upside-down dugout and clutching his Winchester. He was swirled off and hammered under the whitewater, "and when he rose at last he was almost drowned."

The wet dog Trigueiro found Rondon and Lyra, who ran to the river to find Kermit climbing the bank. The rifle was lost, along with more than 10 days' food and a box of boatbuilding tools, but at least the pouch with Belle's letters was still around his neck. Simplicio was not so lucky. "He never rose again, nor did we recover his body," said Rondon, who carefully noted the full name of the young caboclo, Antonio Simplicio da Silva. The next morning they erected a post and carved the words, AQUI PERECEU O INFELIZ SIMPLICIO. "In these rapids died poor Simplicio," as translated by Roosevelt.

His report of the incident in *Through the Brazilian Wilderness* skipped
the details that fingered his son. If Kermit felt any remorse over the consequences of his recklessness, he buried it. In his diary, he wrote merely,
"Simplicio was drowned." Later he had the opportunity to tell his side of
the story in his book *The Happy Hunting-Grounds*, which included a chapter
on the Roosevelt-Rondon expedition, in which he wrote warm and moving
words about Father's strength and courage. But he never mentioned poor
Simplicio.*

◆

When the Rio Roosevelt rafters got to Simplicio Falls, Joe Kaminsky fer-
ried his kayak across the river above the island, to view the far channel.
He paused above a hydraulic, staying in place by surfing on the face of the
wave. He saw an eddy on the far bank, slipped in at a 45° angle, beached
the kayak and disappeared into the forest across the river.

Four boatmen walked along the near bank as Joe Willie looked down
from the trees, on the same Cinta Larga trail that was Rondon's vantage
point. He saw the lush island splitting the river, with whitewater in the
near channel and fast water in the far one. The others waited in the rafts,
swatting horseflies and bloodsucking piums.

Kaminsky came out of the forest, shouted that the far channel was run-
nable, and paddled back to the near shore. He couldn't see a line down the
channel, he said, but it looked fast. The boatmen returned and agreed
the best approach would be to run a short section of stiff rapids along the
bank before the island, pause in an eddy there, then cut diagonally across

---

* In *Into the Amazon*, author Larry Rohter mentions "the inquest Rondon quietly
ordered." In *Colonel Roosevelt*, the final book in Edmund Morris's massive Roosevelt
biography trilogy, in one of two chapters on the expedition, Morris writes: "It was
clear to the Brazilians that Kermit could, or should, be prosecuted for manslaughter."
Morris doesn't say which Brazilians. Rondon? Never. Lyra? Would never go against
Rondon. Dr. Cajazeira? He and Kermit had become close. Morris doesn't attribute a
source, so it might have been the author's speculation. If so, given Brazilian law, and
if left at the camaradas, it's a reasonable conclusion.

the river above the island and shoot into the far channel. It probably wasn't any worse than Class IV, said Slade, adding that there was also the chance of not making the island and getting washed down the near channel and over the falls (like Kermit).

Slade went first, while the others waited on foot at the bottom; he said there wasn't much to dodge, and if there were holes he never saw them. The other boatmen hiked to their rafts, and Boyle, Kelley, and Mario, each with one passenger, went one by one, cheered at the bottom by the others.

Joe Willie explained more about holes to the Candirus. There were two types, he said, "There's a keeper and a stopper, and the difference is if you flip over in a keeper you might stay under for as long as the river wants you. It's like being stuffed in a washing machine in the spin cycle. I've been down in a keeper before, wondering when and if I was going to come up—or even which way up was."

The Candirus paused at the eddy and moved out into the river above the island, then paddled in reverse to hold the raft in place while Joe Willie looked for a line. There were few whitecaps and no visible boulders, but it was clearly steeper and faster. Cinch your life jackets tight, he said. We paddlers were mostly along for the ride, but the river demanded our eyes, as the turns came fast. Working his paddle like a rudder, we could hear Joe Willie grunting and directing himself with colorful commands. Once we carried big speed into a curve, and it might have been a moment . . . but he perfectly skimmed the berm of bubbles around the outside, to our cheers. It was basically a solo run and he nailed it.

◆

Rondon's men began their portage around the rest of the rapids. The *Aripuaña* and two cargo dugouts were unloaded and dragged 600 yards through the forest, while the two smaller canoes with two paddlers ran the whitewater against the bank; one almost hit a tapir riding the rapids like a body surfer.

The expedition was followed by Indians in the forest much of the way. They heard them, and the dogs barked at them, but they never saw them. Rondon believed they were Nambiquara who had never seen White men, but they were Cinta Larga, half a century before they had a name.

The Indians were spooked by the White men, and believed they were spirits, or else they would have killed them; and the Cinta Larga were said to be cannibals, sometimes, who ate the leaders of an enemy tribe. Watching from the forest, they could see that Rondon and Roosevelt were leaders.

The next day they were stopped again by rapids. As camaradas carried loads and guided the empty canoes along the shore with ropes, Rondon went hunting with his dog Lobo. (Rondon loved his dogs more than he loved his men, and his diaries prove it. One time he lost his patience with the Nambiquara when they killed his dog Rio Negro with arrows. "Traitors!" he called them in his diary.)

They were on a path made by Indians. There was a long squeak like a spider monkey, and Lobo ran after it. It was Cinta Larga luring their prey with a gift for mimicry evolved over centuries. Lobo yelped, and Rondon heard short energetic shouts, "with a certain cadence peculiar to Indians when they're ready to commence the attack." Lobo came back with two long arrows clear through him, and died at Rondon's feet.

Rondon fired two shotgun blasts into the canopy and ran. When the Indians didn't chase, he went back to bury Lobo. The six-foot arrows with barbed bamboo tips and hawk tailfeather fletching were like none he'd ever seen. He left beads and two axes at a spot on the trail where he found crossed sticks telling him to keep out. He heard them talking, probably about whether or not to kill him.

Cinta Larga oral history says that is indeed what they were talking about, and that they decided not to kill Rondon because they had watched him at the ceremony for Simplicio, and his mourning of the dead showed his good heart.

If losing Simplicio and Lobo weren't enough, when Rondon got back to camp he learned the *Aripuanã* was gone, too, its weight breaking the rope guiding it over the shallow rapids, nearly drowning the canoeiro Luiz. They'd spent more than two days building it, and got less than two days' use out of it. Roosevelt said it was made of wood that wasn't buoyant. Rondon said that was because Roosevelt didn't want to send a party into the forest to find the better wood, fearing Indians.

They discussed their situation around the campfire late into the night, raising their voices to be heard over the roar of the whitewater. Raising their voices in debate. They knew more rapids lay ahead. Gone down with the *Aripuaña* were the block and tackle, so it would be impossible to hoist the dugouts out of the water on the banks around rapids. They needed another canoe, since they couldn't fit all their gear in the four remaining boats, but there were no suitable trees nearby to build one, and they had few boatbuilding tools anyhow, at the bottom of the river with Kermit's rifle that hunted food.

Cherrie called it a "camp of ill omen." He said it was doubtful they would get out alive. Roosevelt had been carrying a fever for two days, from a type of malaria called Cuban fever that he'd brought back from the Spanish-American War. "We had been gone 18 days," he wrote. "We had used over a third of our food. We had gone only 125 kilometres, and it was probable that we had at least five times, perhaps six or seven times, this distance still to go. So far the country had offered little in the way of food except palm-tops. We had lost four canoes and one man. We were in the country of wild Indians, who shot well with their bows. It behooved us to go warily."

Having lost the *Aripuaña*'s storage space, they left as much as they could behind, including two tents and a box of surveying instruments—Rondon had relented on the survey, but not without an argument, and not completely. They lashed the canoes together in two pairs, carrying Roosevelt, Dr. Cajazeira, three paddlers, and three camaradas whose feet were too battered to walk. The other 13 men, including Rondon, Lyra, Kermit, and Cherrie, began walking single file along the bank.

◆

Where Rondon found Indians, Haskell found children. That afternoon the explorers were startled to see a farmhouse in the forest at the end of a lush path, about 150 yards from the west bank. They beached their rafts and a party of 12 moved on the house in a media assault. We strode past a small sickly cornfield, an impressively sloppy pigpen with a bevy of heavy-lidded hogs, and the scampering offspring of a turkey and cartoon character.

Sitting in the dirt at the doorway of the shack were three children home alone, about nine, three, and two years old. The explorers surrounded them and fired questions like arrows over the click of shutters and whir of camcorders, as the research raged on.

The oldest child was a girl of unique beauty, with high cheekbones, flowing chestnut hair, haunting brown eyes, and gaps between her teeth. Cabral asked her how old she was, and she said she didn't know. "Can you do arithmetic?" he asked. "Claro," she replied. "How much is two plus three?" "I'm not sure."

She sat on the hard ground and sifted beans through her fingers, alternating her gaze up at Cabral and down at the beans. They were store-bought, she said, so they had stones in them. It was the chore her parents had assigned her while they were away at church. "Where is the church?" asked Cabral.

"Oh, there's a city out there," she answered, vaguely waving a thin, delicate, and dirty arm toward the jungle behind the house, past a green garden with tall manioc sprouts. He asked her the name of the city, and she said it was called *Espigao*. He asked if she'd ever been there, and she had, once. She remembered the school, she said.

Her blue-eyed little brother was lively and talkative, a three-year-old cheerfully babbling as he scooted around in bare feet and baggy jeans with rolled-up cuffs full of dirt. But baby sister was the deadpan queen of comedy. She sat unmoving with a fixed bemused expression on her dirty chubby face circled by curly blond hair, snot running over her lip—like guacamole, Mario would still remember 30 years later. She was wildly bottom-heavy, with a big belly that grew over her thighs and toward little feet where her knees should have been.

Tweed gave the boy a blue rabbit's foot, explaining that it would bring good luck; and photographer Clifton gave the beautiful girl a small green stone. But the boy wanted that, too, and snatched it from his big sister, who grabbed it back, and a fight broke out. The explorers were mortified; in a mere 10 minutes, they had disturbed the natural order by enabling envy and greed, corrupting the natives with material things. They cut out down the path, hopped in their rafts, and rowed on.

CHAPTER 20

Dinner

And didn't they get the head and the tripes?
—Jean Chiappino, French ethnologist

Chief Oitamina led a parade of 18 sunburned White people in yellow life jackets onto the FUNAI outpost on the Roosevelt River. Cinta Larga women with high cheekbones, graceful arms, thick waists, and long black hair with streaks of light stood in the doorways of their wooden shacks and giggled sweetly at the colorful train chased by green butterflies. Many were nursing babies or holding them on a hip, as more children clung to their mothers' cotton dresses and stared at the explorers with big dark eyes.

The men were out working in the rice paddies, manioc gardens, and pastures. Pigs roamed between mud puddles and through garbage. There were about 16 wooden shacks with rusty tin roofs, some with concrete floors and some with dirt floors, some open and some with padlocks, built by loggers in unequal trade for mahogany. There were three masonry buildings, one with Deus spray-painted like graffiti on the side, another, the school, having a tile floor splattered with pig shit—it had been weeks since the FUNAI teacher was there, said a boy. The blackboard had a child's drawing of an Indian with long hair feeding a rooster and a fish, and wearing a skirt with a pointed penis peeking from the hem. Potty humor.

Tweed went off in search of the FUNAI director, hoping to use the radio to patch a call to *Good Morning America*. He said he felt pressure to bring back favorable media exposure, that's why he was trying so hard reach *GMA*, "to keep us all from looking like fools." And there was also his notch on the Roosevelt measuring stick, the metaphor that TR used before he went off to the Spanish-American War.

Haskell went in a truck to try to buy rice and beans from the tribe, since so much of the explorers' food was spoiled by gasoline. Tatare led some of his buddies away, a Pied Piper with a Walkman. There was only one old person around, a woman with beautiful long hair having just a few gray strands; Oitamina said she was his aunt, about 90. His brother was there, wearing a cap that said TONKIN GULF AERO CLUB. According to Tatare, he was the so-called "jawbone killer" (he broke their jaws with a club) of the FUNAI director and journalist, some 20 years earlier.

A few men and older boys returned on a flatbed truck carrying stacks of 10-kilogram bags of rice, and unloaded them into a shed. I asked Oitamina if I might interview them, and he led them to a long table with benches, where they perched as he evasively fielded questions. They passed around and drank from an aluminum pot containing *cauim*, a thick white drink made from manioc; Beth took a game gulp and laughed when Oitamina said it was made from larvae and spit.

Mario translated into English what Oitamina translated into Portuguese what the Indians said in Cinta Larga. They said life on the FUNAI post was more convenient and comfortable than it had been in the forest, especially with electricity from the generator. But life was also more complicated and stressful, and they didn't eat as well; now there were hassles and arguments over food. And they were sick a lot, catching colds and diseases all the time. The FUNAI nurse doesn't visit very often. She's in Riozinho, eight hours away.

Oitamina said the best man to ask about the tribe's history was his Uncle Rondon, the pajé, medicine man. He was more than 100 years old, he said, married to the old woman with the young girl's hair. But he was away. Later, with Mario, I got a chance to chat with him in the one-room schoolhouse, stepping around the pig shit. He looked about 70, and said a cobra had given him one of his eyes. As pajé, he knew rainforest secrets that science wanted and the outside world needed, he said. Rondon also was the chaplain, wearing a shiny black suit and tie to the church with DEUS spray-painted on the cinderblock, chanting "Yee-zoose! Yee-zoose!" He used a PA system to broadcast sermons to his indifferent flock. The missionaries were evicted by FUNAI years ago, but their strokes last like scars at the whipping post.

Mostly, Rondon appeared to be a crazy old man who had conversations with his imagination, and whom the others laughed at.

Tweed found more than the radio. It was a giant satellite dish, erected next to a distant shack out by the diesel generator. Six Cinta Larga sat on the dirt floor inside the shack, staring slack-jawed at a television showing *Star Trek*. Captain Kirk and Mr. Spock were speaking Portuguese as they fired up the Enterprise to escape a threatening planet. Assis said that most of the time they watch telenovelas, Brazilian soap operas.

Oitamina said the satellite dish was purchased with money from farming. Assis said it was mahogany money. At first there were six television sets, Assis said, installed in living quarters, but five were sold because of the fighting over them.

Tweed and Chip woke the FUNAI director from his siesta—Oitamina said he lived in Riozinho, where had a new car and sometimes invited Oitamina and his family over for steaks on the barbecue. Grumpily, the director unlocked the door to the clinic/radio room. Chip made a couple of calls trying to reach FUNAI in Cacoal and Vilhena, to help patch a call through to New York. He might as well have been trying reach the starship *Enterprise*.

Dr. Walden looked over the medicine in a cabinet. Having spent years working with Amazon Indigenous people, now dividing his time and practice between West Virginia and Ecuador, he was dismayed but not surprised by the small supply. He said the Cinta Larga were in better health than might be expected. "I see no distended bellies from worms or other parasites, no signs of serious malnutrition," he said, "although the light streaks in their hair is one indication of a significant long-term diet deficiency. I suspect that many of their problems are a result of the drastic change in their lifestyle over such a short period of time. An event like that causes a loss of spirit that's contagious to the body's immune system as well. It's really quite depressing. It's my second-worst nightmare."

His worst nightmare? He paused and sighed. "Total embarrassment at being involved with this expedition."

The director told the doctor there was a snakebitten boy who'd been to the hospital in Cacoal but wasn't healing. Bring him here, said Dr. Walden. His eyes bulged at the boy's fang marks, widest he'd ever seen, three inches apart and two feet up the boy's swollen leg. "That goddamn snake must have been huge," he said. The boy said that recently a snake killed a horse there. Walden told the boy he needed to return to the hospital as soon as possible or he would probably die. The boy calmly accepted the prognosis, thanked the doctor, and said he'd try to find a ride.

Late in the afternoon, a big rain appeared imminent. It was assumed we would camp on the riverbank at the post, as Oitamina had arranged an invitation to dinner. But to everyone's dismay, Haskell and McKnight wanted to move on, to respect the "Indian people's privacy," they said.

"We have the opportunity to have a pig cooked for us by an Amazon Indian village, and Charlie wants to run down the river and eat fucking Spam out of a can!" Tweed exclaimed, incredulous, disgusted, and loud enough for Charlie to hear. "He has no imagination when it comes to eating."

We all had to use some imagination at our late lunch, eaten in the grass like a picnic before a gawking audience. We spread our rationed peanut butter and jelly on small pieces of cheese, since finding an uncontaminated cracker was impossible. We mostly missed the noodles and coffee, dumped in the river.

Oitamina was asked if he was certain the explorers wouldn't be imposing if they stayed the night. He went to the tribe and they said no problem. Hang a hammock wherever you like. Many of us liked the community center, a large grass maloca with a wooden frame boasting graceful, curved rafters under a thatched roof. Big ugly chunks of meat burned black on the coals of a fire in the dirt, parts of what looked like a boar, armadillo, and anteater, with coarse black hair, thick plated skin, and wicked curved claws.[*] A man and his wife kicked the fire and turned over the meat now and then, and when a piece was charred crisp they cut it off with a machete and munched on it. They gave their toddler a piece and he carried it around and gnawed on its gnarly fingers like a baby teething on a rattle.

Four piglets came into the maloca looking for scraps, and the father with an ax handle whacked one cute little black pig on its lower back so hard its rear legs collapsed. The pig squealed in pain and dragged itself out on its front legs as the man laughed, with others laughing outside the hut. For 10 minutes the little pig struggled to support itself on its limp hind legs, and finally regained some use of them. Later, a young boy began chasing pigs around with a stick, beating them and laughing. A woman stepped on a dog's tail just to hear it yelp. Pitifully scrawny dogs cowered and slunk in the shadows, snatching and running with scraps when they could.[**]

About two dozen people joined the hunting party for a pig for the upcoming feast. Oitamina led the way with his bow, made from hard black ipe, bowstring woven from vine, shooting a seven-foot-long arrow with a barbed bamboo tip and hawk tailfeathers. He stalked one of the giant free-range hogs and let fly with a weak shot to the hip. After years of having the

---

[*]   I'm no naturalist.

[**]   "The casual Indian callousness toward animals is not unknown to us, and we are willing in theory to accept that cultural difference without blaming the Indians," wrote Wallace Stegner in his beautiful book of essays on the American West, *The Sound of Mountain Water*, during his 1946 visit to the Havasupai reservation within Grand Canyon National Park. His description of nine skeletal dogs chained to posts and used as scarecrows, howling in desperate hopefulness at his passing, was even sadder than this sadism toward the piglet.

run of the place, the shocked pig lumbered through the village dangling the long arrow, chased by Indians. Oitamina fell behind, slowed by his belly bouncing over the waistband of his jams. The pig made it to the edge of the forest and hid as the giggling hunters sneaked up on it.

Someone fired another shot and missed, and the pig broke out of the bush and sprinted back through the village chased by yelping and laughing boys, as panicked poultry squawked and scrambled out of the way. Oitamina dropped out, replaced by a muttering pink explorer in swimsuit and sneakers, dangling cameras around his neck that swayed and smacked him in the stomach as he ran.

Finally the pig was cornered and several arrows fired into it. A 10-year-old boy delivered the final blows, using a short bamboo spear. He walked up to the panting pig and stuck it in the side three or four times until it fell. The boy stepped back jubilant and raised his bloody hands to cheers from the other boys. As the pig panted its final breath, a squall came with heavy dark clouds and a gusting wind, exciting the animals and blowing leaves and garbage around the outpost.

That night the explorers sat at a long table as the Cinta Larga served them grilled and boiled pork with rice and manioc, watching them eat from the dark corners. The table was lit by a bulb on a post, until a beetle the size of a baseball crashed into the bulb and knocked it out; the bug landed on the ground, got up, shook it off, and walked away. With little light, the shadowy shapes of the Indians became hungry eyes from the darkness.

It wasn't the first time. McKnight's research, which she shared with me, included a report written by Jean Chiappino, a French physician and ethnologist, describing the scene at dinner during a stay at the Rio Roosevelt outpost in 1975: "Sometimes there will be game, if it is a feast, but then the Indian is nearly always sitting at the end of the table. He gets the scraps, a bit of fat, the bones, although it is he who has done the hunting. But aren't these the delicacies of the native population? And didn't they get the head and the tripes? This is said openly, the behavior is explicit enough, and the Indian chews his bones. The next time he will hunt monkeys, because he knows that Whites don't like monkeys."

When we explorers were sated—Kelley alone refused to eat more than one modest helping—the Cinta Larga gathered the leftovers and carried them back to their shacks.

In the morning after the rafts were loaded, Haskell gathered the group to say that the whitewater ahead would be the most treacherous and remote of the descent. It might be as much as two weeks before they reached the next trace of civilization, a large fazenda where Fabio and the Jeeps would be waiting. No rescue in case of emergency. The EPIRB was doubtful and radio useless. Chip had been sending out unanswered calls almost daily, climbing trees and stringing a metallic ribbon antenna between branches in increasingly discouraging attempts to be heard. The air force received one early message, but none since.

Haskell stood hulking on the bank as about a dozen Cinta Larga boys watched. "If anything happens to you, you get snakebit or anything like that, you're gonna *die!*" he boomed. "That's just as plain as it is. This is your *last chance*. If you don't want to go any further, you can get out here."

Mike Boyle had a question for Dr. Walden. "Uh, if we get bit by a snake, how long do we have?" he asked.

No one was inclined to grab their duffel and move into the maloca until they could catch a ride to the city along with the snakebit boy, so the offer went without takers. Other options were discussed. Haskell said that maybe Vilhena could be contacted and the satellite phone driven up from the Mirage Hotel, but it would take three days; he was willing to wait if the others wanted to, he added. Tweed said that if someone should die from snakebite because no rescue was possible because the expedition wasn't carrying a telephone because they didn't want to wait three days, it would be a heavy burden of guilt. McKnight countered that waiting three days would be a heavy burden on morale, considering it was so low already, and lower spirits might contribute to an accident. She held the door open for others to leave. "All I know is *I'm* going down the river," she said.

Quiet Mario Peixoto was last to speak. He put it into perspective, saying, "This is nonsense. People have been traveling down this river for decades. Indians have been living here for centuries without satellite telephones.

I've been on dozens of climbing expeditions far more dangerous than this, without EPIRBs. Let's just get on with it."

The EPIRB was designed for vessels lost at sea, sending a coded signal to a satellite. A battery test was suggested. Chip took it out of its box and put his finger on the test switch. He was asked if he was certain that flipping the switch wouldn't set it off. "Impossible," he said, as he triggered the switch and a green light flashed.

One more thing. The bill for dinner remained to be paid. Joba had negotiated the price to 80,000 cruzeiros, about $3 per person, but Haskell and McKnight didn't have the money handy. They asked the others to contribute 20,000 each, but few carried currency, and only 68,000 was collected. McKnight said she had the final 12,000 but it was in the bottom of her duffel bag strapped in her raft. Haskell, Joba, and Oitamina went back to the maloca and negotiated some more, and when they returned Haskell said it was handled, as the Cinta Larga had settled for 50,000 cruzeiros, or about $1.90 each for the all-you-can-eat pork dinner. The explorers moved on toward the darkest part of the river, with full stomachs and a taste worse than gasoline in some of their mouths.

CHAPTER 21

Disputes

He wished to give me his opinion as to how we
should conduct the work of the expedition.
—Colonel Rondon

On their first day without the *Aripuaña*, 13 of Rondon's men walked along the shore for about seven kilometers, the camaradas leading the way swinging machetes and hobbling on feet wrapped in canvas and monkey hides. The two pairs of canoes were unloaded and guided by ropes over an easy section that Cherrie called *Cachoeira de Boa Passage* (Good Passage Rapids), and one of the pairs over a difficult stretch called *Cachoeira de Seite Islas* (Rapids of the Seven Islands).

Roosevelt's pontoon was too heavy to steer, and at the rapids his canoeiros couldn't reach the bank to unload it. "The rapids came just around a sharp bend, and we got caught in the upper part of the swift water, where there were several big curls. We were within an ace of coming to grief on some big bowlders. It was a narrow escape from grave disaster."

They camped just past a fast river, 70 feet wide, flowing into the Duvida over a six-foot waterfall. In the morning Rondon named it Rio Kermit, holding a double dedication at which he also changed Rio da Duvida to Rio Roosevelt, by order of the Brazilian Government. He had carried along a polished oval board with RIO ROOSEVELT carved into it, now mounted on a thick post cut from a tree, as he made a speech with his men standing at attention on their aching feet. Roosevelt was reluctant, protesting that Duvida was an "unusually good" name, however he graciously accepted the honor. The ceremony ended with nine cheers: hip-hip-hoorays for two countries, six individuals, and the camaradas.

◆

Wired on 85-octane sugar, big bees harassed the Rio Roosevelt rafters for 90 minutes while the boatmen scouted Seven Islands Rapids. One giant fierce-looking candy-blue wasp landed between Cabral and me, and we smashed it with wild whacks of our paddles, as Chip watched from the water where he'd back-rolled over the tube. Another wasp landed and Oitamina picked it up and flicked it back into the forest, before an awe-struck audience. He chuckled and said the wasp was harmless.

Mario's raft had been tied under a tree full of red ants, and thousands of the sneaky little bastards scampered in and stowed away under the bilge and thwarts. They waited until the crux of Seven Islands, the turn where Roosevelt was within an ace of coming to grief; as Mario approached the tricky turn in the heaviest raft, the vicious little monsters sprung from their cracks, raced up the long wooden oars and bit his fingers, while more of the sons-of-bitches scrambled over his forearms after his sweet armpits, as Mario frantically brushed ants with hands that needed to be on the oars. Dr. Walden dropped his bailing bucket, leaped from the bow and began sweeping them with his safari hat, but too little too late. The raft hit one of TR's big "bowlders" sideways, and might have capsized if not for its weight. Another narrow escape from grave disaster. Luckily they weren't fire ants, or the bite marks on Mario's fingers would have become welts and blisters.

Slade led the rafts to a spot where he believed Colonel Rondon had held his ceremony naming the Rio Roosevelt. McKnight had a wooden plaque made in Maine that said RIO ROOSEVELT, and had brought it to replace Rondon's. There was no chance of finding the original wood plaque after 78 years in the jungle, but the expedition tried, as promised in the permit.

The rafts were tied next to a stream flowing out of the canopy on the east bank, not much of a river to name for Kermit. And Rondon had been on the west bank. Slade must have missed the detail. It was Rio Merceliano Avila, mapped and named by Rondon and Roosevelt.

Tweed and Slade were discussing whether or not it was actually Rio Kermit, when McKnight said that no one had told her today would be the day for the ceremony, so the plaque was at the bottom of her duffel, and what does it matter where it goes, we can put it anywhere we want, so let's do it tomorrow. Haskell agreed, adding that it was too much trouble to dig the plaque out.

Tweed, poking among the trees looking for the original board, disagreed, citing the importance of authenticity. Haskell jumped out of his raft to argue with Tweed behind the trees, while Slade took out his copy of *Through the Brazilian Wilderness*, and saw that this was not the right place. The expedition moved on. The plaque would be mounted 17 days later near the Trans-Amazonian Highway.

The sounds of the jungle at night changed. The excited and exuberant clicks, caws, whistles, whines, and shrieks were gone, replaced by an unsettling buzz carried on a hot breeze. It was a deep *dzzzzz*, long and slow, like sleeping under a power line. From one side of the camp it would build for a few seconds to a peak . . . *dzzzzZZZZ!* . . . then stop . . . and start on the other side. Back and forth, rhythmically, over and over, closing in.

There was a lonely dying rasp, like one quick turn of a small rusty ratchet, and in the distance a steel spike was being pounded into the heart of a mahogany tree.

We're surrounded now, said Oitamina. It's time to tell about Curupira.

"Curupira is the father of the forest. He walks with the wild pigs at night and protects the forest against intruders and people who disturb the environment. He is very short—shorter even than me—and his skin is warm and dark, sort of greenish in color. The hair on his head is thick and bulky and hangs very far down. Most people say he wears his feet pointing behind him, to fool trackers, but I don't believe that. I have seen his footprints, and they are normal.

"If you see Curupira, it means that something bad is going to happen to someone in your family. Maybe they will die. Also, when you see him you will get hot and feverish and dizzy. You will know before you see him, because a warm breeze will blow where he is walking, and there will be a buzzing sound. Only the paje can talk to the Curupira; sometimes at night, when he has a question about medicine, he will go to the forest to ask Curupira.

"I have never seen Curupira, but I have felt his presence. It was one night when I was hunting for tapir on the *barreiro*, where there is no vegetation, where the soil is very salty and the animals come at night to lick it. This is when I saw his tracks. I'm glad I didn't see Curupira, because I have friends who have seen him. Last year my cousin saw him, and soon after that my other cousin was killed in a hunting accident. He fell down on his shotgun, and it shot him in the stomach.

"But there is a way to trick Curupira. Knots make him angry, because they confuse and frustrate him. If you gather pieces of vine and tie them in knots and surround yourself with them, Curupira will be driven mad by them and will stop to untie them. This will give you time to escape."

◆

Colonel Rondon's men walked eight kilometers on the second day, made edgy by Trigueiro's barking at the forest. "There is no doubt that there are many Indians on all sides about us," said Cherrie, noting their footprints in mud. At camp they decided to build new boats after all, when they saw two nearby araputango trees, like red cedar, buoyant and soft enough for the few tools they had.

Rondon rose at 2:00 A.M. on March 19 and sat with his gun at his side by the campfire, knowing he was being watched by Indians from the

forest. Work began at daybreak, and for three afternoons there were "tremendous downpours" with thunder and lightning; but they ate well, piranhas
and bananas, while Roosevelt enjoyed watching "wonderful butterflies" and
listening to "attractive bird music."

"Work on the canoes goes ahead nicely," wrote Cherrie on March 20.
"One is finished and the other will be by noon tomorrow."

But Rondon wanted to make what he called a "small reconnaissance"
of a tributary they had walked past. He suggested that he and Lyra hike
back for a couple days, pausing the boatbuilding. Roosevelt disputed and
Rondon gave in, because as he put it, "it was necessary to attend to the
wish of the chief of the American commission relative to the acceleration
of our voyage." But Rondon surreptitiously sent Lyra back to establish
the longitude and latitude of the tributary, "by the sun and by the stars,"
Roosevelt wrote, murky about the details. With Lyra gone for two days,
work on the canoes stalled.

Roosevelt, Kermit, and Cherrie confronted Rondon, who admitted
the ruse but stood by the necessity of the river's measurement. Tempers
were stretched. Cherrie added Rondon to his short list of incompetents.
"We expected to get away today, but work on the canoes was delayed and
finally Col Rondon declared it necessary to take some more observations
for latitude, etc.," Cherrie entered on March 21, vague words that concealed
his anger over Rondon's deception.[*]

To Rondon, this expedition was no more dire than others he'd experienced. "Death and danger should never, no matter how much suffering
they may inflict, interfere in the duties of expedition members," he wrote
in his memoir. If it hadn't been for Roosevelt's big hurry, he suggested,
"these hindrances would constitute, for us, a good occasion to extend, with
greater leisure, our explorations into the interior of these lands, which in
reality greatly interested us in virtue of the exuberance of its formidable
vegetation."

---

[*]   In his 1994 book *My Last Chance to Be a Boy*, author Joseph Ornig first uncovered
       this issue. He had transcribed Cherrie's penciled diary, in 1975.

Describing the many portages, Rondon said, "These repeated stoppages, although they did not succeed in overcoming the resistance and the vigor of our admirable canoe-men, were however, now trying the patience of the members of the American Commission.

"Having pitched our tents, Mr. Roosevelt asked me for a chat as he wished to give me his opinion as to how we should conduct the work of the expedition."

Roosevelt told him they should abandon the survey, as a simple matter of survival. Descend and survive the river this time, come back later to chart it. Rondon told him that was not possible. "Mapping the river is indispensable, and without it the expedition, as far as I am concerned, will have been entirely pointless." It was surely on his mind that this was his only chance to chart the river, because of money.

But he did budge. "I replied that we were there to accompany him and take him across the wilderness, and that therefore, we would execute the services in accordance with his wishes; we would employ our greatest efforts to give him the satisfaction of seeing reduced to a possible minimum, the time which he had still to spend on this expedition." He changed the method of mapping to something quicker and less precise, and agreed to move Kermit out of the lead canoe, where he was bullseye for the barbed tip of a long arrow.

March 20 was a busy day in Cherrie's diary: "It was discovered today that someone or ones of the camaradas has been stealing our emergency rations! Fifteen of the boxes have disappeared!" It was the tin boxes that the quartermaster Anthony Fiala had packed in New York—each box with food for six men for one day. "For some time we have been on a trifle more than half rations," wrote Cherrie.

On March 22 they made 10 kilometers, carrying loads around rapids for seven hours, while the canoes were either paddled empty by the best canoeiros or guided down by ropes. The exhausting day ended at sundown, and they pitched their shelters in darkness.

The *New York Times* got a telegram that day from Anthony Fiala, saying, "We have lost everything in the rapids. Telephone my wife of my safety." That's all.

The *Times* assumed that Fiala's "we" included Roosevelt, not knowing that there were now two parties. On March 23 they ran with Fiala's few words and hundreds of words their own, under the front-page headline: ROOSEVELT PARTY LOSES EVERYTHING IN RAPIDS OF A BRAZILIAN RIVER, MEMBERS OF PARTY PROBABLY SAFE. MAY BE ON UNKNOWN RIVER.

"Probably" safe probably gave Edith her own near–heart attack.

On that day they actually made 13 kilometers, with two hours in the canoes, in swift, smooth water that Roosevelt said was "very lovely"; and seven hours carrying loads, including one stretch for three-quarters of a mile, a "long carry," words that TR, Cherrie, and Kermit found themselves using often. Roosevelt was upbeat as always. If only the *Times* readers could have read his words that day, describing "red splendor that changed first to gold and then to molten white. In the dazzling light, under the brilliant blue of the sky, every detail of the magnificent forest was vivid to the eye."

Cherrie's view was darker. "Our position every day grows more serious."

The *Times* reached Fiala that night, and he sent a cable the next day that clarified things, naming the Duvida for the first time. ROOSEVELT IS SAFE; WASN'T WITH FIALA, said the March 24 headline. But "safe" was speculative, since it had been nearly two months since Fiala had last seen him. The Bull Moose was still lost to the world on the River of Doubt.

Rapids held them to a mere nine kilometers in the next five days, carrying loads and guiding the canoes with ropes. They found honey and Brazil nuts but not many, an "off year" for Brazil nuts, said Kermit.

On March 27, while guiding the canoes through rapids with ropes, the pontoon got pinned against a boulder, and Roosevelt charged into the water up to his chest to help. "His rushing into the water to assist was entirely characteristic of him," said Cherrie. "And he did this after many days of suffering from fever."

Struggling on slippery rocks in fast-moving water, Roosevelt gashed his shin against a rock. It was the same leg he had injured in a tram accident in 1902,* which never healed properly. "From that time on," said Cherrie, "he was a very sick man."

Said Kermit, "He knew well that the chances were against his coming out."

◆

The Rio Roosevelt rafters camped above the nine-kilometer stretch of rapids that Rondon and Roosevelt suffered through for five days. After a two-hour scout of the first section in the morning, the boatmen said there was a narrow line through continuous Class IV rapids. On the right side against the bank were big branches, on the left big boulders, and between them there was a wide hole under a steep standing wave. The line was on the edge of the wave, if you could hit it, but through the wave might work, too.

Boyle hit the line without trouble. Kelley stood to row in her "slug" of a boat, and turned backward to gain speed, ballast forward to keep the nose down to avoid the buckle of the bow that brings a high-side, as Carr Clifton bailed like mad. She missed the hole and shot through the wave like an arrow from the forest.

Tatare rode with Mario. He had walked around the prior rapids, but the boats proved they could take it, so he was ready. Mario spun the raft, stood, and went backward, Tatare's face went into the wave, and he came out bursting with adrenaline and hooked on whitewater rafting.

---

*   It was a serious crash with a train in Massachusetts. Roosevelt was riding to a speaking engagement in the rear of a luxury carriage drawn by four horses, and the coachman turned in front of a trolley on railroad tracks passing from the rear, speeding because it was late for Roosevelt's speech. His Secret Service agent riding in front was crushed and killed by the wheels of the train, and Roosevelt was thrown 30 feet face down into the mud. He got back on his feet spitting blood and had to be restrained from fighting the trolley driver, who would serve six months in jail as the fall guy—trolley-line bigshots had been backseat driving, telling him to speed up. Roosevelt didn't take care of his injured leg, too busy campaigning. The wound got infected and required two surgeries in the next month.

We Candirus recruited Charlie for his power, like having a big-biceps home-run hitter in your lineup. Psyched by our own *ooh-oohs*, we skimmed the hole and blasted through the wave. Charlie was a good fit; he'd found his happy place, on a sports team.

The technique for a standing wave is to hit it head-on and at top speed, hoping you don't high-side. Bury the flat nose of the raft in the backwash (face), cross the boil line (heart), and come out the outwash (slope). Weight up front was more important than maneuverability. Slade chose Beth and Geraldo as passengers, the two lightest. Kelley suggested he carry heavier passengers, but he dismissed the advice from the girl. Who knows why he wanted Beth, since the tension between them crawled around camp like a snake. Their problems went back to the previous May, that trip to the wrong headwaters at the pig farm, and their long hike out after a night in the bed of the truck.

Slade avoided the wave. "Basically I hit the hole where I wanted to, but my load was probably too light, and I needed more power and momentum," he said. "The raft just sort of surfed into the hole and got spun around. I dropped both oars—at that point they're useless anyhow—and spread-eagled myself on the back, to try and keep it from high-siding. There was no point in trying to get Beth and Geraldo to do the same."

Let's go to the chief's videotape: three confused people are in a spinning raft under a crashing wave on the high seas. A blonde and a diminutive Brazilian are crouched on their knees, clutching the tubes at the bow, at the mercy of the force of nature, waiting to be sucked to the bottom while praying to be spit out. The boatman is crawling around at the stern of the boat, trying to catch the slamming oars.

In slo-mo: the raft hits the hole at a slight angle, the two passengers leaning over the bow like mastheads and gamely breaking the wave with their faces. The boatman is bucked forward, losing his grip on the oars. As the raft is spun to the left and around 180°, the left oar whizzes inches over the woman's head like a baseball bat whiffing a screwball. The raft is stopped in the hole stem first, and the boatman dives and sprawls there, trying to prevent a high-side.

The only sound on the tape is the roar of the rapids. Beth says that Slade was shouting at her to grab the oars, which she didn't do because earlier he had yelled at her, "Don't touch the oars! Don't touch the oars!"

The attitude dialog went something like this. Boatman: *I don't want your help because you're useless.* Blonde, arms crossed over chest: *Well, you're not going to get it because you don't like anything I do.* Finally the raft is spit out of the hole.

Slade had said that if a hole was a Class V keeper, you die. But this hole was only a stopper.

CHAPTER 22

Riozinho

Their blood is thicker than their misery.
—Nurse Judite do Nascimento

A network of logging roads ran under the canopy within the Roosevelt Indigenous Territory, one of them 80 miles from the river to Riozinho, where Piu, Oitamina, and Tatare lived. Riozinho was a few dozen houses, some markets, and bars on dirt streets along BR-364, along with the Riozinho Indian House, as it was called locally. The two-lane blacktop carried a stream of smoking trucks, straining under their loads of logs going south to mills in Espigao d'Oeste and Pimenta Bueno.

The logging roads were visible from the river in places. As the rafts passed a dusty red tributary coming from the forest, Assis pointed a condemning finger at it, and with a sad shake of his head said that soon there would be a heavy bridge here, built by loggers to carry mahogany off Cinta Larga land, with the chiefs' approval. "All of the Cinta Larga regions are involved in selling timber," said Assis. "It's not only Piu and Roberto, it's other chiefs, too. At least Piu and Roberto, Tatare, too, are investing their money. They're smarter with money than the other chiefs. They don't fall for bad deals from scoundrels."

Chief Piu's house was built on the best lot in Riozinho, away from the noise of the highway. It was peaceful and tasteful, furnished with leather couches, carved mahogany doors, and cabinets of *cerejeira*, called blonde mahogany. He lived with his beautiful second wife, their new baby, and his nine-year-old daughter from his first marriage, who served Mario and me black coffee in small, delicate China cups.

Piu spent elegant afternoons on his porch, an Amazon gentleman caressed by the humid breeze, relaxing in dapper white slacks and his white rattan rocker, listening to the sweet calls of tropical birds and smoking a Carlton. Maybe he thinks of the days when he had to eat rats to survive. More likely he thinks of his next scheme.

Over his shoulder, the rainforest rose beyond a white picket fence and the small Riozinho River. Two black barbed wires ran across the pickets around a grassy yard with two growling German shepherds chained to trees. It made him look like a cocaine smuggler, but no thanks, he said, being a mahogany chief was difficult enough, and it paid nearly as well. He said it was a dirty and dangerous business, shuttling Bolivian *cocaina* down BR-364.

Having different tastes, Chief Oitamina and his wife and two children lived in a drab green cinderblock house just across a scruffy soccer field from the highway, with trucks rumbling 24/7, braking and accelerating, braking and accelerating, at speedbumps and potholes in the road. Down their dirt street was a ramshackle roadhouse where Indians hung out on stifling afternoons shooting pool on a rocky table, and drinking beer when they could afford it. "It's mostly the Surui who have a weakness for drinking," said Assis. "The Cinta Larga have a weakness for automobiles and fast driving."

Oitamina's wife Regina was a princess in tight pressed bluejeans and blouses, toucan feather earrings, and hot pink fingernails. She studied Portuguese at night school and did her homework with a flair, dotting her *i*'s with circles and drawing perfect triangles for her *a*'s. She watched novelas on television in their air-conditioned bedroom, and had just ordered new drapes from a door-to-door fabric salesman who spread out his samples on their mahogany dining table. They had a maid who came every day to sweep the polished cement floors, wash the dishes, and do laundry by hand, hanging it up to dry on a barbed-wire clothesline in the dirt yard with chickens pecking at bones thrown out the kitchen window. A pet anteater had the run of the place, lumbering around the house in slow motion, sleeping in a low-slung hammock on the porch while the other pet, a sickly starving kitten, was tied to a basket under the house.

The center of attention was their three-year-old daughter Paula, a beautiful child with dark eyes, pierced ears, and an impish spirit that came from knowing she was hot stuff. She paid more attention to her baby sister Ana than their mother did, sweetly wrapping the naked infant in a blanket and wiping papaya off her plump cheeks. She carefully changed her clothes, fed her cookies, and pushed her through the house in a stroller, steering around the anteater lolling in the sun on the floor.

Oitamina and Regina were probably not made for each other. Oitamina wanted a second wife but Regina wouldn't have it. "I asked her, but she said to me, 'Now you are married so you have to forget other women. If you don't want to live with me you better give me back to my parents.' So I have agreed with that, but my cousin is a chief, too, and he has two wives who share the work."

Chief Tatare lived with his wife Julia and their three children on one of the dirt streets between Oitamina and Piu, in a *cerejeira*-sided house that had been built for him by loggers. "This is where I hide from people," he said, laughing and pointing a store-bought crossbow at me when Mario and I visited. The house was surrounded by a covered tile porch, and just outside the kitchen door were two long benches for Tatare's buddies. The dirt yard was surrounded by a six-foot-high spiked iron fence, containing a snarling German shepherd. Tatare said the dog was to protect his family when he was away on business.

The children included a baby daughter, a 4-year-old son, and 12-year-old Elizabeth who was known in school for being stuck-up because she had nice clothes that other girls couldn't afford, and generally acted like she wasn't an Indian, down to her painted toenails. She had a White boyfriend her parents didn't know about, and a stereo in her bedroom where she liked to go and draw the leopard-skin curtains and listen to rock music.

The family enjoyed the big color TV in the living room. The four-year-old was captivated by *The Flintstones*, while Tatare liked *Miami Vice*. He'd recently watched the movie *Spartacus*, and was impressed by the scene where Kirk Douglas fights a Black slave in an arena before a cheering audience of bloodthirsty Romans, for the entertainment of two rich women. The slave wins but spares Spartacus's life and is killed for it. Tatare wondered if that's how it was for Indigenous slaves.

Just down the street from the chiefs' homes, there was a compound of eight small wooden structures, headquarters for the *Associacao Pamare*, Association of the People; two were used to lodge guests, another was a shop selling Cinta Larga crafts, and the rest were for meetings and events. Piu had bought the land, built the buildings, and founded the association to sell mahogany in a more businesslike manner, and to try to include the tribe in the process and proceeds. The financial structure was like that of a one-person corporation, as the loggers paid the chiefs and the chiefs financed the association. Piu had recently resigned as chairman when the job became too much of a hassle, but since he was the best and smartest businessman, knew the loggers, and understood the mahogany trade better than anyone else, he remained involved and influential.

His replacement was a quiet fellow named Antonio who wasn't very bright. He was soon removed from office for breaking another Indian's arm in a fight, withdrawing money from the association's bank account, and cutting secret deals with loggers. He was rejected by the tribe, and his pregnant wife and three children left him and moved in with a White girl from Cacoal.

Oitamina was chairman and treasurer now. He had an administrative secretary, an earnest and intelligent young man of 19 who read and wrote documents and letters. He got in trouble when he showed up with a new motorcycle and couldn't explain how he paid for it on his $250-per-month salary. Oitamina wanted to fire him but some loggers threatened to stop buying mahogany if he did, so the young man and his new Yamaha 660cc Ténéré dual sport stayed.

Two girls worked in the store selling arrows, necklaces, bracelets, and baskets made by Cinta Larga women. The association employed non-Indians because Indians didn't do arithmetic, and the few customers were non-Indians. Sometimes the girls raised the prices and pocketed the difference, but Oitamina needed them.

When there was an issue or dispute, the association held a meeting to resolve it by discussion. As chairman, Oitamina saw himself mostly as mediator: "When there are conflicts I resolve them," he said. A chief doesn't decide, he advises. Oitamina's wealth gave him power but didn't assure respect, as some of the others couldn't see how his lifestyle benefited them. Sometimes that's what caused the conflict. Envy within the tribe had to be dealt with. Oitamina's life was one big conflict of interest.

Although he felt harried and burdened by the responsibility, Oitamina was proud to be head of the *Associacao*, exceptional in that it functioned without help from the government. "It was created to help the Cinta Larga get off the reservation and make them independent of FUNAI," he said, "and to show them that we are capable of dealing with the outside world without their interference."

Sitting at his big mahogany desk, Oitamina pushes aside seven stamps for documents, to find a plaque given to him by the Rio 14 de Abril outpost, for his leadership role in a protest that succeeded in evicting loggers and settlers from their land. He opens a drawer in a file cabinet and pulls out a book with notes from meetings, and letters and documents regarding the Rio Roosevelt expedition. Soon there would be a fax machine, a gift from New Century Conservation Trust.

The ideal chairman for the *Associacao*, as IBAMA in Rondônia saw it, would be a chief to negotiate fair prices from the wood buyers, and use the money to buy food for the tribe and build schools and clinics. "But it would be a very risky job," said Hamilton Casara, the head of IBAMA, when I interviewed him.

"The biggest problem we have with the current situation is that it is only a few Indians who profit," he said. "If Roberto Carlos or Piu ever came to IBAMA with a proposal that proved the whole tribe would receive benefits from the cutting of mahogany, and not just a few of them, then I would seriously consider endorsing it, although it would have to be approved by Congress. But it would be better for them, because IBAMA would not allow a sale at a price as low as the Indians do."

"IBAMA wants us to keep records of how much timber we cut," says Piu, with disdain. "I was in Brasilia and met with the head of IBAMA, and he said we should stop cutting so much and have a reforestation project. But nobody seems to want to help Indigenous people with programs like this."

He has a simpler idea. "I have plans for our community to set up a sawmill so we can do the finishing of the timber ourselves. I know we are being exploited by the logging companies and sawmill owners, and this will cut them out. So far we haven't been able to get any financing for this project, but I'm going to really fight to get this sawmill underway. I don't want to work the way we have been any more, with everybody after us. I want to work in a more legal way, with everything approved, so I can sleep at night.

"There's a lot of politics involved, and we don't know what to do," he added.

He knew the catch was "approved by Congress." All it takes is one corrupt politician to betray you. Sometimes it's better not to take the chance. It's so simple to pocket $5,000 or so and let a garimpeiro move his dredge onto the river, or let a logger cut a tree in exchange for a new truck. Piu got a lot of offers. He was thinking about getting into heavy equipment himself, and was window-shopping for a bulldozer.

Meanwhile, some FUNAI agents were selling Cinta Larga mahogany on the side to loggers. It was fairly simple to do, since the trees grew singularly and isolated in the forest; an agent could hike in, find a tree, and lead the loggers back, to cut it down and drag it out.

"I first began thinking that FUNAI was corrupt and not good for us a few years ago," says Oitamina.* "I've spoken to the head of FUNAI four times about taking their people out of here, but FUNAI just keeps giving us the runaround. The government doesn't want us to be independent. They want us to be dependent on FUNAI. But we want to speak for ourselves. We don't want FUNAI speaking for us in Congress. We have to take care of ourselves. Soon the *Associacao* will be taking a bigger step, sending me to Brasilia to have a voice in new laws proposed by the government that will affect Indians."

Oitamina sees that he's onto a significant subject. He raises his fist and drops it firmly on the desk. "My people are outraged that Indians have not been involved in the writing of laws that affect us! The government treats Indians like we are children! They think that we aren't capable of running things for ourselves, or of being good administrators, but we are. This new legislation will help us get back to our ways, because the government won't be able to order us around anymore. We will be more independent, and FUNAI will not even need to exist anymore. This is why we have to change the law. We want some say in our destiny!"

Oitamina boasts that he lives like a White man because he's smart like one. He's not a dumb Indian, he says.

Down the road a bit, past a small piece of forest at the Riozinho Indian House, there was a clinic run by nurse Judite do Nascimento, feeding and treating sick Indian children for nine years. She had hitchhiked from Para when she heard there was work in Rondônia, but found thousands of job-seekers ahead of her. The only work was deep in the jungle where no one would go, as a FUNAI trainee at the Rio Roosevelt outpost. Like her friend Assis she was enchanted, and knew she'd found her calling.

She spent six months there without leaving, and never missed the town of Riozinho. Now in Riozinho, she misses the outpost. "The Cinta Larga

---

* From a 1991 report by Friends of the Earth, "Following illegal contracts signed by FUNAI officials, 300,000 cubic meters of timber were taken from the Cinta Larga's Roosevelt Reserve and Aripuana Park between 1985 and 1990."

women have such beautiful hair, because they wash it in the river," she says with clear longing. "My hair was very nice, too, when I lived there."

She has a husband, two sons, and an adopted daughter, but she's happiest when she's deep in the forest with Indians. She's in love with the Cinta Larga and Surui she treats, and they love her. "*Ingaramunga* is how you say I love you in Cinta Larga," she says, adding that these are the only Indian words she knows. She would like to know more but the women won't teach her, because, she says, then they wouldn't be able to talk about her when she's around.

The Riozinho Indian House looked much like the Rio Roosevelt outpost, 10 small structures with wood walls, tin roofs, and cement floors. Four structures held 11 rooms where Indians could stay. It was built by FUNAI in 1976, and is dedicated to the director who saw to its construction, Jose do Carmo Santana; six years later he took his life, died with a broken heart, as the Indians' quality of life worsened during his time, for reasons he couldn't control.

The situation now pulls at Judite's heart. When she first got to the post there was money from FUNAI for food, some fish and chicken, but now there is none. Rice and beans are about all the Indians there eat, and sometimes it's slim on the beans. "It's a crime what they eat," she says sadly.

The only money that comes from FUNAI is the $230 per month that pays her salary. There's a rusting Volkswagen bus out back that doesn't run for want of a battery. When she needs to go into the forest to treat Cinta Larga, she's often driven in Oitamina's Bronco. Recently she's been trying to vaccinate the children against measles, polio, and tuberculosis, with vaccines from the health department in Porto Velho. Young children and naked coughing babies with distended bellies play in the dirt near their mothers, who are breast-feeding more babies. "Cinta Larga women start having babies at puberty," Judite says. "We have to keep the Surui and Cinta Larga houses separated, because the men like to sleep with women from the other tribe, and there are a lot of fights."

One of the babies scratches a lice-bitten bald spot on his head. A thin young Surui girl wearing a clean cotton dress, Gabriella, stands shyly in the shade at the door of her family's room with one hammock, holding an aluminum pot. She came to Judite with tuberculosis from her Aripuaña Park reserve, where there was a very high TB rate.

Judite's spirit is kept alive by the appreciation and affection she feels from those she treats. "They call me the white Cinta Larga," she says with pride and humility. The only time the expression on her gentle face turns negative is when she laments that she can't get rid of their worms. "It's hopeless," she says. "I just can't get through to these Indians about hygiene. The children shit everywhere, and the mothers don't like us to scold them. We're tired of telling them, explaining that it's the biggest reason their babies are sick."

Another nurse works there with Judite, and a doctor comes from Cacoal with reasonable frequency. "There was a full-time doctor here for four years," she says, "but he left four years ago. Doctors and nurses don't like to work with Indians because they think they're dirty, and because the Indians are difficult; for example they don't give you information when they're sick, and they don't take their medicine unless you watch them. Indians sometimes go to the hospital in Cacoal but they're treated poorly. The staff there thinks they're not worth good care because they don't understand about hygiene."

Sometimes medicine is purchased by sympathetic loggers. "A couple pharmacies in Cacoal help, too," she says, "but FUNAI owes them so much money that they can't carry the credit anymore.

"People in Cacoal won't help the Cinta Larga because they know how much mahogany money is floating around in the tribe," she continues. "It's a lot more than they have, and they resent it." She doesn't really want to talk about the obvious, but some of her disgust toward Oitamina, Piu, and Tatare can't be hidden, especially since Oitamina and Tatare bring their children to her for treatment. She's mad because recently a Cinta Larga baby needed medicine, and it was hard to get the money out of Oitamina. She can't understand it, and she quietly holds it against him.

"We at FUNAI don't get involved in this mahogany business," she says. "FUNAI doesn't want us to. Even if we see the Indians are being robbed and exploited, we say nothing because then the Indians get upset with us and take the sides of the loggers even more, because the loggers have money and we don't. The loggers are very clever in the way they dole this money out a little bit here and there, and make the Indians think they are their friends. They're always telling the Indians not to listen to FUNAI, that FUNAI doesn't care about them, FUNAI can't help them. And the Indians believe them because money talks.

"As for trying to tell the other Indians that their chiefs are causing them to suffer, it's always a mistake to criticize one Indian to another. Their blood is thicker than their misery."

Back at *Associacao Pamare*, Oitamina conducts a tour mostly for the benefit of Mario and me. His group includes young men and boys showing amusement, fascination, or boredom, women breast-feeding, and two pleasant punks who are Oitamina's bodyguard and driver. One carried a concealed weapon and the other wielded an automobile—Cinta Larga drive fast and at the edge of control, so carnage is high. Oitamina mostly used drivers for his high-performance Bronco, one of whom was a spy for the loggers.*

Oitamina sits in a heavy mahogany chair at the end of a long conference table and puts on his chief's *cocar*, a feathered tribal headdress neatly culture-clashing with his tank top that says CROCODILE BEACH. Rubber flipflops dangle from his toes and stretch to make contact with the floor, dropping off as he swings his bare feet. There's a big map of Brazil tacked on the wall behind him, over an illustration previewing the plan for the tribe's next step toward independence.

It's a drawing of an Indian carrying a long bow and quiver of arrows, wearing a camouflage uniform with blood-red fringe across the shoulders and down the arms. He wears combat boots and a bush hat with the brim pinned at the side. His pants are very tight around his buttocks. Under the drawing it says *Guarda Foresta Indigina*.

Oitamina explains that the *Associacao* intends to form a forest police force, and this is what its patrolmen will look like. On the wall there's also

---

* Mario found most of this out, including about Tatare's daughter's White boyfriend.

a chart showing the chain of command from general to private. The force will stop the loggers from cutting mahogany without contracts with the *Associacao*, and keep the forest free of nonpaying garimpeiros, seringueiros, pig farmers, manioc planters, colonists, and other intruders. FUNAI doesn't know anything about this planned project, he adds, so please keep the secret.

Oitamina smiles when I ask him about the tight pants. "That's to show how physical and strong the Cinta Larga man is," he replies.

About a year earlier, near the Cinta Larga FUNAI post at Serra Morena in Mato Grosso, five loggers were killed by 35 Cinta Larga, for cutting wood they hadn't paid for, and after they'd been told to get out. Their skeletons were discovered months later. "We used arrows because guns make noise," said Oitamina.

"Indians don't invade the cities, so why do white men think they can invade our land?" he asks. "We can justify killing them. Piu and I complained about these loggers to FUNAI, but FUNAI did nothing. The Brazilian government has set this reserve aside for us, and now they can't take it back. If they try, it would be a crazy thing to do. There will be a war."

Back in his bedroom, tacked on the wall above the VCR he bought to show his expedition video, there was a striking poster. Glaring down at home theatergoers was Sylvester Stallone, alert in the jungle, carrying a crossbow at the ready and a quiver of arrows in a sling on his back. Hair like Roberto Carlos, camo attire, sleeveless, muscular arms, tight pants around powerful thighs. Under the actor in blood-red letters, RAMBO: FIRST BLOOD: *"No man, no law, no war can stop him."*

CHAPTER 23

Morphine

There was only one thing for me to do.
—Theodore Roosevelt

As Dr. Cajazeira wrapped Roosevelt's leg to compress the bleeding, the sky began to gush. For four hours, all they could do was huddle and wait. They got on the river for 10 minutes and hit more rapids, so they camped in the rain with no fire. By morning Roosevelt's leg was infected, and his fever had spiked.

The rapids were run by the best canoeiros, as the others carried the gear for about a mile. The camarada Macario chopped a giant tree to fall perfectly as a bridge over a tributary that Rondon named Rio Cherrie.

They were at the entrance of a tall gorge. Rondon and Lyra hiked high along the west bank, to an altitude of 350 feet, measured by Lyra using his barometer as an altimeter. They stood at the edge of a cliff and looked down to see whitewater flowing through a canyon for more than a mile: six waterfalls, the final three dropping 10 meters. That night Rondon spoke to the men.

In *Dark Trails*, Cherrie writes, "I have never forgotten the expression on Rondon's face when he said, 'We shall have to abandon our canoes and every man fight for himself through the forest.' . . . Hoping the stronger men could forge ahead and find aid," Rondon added, in his second speech at the Rio theater.

"Had we done so," wrote Cherrie, "I doubt if any one of us would ever have come through. To all of us, his report was practically a sentence of death.

"Colonel Roosevelt was a very sick man and the effect of Rondon's report on him, with his feeling of keen responsibility to us all, was such that I felt he might not live through the night."

Roosevelt never mentioned Rondon's verdict that night; he barely mentioned injuring his leg. He admired Rondon and respected his commitment, dedication, and strength. "In my life I've known two great colonels," he would say. "The one who solved the problem of the Panama Canal, and Rondon."

◆

It took the Rio Roosevelt expedition less than two days to travel the 39 kilometers from Rio Kermit to the waterfalls, compared to Rondon's 12 days, walking and building canoes. There was nothing the rafts couldn't run. The waterfalls were an easy portage, over a logging road. Lucky it was there, said Charlie.

Slade said we were lucky to be anywhere but the bottom of the river. The waterfall gave no warning, before a smooth edge and long drop. When Kaminski felt the current he yelled back to Slade to row like hell to shore. The rafts squeezed into an eddy, where Slade said if we had gone any farther we would have been swept over the falls and someone would have died.

At camp, Slade and Chip Haskell hiked along the east bank to view the waterfall, and at dinner Slade said they'd seen the "mother of all rapids." He said the waterfall was 30 feet. "Did you see it?" I asked. "It's 30 feet all right," he replied.

At daybreak I hiked downriver to see the mother myself. The growth along the steep riverbank was too thick, but there was a trail climbing to an opening in the green walls. At the top, I found myself walking on a mahogany sidewalk, a chopped tree not taken evidently because of termites. Standing on the five-foot-high log with 100 feet flattened where it had dropped, I saw a steep stretch of whitewater, and distant mountains that looked like the Alleghenies, as TR said.

Back down at the riverbank, the waterfalls were hidden by an island. I picked my way upriver, creeping and climbing through jungle, checking for snakes with each step. I finally got above the island, and looking down could still only see the back of the waterfall, dropping into a howling void. It looked like it might be 30 feet all right.

◆

Kermit told Rondon that his father would never survive a trek. He was sure he could get the dugouts past the waterfalls. Lyra sided with Kermit. Cherrie and Dr. Cajazeira supported them. Rondon doubted it but agreed to try.

Roosevelt had been silently, stoically, suffering for more than two weeks. In *Through the Brazilian Wilderness*, he only mentions his leg injury in a passing sentence. "While in the water trying to help with an upset canoe I had by my own clumsiness bruised my leg against a boulder; and the resulting inflammation was somewhat bothersome." *Into the Amazon* says blood spurted from the wound, and *The River of Doubt* says blood spun from it. Dr. Cajazeira says he used gauze to stem the bleeding.

"He had been ill intermittently since the days spent at Broken Canoe Rapids where we had lost our first two canoes," wrote Cherrie. "His sickness began with fever. A little later dysentery further sapped his strength. Now, in addition, he was suffering from oriental ulcers, and the wound that he sustained when assisting in salvaging our canoes had become infected."

Kermit spent the next day, a Sunday, working with Lyra, fighting the six dugouts through the gorge, getting one canoe past the third waterfall.

"He and Lyra had now been in the water for days," said TR. "Their clothes were never dry. Their shoes were rotten. The bruises on their feet and legs had become sores. On their bodies some of the insect bites had become festering wounds, as indeed was the case with all of us."

Rondon and his men cut a trail "around and up and over the mountains," said Cherrie. They had to go inland because it was "too dangerous to cut a trail along the precipitous sides of the mountains facing the river."

For the next two days Kermit inched the dugouts through the rapids, as camaradas carried loads over the mountain to the camp below the falls. Cherrie too was sick. On the third day Roosevelt had to hike there himself. Two or three times he dropped and couldn't get up, imploring Cherrie to go on without him. Cherrie lifted his friend and held him on his feet as they continued to climb, fearing a heart attack or asthma event with each step and stumble. At the top, Roosevelt snapped back into optimism, enjoying the view of the mountains he likened to the Alleghenies. Cherrie saw "a vast panorama of forest-clad mountain-tops and valleys, with the Rio Roosevelt rushing like an arrow of light straight-away toward the distant hills." It was all downhill to the camp, where Roosevelt collapsed.

Fighting his own malarial fever, Kermit worked for three-and-a-half days from sunrise to sunset, with Lyra and the four best men, to get the dugouts downriver. Kermit engineered and directed the lowering of the boats by ropes, clinging to narrow ledges on the sheer canyon walls, and wearing his father's old shoes, as his had given out. They lost one canoe when it slipped from its ropes as it was being lowered over the falls, "its bottom beaten out on the jagged rocks of the broken water," said TR.

That night Kermit talked his father out of taking his life. Roosevelt carried "a small vial that contained a lethal dose of morphine," writes Candice Millard in *The River of Doubt*, and he called Kermit and Cherrie to his cot and told them to go on without him. He had a code, carried since his cowboy days: If a man was a burden he had to go. But Kermit refused, and TR knew that if he killed himself Kermit would feel that he failed the family and would probably die anyhow trying to carry his body out. He wanted to be buried like Lobo but knew that wouldn't happen. "So there was only one thing for me to do, and that was to come out myself."*

Rondon finally acknowledged the strain. The camaradas were all but finished. "This hard work during four days, caused considerable suffering to our men," he said. "All but two of them broke down, not in spirit but their physical forces were exhausted."

There's no record of Rondon giving Kermit credit for saving the expedition and the men's lives.

◆

The Rio Roosevelt expedition's portage on the opposite side of the river was more than a mile. Assis, called "machete meister," chopped a path from camp to the logging road, past a big mahogany stump and tall mahogany tree that had been cut and left, soft inside. Almost everyone carried three loads, one trip with each deflated raft rolled up and carried on the shoulders of five people. At dinner that evening Haskell asked for our attention and said, "I want to tell you how proud I am of everyone. Before this expedition began there were some rumors flying around that this was nothing more than a rich person out to have a good time. Well, today has completely disproved that!"

The jungle was a junkyard that night, rusty wheels squeaking and wind chimes made from old car parts clanking in the breeze. A carpenter checked the distance between trees, shaking the metal ribbon of his long tape measure.

We finished the portage by noon the next day, and Charlie gave us the afternoon off to catch up on our work. Kaminsky and I had been having creative differences over the would-be PBS *Nova* film, and Charlie attempted to mediate but the differences remained, so he fired me. It was all he could do, since Joe had a contract and owned the camcorder. I fully supported his decision, liberated by a lighter load.

---

*   He confided this to a friend, according to *The River of Doubt*.

Maybe because that firing went so well, Charlie and Beth tried another. They quietly approached Joe Willie and Kelley, offering to make them co–head boatmen. If they were willing, Charlie said, he would exercise his authority and tell Slade he was no longer in command on the water. Joe Willie's jaw dropped. He explained to Charlie that Slade was the best man to guide the group down the river because he had prepared for the expedition responsibly and professionally; he had done his research and knew what to expect. He told Charlie that dumping Slade and Boyle while promoting himself and Kelley would not bring harmony to the river.

Carr Clifton went location scouting with Chief Oitamina. They were buddies. Oitamina connected with Carr's silly sense of humor, and laughed at Carr's teasing him. He was intrigued by Carr having hair everywhere on his body but his head. Carr had been teaching Oitamina English. It started with a rooster crow "Cock-a-roo!," and then "okey-dokey," and "real food," to describe what the Indians ate, compared to the Spam and jelly on fuel-flavored crackers the White men offered him for lunch every day. Oitamina picked up "wow" on his own, repeating the expression of wonderment he'd heard one evening when a bird flew over the camp sounding its siren.

After that handful of words, came the corruption. Carr started it with "fuckin' A," which Oitamina got the gist of. The fun grew to short flippant sentences such as "Pull the EPIRB!," which had become a tongue-in-cheek call in times of trouble. Oitamina strung them together. "Okey-dokey, real food," he said at dinner as he extended his plate to be served. When the petrol-infused noodles were plopped on, he responded with, "Wow. Fuckin' A. Pull the EPIRB!"

Oitamina was stunning when he exercised his genetic gift for mimicry. Without any prompting or coaching, he started to sound like Charlie. Oitamina would paint his face with intensity, point a stubby index finger, and boom out, "Lemme tell you sumpin! Iz dat uh . . ." Carr considered teaching Oitamina to say, "Get bit by a snake and you're gonna die!" but thought better of it.

CHAPTER 24

Murder

We felt that he had run amuck and was probably
determined to kill as many of us as he could.
—George Cherrie

As Roosevelt and Cherrie feared, the arrow of light they saw from the summit flew into a "chasm between two mountains." Rondon, Kermit, and Lyra scouted and saw continuous rapids for three kilometers, and came back with the same plan. Two canoeiros would run the early rapids in empty boats one by one, then six men would lower the boats with ropes over the heavier rapids, then they would cut a trail and drag the big dugouts around the final falls.

"We had been exactly a month going through an uninterrupted succession of rapids," said Roosevelt. Added Cherrie, "A sense of gloom pervaded the camp." It wasn't a good camp, hastily made on rocks along the chasm.

The current was too fast from the start, and the two camaradas—not the ace canoeiros Luiz and Antonio the Paresi, but two others—failed to put a tie-rope on the first canoe. They grabbed at branches to slow it, but couldn't hang on so they rolled into the water and swam to shore, as the dugout was "crushed to splinters in the whirlpools and rapids below," said Cherrie. They were back down to four canoes, including two they had built.

Another camarada, Julio de Lima, helmsman in Roosevelt's canoe, shouldn't have been anywhere near the ex-president. Roosevelt called him "utterly worthless, being an inborn, lazy shirk with the heart of a ferocious cur in the body of a bullock." Whether he was chosen by Rondon or Lyra, it was a wonder how he stayed in that position. Roosevelt was probably too nice to complain to Rondon, who said they realized Julio's bad character too late.

Julio was a tough White guy from Bahia who'd been hired in Tapirapoa to work with the oxen for the march over the Highlands—he pleaded for the job, because of the double pay, said Rondon. Along the way he attacked another camarada with a knife and might have killed him if not for the intervention of two of Rondon's lieutenants. He somehow made it not only to the final 16 camaradas for Rio da Duvida, but also into Roosevelt's dugout with two other paddlers. Rondon said he hadn't been told about the knife incident, although surely he saw the same things in Julio that Roosevelt had.

It was Julio who had stolen the Americans' tin boxes of food. "On such an expedition the theft of food comes next to murder as a crime," said TR. "He stole their food as well as ours." Julio was caught red-handed stealing dried monkey meat, during the long carry. Sergeant Paixon, a "huge negro" and "stern disciplinarian," said Roosevelt, confronted Julio and "smashed him in the mouth." (Paixon means "passion" in Portuguese.)

As Paixon continued with a load on the trail, Julio grabbed a rifle, followed him, and shot him in the heart. "Under such conditions whatever is evil in men's natures comes to the front," said TR.

A gunshot in the forest often meant meat for dinner, so there was no immediate alarm. But when camaradas found Paixon's body and came back yelling, "We felt that Julio had run amuck and had probably determined to kill as many of us as he could," said Cherrie. Roosevelt leaped up, grabbed his trusty Springfield, and dragged his bad leg into the jungle chasing a shootout with Julio, after telling Kermit and Cherrie to stay and guard the supplies. Dr. Cajazeira followed with a revolver, reminding Roosevelt that he was half blind, so if they spotted Julio, the doctor would tell the Rough Rider where to aim.

When camaradas found the murder weapon, a .44-caliber Winchester, there was great relief. Julio had fled in a panic, leaving the rifle behind.

In his 1969 doctoral thesis at New York University, titled *Rondon: Biography of a Brazilian Republican Army Commander*, Donald F. O'Reilly wrote, "Roosevelt was enraged, insisting 'Whoever kills ought to die,' wanting Julio hunted down and shot without a trial, viewing the case as one of military law on a field of battle." Rondon's diary agrees, adding that Roosevelt told him, "That's the way it is in my country." Rondon replied they would never find him, and if they did they would have to abide by Brazilian law and bring him back to trial. "In Brazil, when someone commits a crime, he is tried, not murdered."

The two men agreed that capturing Julio, feeding and guarding him on the way back to civilization, if they made it at all, would further risk their lives. So Roosevelt wanted to find and execute him by firing squad, while Rondon wanted to leave him to be most likely executed by Indian arrows. They buried Sergeant Paixon in a shallow grave dug with machetes and knives, under a cross of sticks, wearing trousers that TR had given him, heading downriver so his spirit could find and haunt Julio.

That night's camp was a bivouac in the gorge, hammocks between boulders. Roosevelt found a spot for his broken cot on a slope, and didn't sleep much. "There were a good many days, a good many mornings when I looked at Colonel Roosevelt and said to myself, he won't be with us tonight," said Cherrie. "And I would say the same thing in the evening, he can't possibly live until morning."

Roosevelt stumbled over rocks on shaky legs and buckling knees, to reach the next camp at the end of the gorge, as Cherrie, Cajazeira, Kermit, and Rondon each helped keep him on his feet. Said Rondon, "Such brutal exercise was excessive for his state of health, and made him suffer horribly." He told Rondon to "Move on and leave me!"

That night his Cuban fever hit hard, taking him from shivers to delirium, as hailstones fell from the sky—"tempestuous," he said. Kermit and Dr. Cajazeira stayed up all night with him, watching his temperature climb to 104°. He wouldn't take his quinine pills, so the doctor injected it into his abdomen, using the needle from his jaguar-skin pouch.

"Father was out of his head," said Kermit. He repeatedly recited lines from the poetic fable "Kubla Khan":

> *In Xanadu did Kubla Khan*
> *A stately pleasure-dome decree:*
> *Where Alph, the sacred river, ran*
> *Through caverns measureless to man*
> *Down to a sunless sea*

He drifted in and out of coherency. He asked if Cherrie was getting enough to eat: He can have some of my food, I don't need it. Just before dawn, he called for Cherrie in a weak voice. "Boys," he said, "some of us are not going to finish this journey. Cherrie, I want you and Kermit to go on. You can get out. I will stop here."

◆

When the Rio Roosevelt expedition reached the entrance to Paixon Gorge, as Rondon had named it, Oitamina jumped out of his raft and slipped into the jungle along the river as if he were tracking Julio. Joe Willie took off in pursuit, moving in long stable strides on wet jagged rocks at the edge of the river, and Kelley followed with the surefooted steps of an experienced hiker. I tried to keep up but stopped to watch the sun squeeze between slots and cracks in the rainforest canopy, making patches and speckles of light on the jungle floor.

Oitamina's movement was marvelous. In his orange paisley jams and flimsy flip-flops, he glided over and between the tangle of clinging vines, creepers, and crawlers with an ease that seemed supernatural—a ghost through walls—his economy of movement polished over thousands of years. Joe Willie was using all his long legs and backwoods years to stay with him, but Oitamina was soon out of sight. Dr. Walden said if you want to keep up with an Indian in the forest, find one seven months pregnant with a three-year-old on her hip.

Joe Willie and Kelley continued at a quick but human pace, driven a couple hundred feet up the hillside by the thick growth, then back down to knee-deep pools in the river, where they studied the rapids. They stepped with care on the slippery rocks to keep from bashing their shins like TR.

After about half a mile, at a spot where the whitewater tumbled, tapered, churned, and foamed, we found Oitamina sitting on a boulder; he'd found his filmmaking POV. He told Joe Willie he had run this stretch in a motorboat—the line's down the right side, he said. He'd tried to go upriver, he said, and capsized right here.

Oitamina wasn't comfortable in whitewater, but Tatare now loved the wild rides. It showed in his eyes, big as mangoes when the rafts bounced and flew. He was proud of himself for meeting the challenge. It was very cool, running the rapids of Rio Teodoro in a rubber boat. His buddies would be impressed.

Joe Willie told his Candirus that Paixon Gorge was Class IV. The river squeezed into a 50-foot-wide channel with rock walls, making compression waves three feet high. There was a big hole at the beginning, and a smooth powerful wave that rolled diagonally from the left bank straight into the hole. If you tried to skip over the wave it might surf your raft sideways into the hole; if you tried to blast through the hole, said Joe Willie, there was a good chance you'd flip.

The right side, Oitamina's line, was squirrely and choppy, into a big depression, with a log reaching out from the bank after that. Joe Willie said our best of bad options was to skirt the hole, paddle hard and fast through the squirrely chop to carry through the depression, then surf its outwash while steering to miss the log. The line threaded three needles. The other four rafts, heavier than the paddleboat, would pass to the left side of the hole and take their chances with the wave.

With Charlie the big boss now a Candiru, we felt even more superior. We *ooh-oohed* away from the eddy and blasted through compression waves that rewarded facefuls of water. Fifty feet from the hole, Joe Willie shouted, "Now dig in! Hard!" and we did, clipping the rim of the hole in gnarly foam. Joe Willie shouted "Left turn!" and we swung the raft over the depression and surfed past the sharp point of the log, whooping as we cleared it.

The paddleboat joined Slade's and Boyle's rafts in an eddy and waited for Mario and Kelley. Mario appeared around the bend, coming down sideways; just before he hit the hole he swung the heavy raft backward for power, and wrestling the oars he bounced through. Kelley came through perfectly, on her line and under control, left of the hole against the boulders and along the weakest part of the wave, standing to row forward, pigtails flying, in the worst-handling boat.

"She's the only boatman who hasn't had trouble in the whitewater yet," observed Charlie.

"That's because she's a lot better than the others," said Joe Willie. "I ain't braggin' on her 'cause she's my girlfriend, it's just the plain truth. She's just more well-rounded as a waterman. I've seen her run a lot of things none of them other boys would even consider."

The afternoon was an Amazon idyll. The river widened and flattened, its current lazy. The jungle was quiet, a faint hot buzz shattered by an occasional shriek. The banks grew taller and lusher. A long-legged egret launched from the shallows and skimmed over the river dragging its feet—a *jacana*, the Jesus bird, walks on water, as Roosevelt noted.

Like lightning, the sun shrank into a blinding molten ball torching a hole in the sky that stretched over the emerald horizon and into precise clouds, shades of gray leaping down in 3D.

The hairpins returned and rainforest circled the rafts. Oitamina said this part of the river was full of piranha, so Boyle broke out his rod and began trolling; two got away, but he fly-casted to catch and reel in Tweed's undershorts, fallen off his raft where he'd spread his laundry. Tweed alone had shown the initiative to stake out one-third of a raft, building a bunker behind the thwarts and riding two stacked duffels, as TR rode tin boxes in the back of his long dugout.

When it was time to camp, Slade rowed near the riverbank as Oitamina stood in the bow and studied the shore. He paused at a spot that was dry and not too dense, but Oitamina pronounced it "very bad," and Slade didn't argue when the others told him to listen to the damn Indian this time. Ten minutes later we were hanging our hammocks at a lovely camp with no bees, few fire ants, and hardly any mosquitoes until it rained after dinner.

Oitamina and Tatare went hunting for bait. Tatare threw a stick at a small black bird like a cormorant and knocked it out, grabbed it by a leg and carried it stunned and squirming through camp, then chopped it into big pieces on the riverbank and threw them in the paddleboat with Cabral and Oitamina. They caught four big piranha in 20 minutes, and returned flaunting the fish the way Boyle had waved Tweed's boxer shorts. It was Charlie's own expedition ambition to become the first man, that he knew of, to catch a piranha with a fly rod; but he hadn't found the time to try.

Oitamina had proven himself to be a real Indian. Charlie had wanted to leave him behind in Vilhena after he showed up with neither food nor experience at whitewater rafting, and now the chief had safely guided the expedition through the jungle and saved it grief. He'd been an asset to the research of Cabral, pointing out medicinal plants that Indians use for toothaches, fainting, malaria, heart attacks, liver troubles, menstrual cramps, erections, and crazy spells.

Oitamina and Tatare politely declined the curly little gassy noodles in a tangy tomato sauce, for dinner. They dropped their piranha in a pot of water on the campfire, and when the fish were soft they broke them up into big pieces. Holding his spoon with a firm overhand grip, Oitamina dipped out a piranha head, flopped it on his plate, picked out the glaring eyeballs with his fingertips and popped them in his mouth like Spanish peanuts. He grabbed the head with his meaty hand and bit into it, crunching and slurping and sucking the skin off the skull. He and Tatare scarfed the rest of the fish down, skin and bones and scales and teeth and fins and guts. Real food.

CHAPTER 25

An Indian Matter

Ah yes, but you are in Brazil.
—Rondônia Sheriff

Roosevelt's fever broke at daybreak. The cold rain stopped and the sun came out. Sunless sea no more. The rapids from camp were softer. Kermit made turtle soup for breakfast. TR gave some of his stash of chocolate, melted a hundred times, to the camaradas. "The men loved him," as Rondon had observed, back on the Paresi plateau when Roosevelt was telling campfire stories at night.

After one more day with rapids, the mountains dropped and the river widened. On April 6 they made 36 kilometers, camping at a river that Rondon named Rio Cardoso, for an officer who died of beriberi in Vilhena before they began. Rondon continued to chart the river using the method that he and Lyra devised.

They didn't stop for Julio, who appeared from behind the trees on the riverbank. Roosevelt took aim with his rifle, paused as he thought about pulling the trigger, then put the rifle down, respecting Rondon's position.

Julio called to the other canoes as they passed, but was ignored. "His murderous hatred had given way to his innate cowardice," said Roosevelt.

At camp, Rondon declared that he wanted to bring Julio in after all, while Roosevelt now wanted to leave him to his dark fate. It was the biggest fight yet between the men; even Rondon acknowledged "the clash was tremendous." An exasperated Roosevelt yelled at Rondon, "The expedition is endangered!"

Rondon writes that when Kermit tried to agree with him, TR shouted at him "Shut up!" Kermit said Rondon "vacillated about Julio with 100 lies," accusing him of using Julio as an excuse to spend time charting another tributary. Which is what happened, for two days as a search party tried to find Julio, returning exhausted, hungry, and empty-handed.

Roosevelt was generous in his book, saying that given Rondon's responsibility to his mission and the laws of Brazil, "he must act as his sense of duty bade him." As for Julio, he said, "Surely that murderer was in a living hell. With fever and famine leering at him from the shadows, he made his way through the empty desolation of the wilderness."

◆

It rained for 16 hours, at the Rio Roosevelt expedition's first camp after Paixon Gorge. There was a long debate in the morning about whether to get back on the river or wait. A few hours downriver lay the Captain Cardoso outpost near Rio Cardoso, and Slade argued that since it was such an effort to break and make camp, why bother for half a day? Better to leave the next morning, stop at the outpost for a quick visit, and get in a full day on the river.

Quick visit? That issue again. There was research to be done. There was adventure to be had, gliding down a calm river in a tropical deluge. Dr. Walden reminded Slade that in the jungle you work with the weather, not around it.

Oitamina wanted to wait. He liked the idea of a quick visit. The grass at the outpost was too tall, he said, and FUNAI didn't have a radio there.

With Oitamina in Slade's corner, the waiters won. Then the rain stopped and we had time to kill. Carr taught Oitamina to say "Hey dude," which he shouted from the treetops as he hung the antenna for Chip to make more forlorn calls for human contact. Slade patched some of the three dozen holes that ants had chewed in his tent. Boyle asked Dr. Walden to lance a nasty boil on his butt, pain that was nothing for a man who'd been bitten on a testicle by a tarantula, and for days afterward carried a grapefruit in his crotch. Tweed picked some lime-like *jeniparanas* and made Amazon vodka gimlets. I found a small frog on my big toe when I took off my soggy sneakers, and Tatare used it for bait to catch a piranha.

We woke to whooping birds and screeching monkeys. As we loaded the rafts, furry lightning bolts whizzed past our heads, electric caterpillars dropping from the canopy. More than 20 landed in Kelley's raft as she threw on her hooded poncho and yelled for the others to hurry! The caterpillars were being dropped by the smoke from burning plastic bags rising into their trees. In the campers' rush to escape they skipped cleanup, so litter remained. Monkeys scrambled out of the trees and rummaged through the campsite for scraps, as an empty vodka bottle glared from the ashes of the smoldering campfire.

Giant kamikaze bumblebees dived at Charlie's yellow hat. They looked like little buffaloes, furious black eyes and bulky drumstick legs. The Candirus fought them with their paddles, swinging furiously around each other's heads. The bees retreated when it began to rain. Only Charlie was stung. He said it hurt, a lot.

On the west bank, the expedition passed two patches cleared for ranching. Assis said settlers had been there until about a year ago, when the Cinta Larga killed three of them after repeated warnings and FUNAI's failure to evict them. It might have been the issue that Piu had mentioned to Haskell and McKnight back in Vilhena, when he said that he and Oitamina had been unable to convince some of the downriver Cinta Larga that the Rio Roosevelt expedition would be beneficial to them. Piu couldn't come up with an answer to their question: How?

But now Oitamina added some startling new information: the Cinta Larga at Captain Cardoso wanted to kill us. That morning he'd casually told Charlie he was a marked man.

As the rafts neared Captain Cardoso, Charlie moved from Joe Willie's raft to Slade's, to be near his shotgun. As they approached the outpost, Oitamina squirmed and scanned the jungle, into the "living hell" where the ghost of Julio wandered. Fidgeting and fast-talking, he told Mario to row faster and toward the far side of the river, away from the outpost.

"Oitamina says we shouldn't stop at the outpost!" shouted Mario up to Slade in the lead raft. Oitamina looked over his shoulder and motioned to Kelley and the paddleboat to speed up. He told Mario to take over the lead because Slade was going too slow.

Then he added a new twist, which Mario delivered with another shout across the water. "Oitamina says that these Indians are afraid we're going to kill them!"

The paddleboat pulled alongside Mario's raft, and I asked Mario, "Why do they think that?" Mario asked Oitamina, and replied, "He says they think we're trying to steal their land."

Assis was the one person who could make sense of this. He wasn't the least concerned. "This is an Indian matter," he said simply.

At the outpost there were no signs of life. A dirt road ran down the west bank and continued up the east bank, at a wood bridge bunched against the bank like a boardwalk flipped by a cyclone. The grass was tall, as Oitamina said. Only five or six Cinta Larga lived there, said Assis. "It isn't really meant to be a place for Indians to live. The purpose of the post is to keep White men off the land. Most of the Cinta Larga around here live in the forest."

As the expedition rowed past, Tweed shouted up to Charlie and asked why they weren't stopping. "Because Oitamina doesn't want to," he replied.

Tweed was outraged. He said Charlie had allowed Oitamina to manipulate the expedition past the post. He accused Charlie of being a coward, although not to his face, and said the reason Charlie didn't stop was because he feared for his life. TR had spent two nights at camp next to the mouth of the Rio Cardoso. Tweed was missing another chance to walk in his great-grandfather's footsteps.

A couple miles past the outpost, rapids split into three channels around lush islands. Oitamina, still on edge, wanted to run them without pausing, down the left channel he said. But Slade insisted on scouting, so Kaminsky checked the channels in his kayak, using a radio to report back to Slade, who had to row to the middle of the river to copy—it was the only time during the expedition the handheld transceivers worked. Oitamina's channel was ugly. Kaminsky found an easy path weaving between the islands.

His eyes still on the riverbanks, Oitamina was now fuming and pouting. He said he would have stopped at the outpost, but nobody told him they wanted to stop. His imitation of Charlie had reached a new level.

As Mario and I would learn later in Riozinho, Oitamina's problem wasn't about White men, or about land or gold or diamonds—or a Hollywood movie, which also came up as a possible motive for murder. It was about mahogany, and it was an Indian matter as Assis said, between Oitamino and Jacinto, chief of the Cardoso band of Cinta Larga. Oitamina and Piu were running low on mahogany from their own forest, so they were stealing some from Jacinto's land, by finding trees and showing loggers where they were. It was probably the reason Oitamina had been down the river.

Chief Jacinto sold the Cardoso mahogany to loggers himself, at a less greedy pace than Oitamina and Piu, so he had plenty. He had put out the word that Oitamina better stay the hell off his land. If Jacinto ever caught him there, he would kill him. As for the White men, whatever they were doing there, if they were with Oitamina they were up to no good. Maybe he would kill them, too.

Back in Espigao d'Oeste, the police were watching the logging activity second-hand. A deputy in the Rondônia sheriff's department was working undercover on a drug assignment one night, and saw more than 20 trucks loaded with logs rumble out of the forest under the cover of darkness. It was an average night during the cutting season, he said, sitting on his living-room couch facing the open door to the street, where a conspicuous Jeep Comanche pickup was parked in front of his house. Under a pillow at his side, there was a .45-caliber Remington automatic pistol.

It was a week or so after the Rio Roosevelt expedition had passed Captain Cardoso. All the whitewater had been run, and 14 of the 20 explorers were chugging to Manaus on a riverboat. I had left the expedition at the next fazenda/resupply, taking Mario with me to translate, in the Jeep Comanche that Haskell let us use. We were in Espigao looking into the mahogany trade, and were almost certainly being followed. We looked over our shoulders a lot, like Oitamina had done at Cardoso.

The plainclothes cop heard a noise and sprung to his feet. He slunk through his house with his back against the wall and gun at his thigh, checked each of two bedrooms by pushing the doors open with his foot, then pounced through the kitchen door to the backyard, pointing the gun into the dark. He came back to the living room shrugging and wearing a sheepish grin.

"Must have been the cat," he said.

You can't be too careful, he said. He said the joke in Rondônia was that you could get AIDS from reading the newspapers because they dripped with blood. Last year the sheriff had his face blown off by a 16-gauge shotgun in front of his young daughter in the front yard. His deputy said the sheriff was killed either because he was getting too close to a drug bust, or had done something to piss off the mahogany raiders.

Two suspects were arrested, and before the trial one was killed by police after he escaped from jail. The other was defended by logging company lawyers and acquitted. Later he was convicted of rape and got locked up for that.

The dark tale was confirmed by the new sheriff who was brought in from São Paulo and moved into the dead sheriff's house. He had never been to the Amazon. "I know nothing about Rondônia," he told us in English. "For me, is a very big adventure. Fortunately the problems between the Indians and the White man are not mine. I do not put my nose in this business. That is the job—do you say, jurisdiction?—of FUNAI and the Federal Police. But I know that the Federal Police do not like the laws that protect the Indians. For example an Indian can kill a White man on their reserve, and it is impossible to arrest them. The Indians know this, and take advantage of it. And sometimes criminals pay Indians to hide from the police on their land.

"Anyhow, I think nowadays there are not many conflicts between the Indians and White men. They live as friends, because the Indian sells wood to the White man."

But it's illegal, I said. "Ah yes, but you are in Brazil," he replied with a laugh.

Meanwhile there was a party going on at Piu's place. Not his house in Riozinho, but his weekend retreat, a house on 35 acres way down a dirt road closer to Espigao. It was a chance for some of the players to get to know each other over a churrascaria and good liquor. There were gold miners flaunting the fruits of their labor in chains around their necks. Wood buyers peeling off 50,000 cruzeiro notes and sending young Indians out with drivers for more beer and soft drinks. There were neighboring fazenda owners, sawmill operators, and cattle ranchers. The FUNAI agent from Cacoal was there. The heavyweight guest was the godfather of mahogany buyers, a man they called *Caixa d'Agua*, or Box of Water, the name of his logging company.

Piu had hoped to have his own big box of water, his swimming pool, finished in time for the party, but its excavation was delayed by rains. The corners were staked, so he walked his guests to the center of the future pool and invited them back for a pool party when it was finished. It would be dry season by then, and the mahogany cutting would be going full swing again.

CHAPTER 26

Turtle Soup

The only thing senior about them boys
is their age and attitude.
—Joe Willie Jones

The camp after Cardoso was lush and spooky, snaking vines and bending ferns with razor fronds like shutters. Oitamina and Tatare said stay out of the water, stingrays on bottom. Cabral chopped the head off a fer-de-lance, and hung his ace-of-spades trophy on a vine glaring down and flashing its fangs at the explorers during dinner.

Roosevelt said it was "hot, wet, sunless" here, and our night was thick. A quiet drip came out of a cave, and a dull whistle moved around camp, first here then there. Boars in the dark, grinding their teeth—Oitamina said they do that. A spooky rustle, stalking us. I hung my poncho on a fern at the end of my hammock, and woke in the night startled by the Grim Reaper at the foot of my bed. In the morning Boyle swore he'd seen the silhouette of two men paddling a canoe downriver under the three-quarter moon. He ran to the bank, but they were gone.

The day got hot fast, the river wider and flatter but still bumpy. A baby-blue sky with sweet puffy clouds rode on an emerald rim of the rainforest. Purple blossoms rose from ipe trees like fireworks over the canopy. The sky grew still and heavy, then collapsed from its weight with a deluge building for 24 hours. Fierce splashing on calm water made the river smoke. The four oarsmen reversed their rafts and put their backs into the weather and their work, while the Candirus stroked heads-down into raindrops big as marbles.

When the rain stopped the macaws started. Two of them, flame red—until now they'd been blue and yellow—flew up behind the rafts and sounded a few raspy croaks, followed by seven more, flying in formation: two-three-two, the trailing pair down a bit. They croaked their warning at us and continued their chase of the outlaws.

Then the mother of all birds called from the distance with her internal-combustion drone. With a wingspan of 30 feet she could fly 100 miles per hour. She appeared skimming the treetops and dipping her wings from side to side, then climbed, banked, circled, and spit a small projectile at the explorers.

Boyle rowed over to the bobbing thing, and Tweed picked it out of the water. It was a plastic bottle with a note inside that read: "Do you need to be rescued?"

No one had a clue. Except . . . that one time, at the Rio Roosevelt outpost. That little switch Chip had flicked. It only tested the battery. It couldn't have actually signaled a satellite to send out the Brazilian Air Force. Could it?

The mystery plane made a couple more passes, its pilot and passenger looking down for signs of distress, as the explorers cheerily waved and threw thumbs-ups.

That night a big moon lit the river, as little people played out-of-tune xylophones and vibraphones until 2:00 A.M.; one plinked on, the Lionel Hampton of frogs. Up the hill behind camp, an early-rising artist began his day's work, delicately chinking a steel hammer and chisel on a mahogany carving of a black jaguar, like the one Mario and I would see driving out in the Jeep.

The blistering day didn't slow the Candirus. Boyle had said something smartass about the paddleboat always lagging behind, and Joe Willie scoffed. "A couple days ago Slade said we weren't supposed to pass the 'senior' boatmen," he said. "Shee-oot. The only thing senior about them boys is their age and attitude."

There was a lot of river to run, to reach Fazenda Muiraquita. The rafts took their assigned positions, paddleboat last. In the lead, in the fastest boat, Slade began pulling away. Joe Willie let him go for an hour, then told his boys it was time.

With Charlie's big biceps pumping, and Chip cheering his dad on, the Candirus stroked firm and steady, picking off the other rafts one by one. Slade in our sights, we closed the gap and casually paddled past without giving his raft a glance. We stopped in an eddy and waited for the others to repass, then dutifully brought up the rear.

Mangroves appeared, a maze of channels and choices. Slade led the rafts into the widest path, but Joe Willie kept going and plunged the paddleboat into a small hole in the mangroves. We weaved for about ten minutes, calmed by his confidence, and came out downriver, no sign of the rafts. Maybe they've come and gone, one Candiru dared suggest. "We'll just wait here a while," said Joe Willie.

Five minutes later the other rafts straggled out of the mangroves. Slade was not happy to see Joe Willie. Later he grumbled something about the paddleboat's insistence on rushing out front. Joe Willie just lowered his head and grinned at his feet.

◆

Kermit's turtle soup was the turning point for his father. The 36-kilometer day brought momentum to another week of diminishing rapids. The canoeiros Luiz and Antonio could run them, and the men had less to carry now. Kermit shot three monkeys and a couple of curassows, and there was plenty of fish—they caught 28 on Easter Sunday, April 12. They feasted on a catfish more than three-and-a-half feet long, with a monkey in its stomach; the Brazilians told TR that in the Amazon River there's a man-eating catfish that grows to nine feet.

But Roosevelt's leg wasn't healing. He told the doctor the infection would go away on its own, dismissing it as he did the bullet he carried against a rib, and as he had the leg wound from the trolley crash.

In the next two days they made another 36 kilometers. Roosevelt called April 15 a "red-letter day," as they found a post with a board marked J.A., indicating someone had come upriver that far. They "cheered heartily" when they saw a hut with a thatched roof in a freshly planted clearing with three dogs, but nobody was home. "Another hour brought us to a similar house where dwelt an old Black man, who showed the innate courtesy of the Brazilian peasant." He told them the Aripuaña was just downstream.

At a third house, a woman saw them coming and ran with her two children to get her husband, who came back with his gun, but Rondon introduced him to the former president of the United States—who could no longer walk, and had to be carried from the canoe. After a modest meal, Cherrie and Kermit downed the last of three bottles of Scotch they'd been sharing for six weeks. Kermit liked the chicks pecking on the dirt floor. "How nice it was to see them!" he wrote. "How it made me think of home."

Roosevelt had been stalling the doctor about operating on his leg wound, now hosting flesh-eating bacteria. Cajazeira was still shooting quinine into TR's abdomen. "Day by day his condition worsened," he said, "and we were seriously concerned." Cajazeira had been urging TR to let him lance the wound, but TR still hoped it would heal itself. Not likely, said the doctor, more likely you'll die. Blood poisoning was imminent.

In the morning in the grass outside the hut, with no anesthetic for the slice of the hot knife, Cajazeira lanced the infection. Any screams didn't make it into history. "Without a murmur he would lie while Cajazeira lanced and drained the abscesses," wrote Kermit, suggesting it happened more than once, and calling it "a veritable plague of deep abscesses." Added Roosevelt, dry as can be, "An added charm was given the operation, and the subsequent dressings, by the enthusiasm with which the piums and boroshudas took part."

"Father's courage was an inspiration never to be forgotten by any of us," Kermit would write years later. "With it all he was invariably cheerful, and in the blackest of times ever ready with a joke. Nothing but Father's indomitable spirit brought him through."

Even before Roosevelt got back to New York on the steamship *Aidan* on May 19, ridicule arrived from England over his reporting the descent of Rio da Duvida, now Rio Roosevelt, and putting the 472-mile-long previously unknown tributary of the Aripuana and Madeira Rivers on the map. Two days after he got off the river, a disparaging article appeared in the *London Times*, suggesting that Roosevelt had no idea where he'd been, that his accounts of rapids and waterfalls were exaggerations if not fabrications, and that the ex-president had actually descended a tributary of the Tapajós River hundreds of miles away, a theory promoted by two prominent British explorers and one respected geographer. The charges were quickly countered in the US with facts from all the best and credible corners, calling them "absurd" and "preposterous."

Anthony Fiala said it best. Arriving back in New York on May 1, he gave a beautifully colorful and articulate—and in parts wacko—interview to a lucky reporter from the *New York Times*, on his ship as it was towed into harbor. He called the accusations from England "profoundly ignorant."

"The positions on these maps were astronomically determined with a six-inch Hyde theodolite, fitted with micrometer adjustments—the latest construction," he said. He should know, he was the gearhead who bought the heavy brass instrument, like a surveyor's transit.

The British critics were jealous. Their own Lieutenant-Colonel Percy Fawcett had explored the Amazon in 1906, 1908, and 1911, when he famously found the "lost city of Z." Fawcett brought back stories, but Roosevelt delivered science. He had charged into British territory and come out a star.

PART III

LEAVING THE RIVER

CHAPTER 27

Fazenda Muiraquita

Excuse me?
—Chip Haskell

Fazenda Muiraquita was a cattle ranch growing out of a quarter-million acres of jungle, the oldest ranch on the Rio Roosevelt. The Brazilian government in 1974 offered free land to settlers if they made it agricultural, and a small São Paulo construction company owned by a gentleman named Sergio Prandini claimed the parcel and built the ranch. Prandini said the word *muiraquita* meant either magical frog or big vagina, with a roll of his eyes over his language that speaks in metaphors.

The fazenda's staff of 21 people scrambled to get rooms and meals ready for the Rio Roosevelt expedition, coming through, two days early. Maids and cooks were thrown into a spin. It had taken just two days for the rafters to travel the 87 kilometers from Rio Cardoso, not four days as scheduled.

Haskell, McKnight, Slade, and photojournalist Greenberg had visited Muiraquita the previous May on their flyover of the river. They landed on its airstrip and looked around, but left before the foreman could be brought from the house, because Haskell feared rain that might get the plane stuck on a muddy strip.* They'd stayed long enough to see that Muiraquita would be perfect for their needs, as the final resupply. They arranged the details by fax to São Paulo, where Prandini lived with his wife Marta.

The main house of the fazenda—Charlie called it "facienda" until the others wanted to strangle him—had three bedrooms and a living room with rich paneled walls, shiny terracotta floors, plush leather sofas and chairs, a stone fireplace, television, and a bookcase boasting a rare old copy of *Through the Brazilian Wilderness*. A screened porch became the mess hall, where explorers enjoyed their first real food since the feast at the outpost nine days earlier.

Drained, disorganized, and dragging dissension, they crashed all over the house that night. Muddy shoes, soggy clothes, and piles of gear were spread and hung around, and the single small bathroom was overwhelmed. Charlie, Beth, and Charlie's shotgun slept in the master bedroom, while others bunked where they could, most on the porch. Hammocks hung in the soft glow of the full moon, birds whooping through the screen.

Since the Jeeps driven by Fabio, Darcio, and Telmo wouldn't arrive for two more days, there was time for eating, sleeping, and sightseeing, while the maids and cooks worked dawn to dark, facing mountains of laundry, dirty dishes, and fresh food to prepare. They were meeting the Brazilian standard of hospitality, Sergio and Marta's standard.

---

* Mark Greenberg recalls, "We were in a twin-engine Piper Navajo, known by pilots as 'Navahog.' The airstrip was fairly wet and the ground soft in spots. The rear door had been removed to facilitate photography and to give Slade a full view below. Also in the rear was a full 55-gallon drum of fuel that wasn't even close to the center of gravity. The airstrip had a distinct slope. There was no wind at the time of takeoff. The pilot made a near-tragic mistake deciding to take off going uphill on the soft turf. The takeoff roll was excruciatingly long, and near its end, Charlie screamed at me, 'Don't lean out the door!' because the pilot was afraid I was putting drag on the airstream. I watched trees go by the wingtips. We were spared crashing only because there was a couple hundred yards cut out of the forest past the runway."

Paulo the fazenda foreman was a rangy fellow with a thick mustache, frayed straw cowboy hat, ankle-high pointy-toed boots, and no socks. Strong and silent, he could do everything. Having grown up in Vilhena, he knew an easy route to the headwaters. Haskell had flown away in his turboprop before they could meet. Too bad, said Paulo, I could have saved the expedition a week of grief.

When his Bandeirante rolled up, some of the explorers jumped on the bed to explore the fazenda, weaving through small houses, shacks, barns, offices, and employees' quarters. Vultures cruised in slow circles and strutted on rooftops, spreading their wide dark wings, lined up like crucifixion row. The afternoon sky turned leaden and exploded in big booms, blasting raindrops from clouds seeded by dynamite.

Only 7,000 of the fazenda's 100,000 hectares were cleared, just 2,500 remaining in pasture, the rest scrawny second-growth forest. About 1,200 cattle made it to market each year. There were some pigs, but attrition was high, as jaguars lived in the nearby caves.

If it weren't for government subsidy, said Prandini, fazendas like Muiraquita couldn't survive. His investment was in real estate, not production. The wood, worth millions, was getting more valuable every year. He wasn't in a hurry to exploit it. He had enough in life.

"In the whole forest we have few mahogany," he said. "We have something like three-tenths of cubic meter per hectare, but we have 150 cubic meter per hectare for all kinds of wood. Mahogany is very rare and very valuable. But you need to exploit the other kinds of wood you have. The money that you can earn from mahogany is very few if you compare to all of wood you have. Some companies want us to exploit mahogany. We don't want to exploit only mahogany. This is Indian activity. Indians are not good businessmen. That is the reality. They don't know what is the value of the things they have in their hands. Mahogany is like diamonds. If you take out diamonds from your property you make depreciation."

In the early years cattle were driven more than 100 miles over a trail through the jungle, and they swam across the Rio Roosevelt. Now water buffalo were herded along the road; they thrive in swampy pasture, and the meat is lean.

What Prandini wanted to do was build an eco lodge at the fazenda. A bright vision, ahead of its time: eco adventure tourism. Rafting trips down the Rio Roosevelt, guided by Indians and ending at Muiraquita. Fixed campsites along the way. Income for the tribe, to build schools and clinics. The rainforest would be watched closely by sporty environmentalists from around the world. Prandini would love to have guests like that at Muiraquita. Triple win.

Muiraquita had built a 200-kilometer road to Espigao d'Oeste, approved by FUNAI, crossing Zoro territory. There was an iron gate with armed guards hired by Muiraquita at FUNAI's request, to keep out mahogany raiders. The raiders had guns too, and there were more of them. The latest incident was 20 settlers, fueled by raw white rum *cachaca*, shooting from the back of a flatbed truck as it crashed through the gate.

When Fabio reached the gate in the leading Jeep Comanche with a load of beer on ice in the bed, the guards insisted they escort him to the fazenda—there were bandits on the road, they said. Fabio dissuaded them from joining the party by leaving some Brahma behind.

The beer and the guns arrived together. Fabio drove up in the Comanche with its bed full of ice flashing bright gold cans of Brahma. Darcio and Telmo drove the other two Jeeps with three passengers: Piu and the guys with the guns, a young FUNAI agent and a sergeant with the Policia Federal Floresta. Piu appeared to carry the two armed men in the pockets of his white jeans. The young FUNAI agent carried a .38 on his hip, and the Federal sergeant wore camo and carried a small machine gun, a "grease gun" fired from the shoulder.

The party lasted well into the night, jungle sounds now including snaps and whooshes from popping cans and spraying suds. Piu stripped off his shirt and donned every Cinta Larga badge he had. Around his neck were strands of Brazil and palm nuts, panther and monkey teeth, toucan and macaw feathers, turtle bones. Slung over his shoulder and across his smooth chest was a black ipe bow; in one hand he wielded a fistful of long arrows with blood-encrusted bamboo tips, the other gripped an icy Brahma, as he strutted his tribal stuff. Under the disapproving eye of Assis, Piu's FUNAI friend hung at his elbow, matching him beer for beer and laughing at Piu's every superior observation.

The Federal sergeant with the grease gun seemed edgy, watching from the fringes. Charlie was not comfortable. These men with guns, who he didn't know and couldn't control, drinking his beer . . . it didn't fit into his picture. He told Fabio to get rid of the agents, or at least disarm them. Fabio went to Oitamina with Charlie's request. It might have been a demand. Offense was taken. An angry chief with armed men at his elbow and a few beers under his belts went looking for Charlie, who carried a shotgun and a temper.

Oitamina said he needed the guns around him for protection. Charlie said the guns had to go. The standoff was scary. They reached a compromise: the guns would be stashed out of sight in a Bandeirante. Oitamina stayed angry, and could still reach the guns, but at least now the grease gun was separated from a beer-drinking Federal's finger.

There were other confrontations in dark corners of the party. Boyle unloaded on Chip, calling him a young man with too much education and not enough brains, and mild-mannered Mario unloaded on Boyle, for expecting too much work without providing the time and tools to do it. Chip had a word with Beth. She had complained to the explorers that the cost of the expedition had reached half a million dollars, and when she called it "our money," he reminded her that the money being pissed away in the jungle was Haskell family money, not hers, pissed away in large part by her misguided leadership of his trusting father, for example trying to demote Slade.

At dawn, half a dozen vultures perched in a row on the peak of a shed, silhouettes like the Grim Reaper I'd seen at the foot of my hammock.

CHAPTER 28

The Cause

Truth, lost in translation.

Much of the next day was spent jostling for the satellite phone. First, Peter Riva was called. He said the missing tape from the headwaters had been found, in an ammo can inside the Wrangler where Kaminsky had put it before forgetting. Fabio shipped it to *Good Morning America*, which had just aired Tweed Roosevelt waving goodbye as the explorers floated off into the jungle and rapids, where lurked panthers, pythons, and piranhas.

NPR and Voice of America wanted to talk to Tweed. The media only had eyes and ears for Theodore Roosevelt's great-grandson, which irked Haskell and McKnight. In Tweed's interviews it sometimes sounded like he was leader of the expedition, which didn't help.

Riva answered the mystery of the rescue plane. A coded signal had been sent from the EPIRB up to a satellite, which bounced it down to EPIRB mission control, which called the Brazilian Air Force, who declined to respond because the signal had been a single short beep, sure sign of accidental engagement. Having no word from the expedition for more than two weeks, Riva called the air force and asked if they'd heard anything, and they told him about the beep. Choosing safety over sorrow in the Amazon, Riva called Fabio, who hired a small plane to fly over the river and locate the explorers.

There was attention from the Brazilian media. *Manchete*, the giant weekly news magazine, sent a reporter and photographer who traveled 24 hours by plane, bus, and jeep to Muiraquita. They wanted to go down the river with the expedition to the next fazenda, which wasn't far; but Greenberg nixed the notion, having an exclusive contract for photography on the river. A photo of my raw, red, knee-to-ankle would appear in the magazine, disgusting with pustules. I think the intolerable itching for days, as TR described it, was caused by brushing against the wrong leaf while riding a mule in shorts.

There was a team meeting in the living room. *Manchete* was big, so Haskell and McKnight wanted to discuss what the expedition should and shouldn't say to the reporter. The discussion quickly bloomed into full-on spin control. I was bewildered, since my job was to uncover the flimflam, not create it; and there I was in this meeting, wondering if they forgot to lock me out.

The expedition was nearly over, and it was still searching for a cause. The meeting evolved into a specific purpose: determine the objectives of the expedition and fit them to the results. The hard part was getting 20 people to keep their stories straight. Another problem was nobody cared except Haskell, McKnight, and Tweed. Slouching apathy filled the room. Getting on the list for rides over the rainforest in Sergio's airplane, in which he and his wife Marta had just arrived, elicited more enthusiasm.

However, it was decided that three expressions that had been used in the past were now taboo, since the expedition couldn't back them up: "biometric sampling," "scientific" expedition, and "explorers," although by the end of the meeting explorers would be back by default. Biometric sampling, a biological field examination, had to be dropped because the scientist Joao Ferraz never had the time to do it. Ferraz, whose position at

INPA was higher than anyone had realized, also said the expedition had to stop using the word "scientific." Haskell said that couldn't be done because the permits said it was a scientific expedition. Ferraz argued that all three scientists were coming back empty-handed with the expedition two weeks early, time that should have gone toward science.

Haskell replied that this was the first time anyone had complained to him about not having enough time. He wasn't going to yank the stated purpose out from under the expedition just like that. It was a tense stalemate for awhile, until Haskell suggested they change the word from "scientific" to "scouting." He recited it aloud, and it sounded good. They would say the expedition "took some samples" and did some "very detailed scouting." This was accepted by Ferraz, although he still seethed.

Finally, what would the explorers call themselves if they weren't explorers? Tweed suggested the word "explorers" was an inappropriate stretch, and he believed the best alternative was "adventurers." But Haskell said that sounded too much like a rich guy on vacation, and McKnight didn't like it because those pesky permits weren't for the purpose of adventure. Haskell liked "surveyor" but no one else did. The word explorer ran out of resistance, so that's what we were.

Dr. John Walden brought up a final word that he said the group had to stop emphasizing: "danger." He said in all his years in the jungle, leading treks and expeditions, he'd never seen anyone on an expedition get bitten by a snake and die. The chances of drowning in the rapids were about the same, with the crack Sobek crew. And the idea of an attack by Indigenous people was ludicrous.

That afternoon there was a big churrascaria to celebrate the Rio Roosevelt expedition. A pig and cow were butchered, big chunks of meat speared and racked on long skewers whittled from branches. Wood was piled into three deep pits for fires to grill the meat. Rice and beans were cooked over a woodstove in the hot and bustling kitchen.

The landing strip began buzzing, as important guests arrived: the new sheriff of Rondônia, a representative to the Brazilian Assembly ("a faithful friend for any occasion"), and two neighboring fazenda owners, one of them a ringer for Rock Hudson in *Giant*. It was a pleasant social gathering, as everyone got along thanks to the energetic grace of the Prandinis, Sergio and Marta.

Piu had a surprise for Haskell and McKnight. He'd invited a man whose business card said he was a forest engineer, and who had driven eight muddy hours from Espigao in order to pitch a proposal to New Century Conservation Trust. It was for a reforestation project, a mahogany farm on Cinta Larga land, which he said would employ 200 Indigenous people while providing timber and preserving forest. It would only cost two million dollars, with a return coming in just ten years.

The dining room was hot and loud. McKnight was seated at the end of the long dinner table, dutiful, looking harried. Sitting next to her, Haskell kept gripping his big head with his big hands and wincing. Piu sat halfway down the long table looking distrustful, his right eye drooping as it did when he schemed. The young forest engineer sat at the far end of the table, raising his voice to be heard. He seemed sincere but sounded desperate.

The pitch had been going on for nearly an hour, while Ferraz was in the living room across the hall unaware of the discussion. When he walked in on it, his eyes widened in astonishment and anger. It was inconceivable to him how Haskell and McKnight could sit down to hear a proposal for a reforestation project without informing the Brazilian scientist whose specialty was reforestation. He'd been a mere 30 feet away, for God's sake!

It was the final straw for Joba, the situation clearly hopeless. He sat in on the meeting for about 15 minutes, and heard enough of what he considered nonsense to get up and leave, his patience snatched by his disgust. Haskell and McKnight didn't appear to notice anything was wrong.

To Piu, McKnight sounded like every White person he'd ever heard talk big, when she told him, "In the US there is much money available for non-profit organizations. But the only way we could get the money for this project is if I could go as president of my company and present this as a project of New Century Conservation Trust." Truth, lost in translation.

Piu was trying to do what the system—the Brazilian government, the environmentalists—wanted him to do, but the scheme was canted toward his pocket. It's all he knew, it was success in the White man's world, all he'd ever seen, learned on the streets of Espigao and beyond. It was White man's capitalism, and it worked.

Oitamina was there, too, pushing for the two million, as if Charlie could just pull the cash from the bottom of his duffel. He didn't laugh when Charlie pointed a finger across the table at him and said, "Lemmie tell you sumpin. Iz dat uh . . . when you ask someone for two million dollars, the first thing they're gonna ask you is how that money is going to help the Cinta Larga in 10 years, 20 years, and you better be able to answer them."

Haskell and McKnight would show the reforestation proposal to experts back in the US, who said what Ferraz had concluded in 15 minutes: unworkable.

Oitamina was confused by conflicting desires. "What I want to do now is take it easy," he said. "There's been so much pressure: pressure from Whites, pressure from Indians. I have to take care of everything. Every time two Indians get in a fight, I have to stop it. And dealing with the wood buyers! I will say it openly, in clear Portuguese: We don't want to keep on this way, helping the timber men get rich.

"Our main concern today is how to acquire financial resources. We own the land but we don't have the right to sell anything that's on it. The White man clears his land and plants rice and beans but we can't do that. If we're going to farm our land, how do we get the money to buy tractors, for example? We can't control our affairs because we don't even have enough money to buy seeds.

"Charlie says to me, 'What do your people need, Roberto?' We need health, we need education, we need a project of some kind for these things. But Charlie doesn't understand anything, because he can't speak the language. From what I've seen, Charlie doesn't even understand English." Oitamina laughs uproariously.

The next morning the explorers continued down the river with one less raft. Oitamina, Tatare, and Assis went back to their homes and families in Riozinho; Cabral went with Fabio back to Manaus; and Mario and I took the Jeep Comanche to Espigao d'Oeste and Riozinho, searching for reality. Driving the Jeep along the jungle road, we almost hit it head-on when we rounded a curve and met a large flatbed truck carrying a bulldozer toward the river.

When the Rio Roosevelt expedition had stated its intention on the permit application to write a scientific report on the state of the forest around the Rio Roosevelt, to be presented at the Earth Summit by INPA scientists, word moved fast from Brasilia. Neither FUNAI nor the Federal Police wanted to be embarrassed by a report that exposed mahogany harvesting in Indigenous territory. The police had sent men into the forest around Rio Roosevelt to tell the loggers to move their heavy equipment out, until after the expedition passed through.

It was one of these bulldozers, already moving back in, that passed our Jeep. The loggers had been following the Rio Roosevelt expedition, lurking from the forest like Cinta Larga stalking Rondon. Our Jeep would pass two more bulldozers coming in, plus three trucks stacked with giant mahogany logs headed to Espigao.

The remaining 14 members of the Rio Roosevelt expedition connected four rafts in the shape of a diamond and attached a 10-horsepower outboard motor to the back of the bulky craft that confined them. Lashed together for the next few days, they chugged down the rest of Rio Teodoro to the Aripuaña River, where they were met by a chartered riverboat to carry them 463 miles to the Madeira River and another 900 miles to the luxurious, mahogany-lined Tropical Hotel on the Rio Negro in Manaus.

Within months of the expedition's descent of the Rio Roosevelt, there would be a dredge at the riverbank digging for diamonds.

CHAPTER 29

The Aftermath

In deepest Amazonia, some modern
explorers discover bugs and rain.
—*Outside* magazine

S oon after Charles Haskell and Elizabeth McKnight returned to
Maine, they began planning the next project for New Century Conservation Trust, a retracing of David Livingstone's fourth and final trek
in Africa, in 1872. "After the expeditions, Mr. Haskell lectured widely
on environmental issues, the need for conservation and the importance of
studying history," said the *New York Times*.

The Rio Roosevelt expedition received substantial publicity, which
Haskell believed made it a success. He and McKnight spoke to a full
house at the Explorers Club, where he was a member. "The expedition *was*
a success," he told me. "No one got hurt. We got to the end of the river.
The scientists did some scouting, sampling, and interviews. Four thousand
slides were taken of the expedition, and 37 hours of video were shot. The

Indians did go with us, they did talk to the scientists, they did agree to let the scientists go back in."

Nova passed on the documentary, selling the rights to Kurtis Productions for a 60-minute show that aired on PBS as part of a series called *New Explorers*. Haskell and McKnight appeared with Tweed Roosevelt on *Good Morning America*, and feature articles were published in *Life*, *Outside*, *International Wildlife*, the *New York Times*, the *Washington Post*, and other major newspapers, in addition to my dispatches along the way in *New York Newsday*, excerpted by more than 50 papers around the country.

The media rolled with the spin, impressed by the adventure. Only *Outside* glimpsed an expedition of doubt, reporting in its subtitle, IN DEEPEST AMAZONIA, SOME MODERN EXPLORERS DISCOVER BUGS AND RAIN. It might have reflected my own point of view, second-hand. The *Outside* writer had called my home in Hood River while I was in Brazil and spoke to my wife.

The American Museum of Natural History presented a Rio Roosevelt expedition display, featuring bugs that Tweed had found in the rain. *Life* magazine published eight pages stacked like slices of baloney around Tweed as man in the arena. "Haunted by his great-grandfather's fateful expedition, Tweed Roosevelt takes on poisonous caterpillars, spiders the size of dinner plates, and piranha-infested pools," the magazine wrote. Haskell and McKnight doubled down on their annoyance over Tweed's sometimes appearing to be leader of the expedition.

Team members became explorers, adventurers, risk-takers, scientists, environmentalists, humanitarians. McKnight was named to the Society of Woman Geographers, deservedly so, further receiving their outstanding achievement award. We all were awarded distinguished service medals from the Theodore Roosevelt Association.

Haskell confessed to me that he'd never been to Vietnam. When I asked why on earth he would tell such a lie, he answered, "Because I was afraid no one would follow me if I didn't have those credentials." It was the skeleton in the family closet that Chip Haskell had hinted at, on the river. I fulfilled Chip's prediction that we would be speaking again by calling him and telling him Charlie's explanation. "Bullshit," he replied. "I grew up being told that lie." In fact they had a big fight about it, on the night before the expedition left Vilhena. "I told Dad that I thought it was behind us."

Charlie and Beth married soon after the expedition. He died in 2004 at age 55, same age as TR when he went down the River of Doubt. His spinal cancer might have grown from a virus caught on the River of Doubt. He died never knowing that his hero Theodore Roosevelt's first child had Haskell blood, and was named for a Haskell. His pure hope, that everyone on the expedition would become best friends forever, didn't make it. That sweet naive dream was Charlie Haskell, heart and soul. "If I were to say I want the moon, Charlie would say, 'Mom, I will get it for you.'"

After the expedition, multitalented Mario Peixoto continued to train Outward Bound instructors on Oregon's Mount Hood, and then became a professional photographer. He worked for Hollywood movie studios at color and lighting, then invested in real estate in Venice Beach, California, where he did well and retired early to meditate and live the life of a gentleman surfer. In 2022 he went back to the Amazon to make a minidocumentary about the Yawanawa tribe's efforts to protect their 780 square miles of rainforest, presented at COP 27, the UN Climate Change Conference in Egypt. In 2023 he left California and moved to Santa Fe, New Mexico.

Joe Willie Jones's distinguished career as a whitewater adventurer, guide, explorer, competitor, and coach now spans four decades over hundreds of rivers on every continent, from the Arctic to Patagonia to Africa. He's been a consultant for feature films and documentaries, and is the current president and chair of the International Rafting Federation, the governing body of rafting, with an international race series. "He's the same Joe Willie," says Carr Clifton, with a small smile.

Dr. John Walden died of a stroke in 2020, saddening thousands who knew him in West Virginia, Ecuador, and the Amazon. Mark Greenberg vividly recalls the doctor lancing a boil on his forearm at Fazenda Muiraquita, "after handing me the foreman's hootch." Walden later treated him for a flesh-eating disease carried home from the Amazon. Greenberg got further treatment in Paris, where he was shooting the funeral of Marlene Dietrich.

Joe Kaminsky, too, picked up a parasite on the expedition, and was treated for leishmaniasis on his leg in Rio de Janeiro. Fortunately it was cutaneous leishmaniasis of the skin, not visceral leishmaniasis of internal organs, which can kill you by eating your bone marrow.

Carr Clifton is today acclaimed for his artistic landscape photography from some of the planet's most remote places. With five coffee-table books and another ten books featuring his pictures, "Carr Clifton has achieved iconic status in the world of nature photography," said *Digital Photo* magazine. Carr says his intention is to create poetic images, and he succeeds, as shown in his 2012 book *Sacred Headwaters: The Fight to Save the Stikine, Skeena, and Nass Rivers*, in British Columbia.

Kelley Kalafatich was stunt double for Meryl Streep in the 1994 movie, *The River Wild*, filmed in Montana. In 2001 she ran the Colorado River in winter with two women, Rebecca Rusch and Julie Munger, on riverboards, which are like heavy-duty bodyboards. For 300 miles over 18 days, they rode rapids to Class IV. With Carr Clifton, she coproduced the award-winning documentary of their inspiring accomplishment and beautiful adventure, *Three Women, Three Hundred Miles*.

In 2004 on an 800-mile trip down the Blue Nile River from Ethiopia to Sudan, she came home with a parasitic worm called schistosomiasis, or bilharzia. Three years later she felt a sharp pain in her abdomen. "I walked into the ER and never walked out," she said in her TEDx talk in Bend, Oregon, in 2013. In the hospital bed, she felt paralysis crawl from her feet to her spine. On the stage in Bend, she fought back tears. "I haven't talked about it much," she explained.

"It's not the chair, it's the pain," she said later. "Sometimes I wonder what it is I've done in my life to deserve all this pain." Some days are better than others. She lives in the fog of painkillers. She has dear friends who love her. Medical bills will follow her the rest of her life.

Thirty years after the expedition I contacted Chip Haskell, now 55, same age as his father when he died. He went back to school and got a Masters in International Finance and Accounting, led asset development for energy companies in Amsterdam and Lima, then founded Vair Companies in

Atlanta, where, he says, "We help companies structure the project deals that allow for infrastructure to be implemented in developing countries." Sounds like Piu needed him 30 years ago.

For adventure, he's a rich guy on vacation, flying and racing vintage gliders. He owns three, and finished fifth at the US Nationals in 2022. "Have also been doing a bit of sailing lately," he emailed me in September 2022. "Just delivered a 42ft sloop from the Bahamas to Florida."

He paid no attention to the expedition for 25 years, until he found that Tweed Roosevelt had been, in Chip's opinion, misrepresenting his role by coloring himself as its leader, sometimes never mentioning Haskell; or, when Charlie was brought up, in one interview at least, called him a fraud and a liar and accused him of claiming he was a Vietnam hero.

It was Tweed's duty to protect the Roosevelt legacy. The media made him the star, naturally, and he might have been too good at it. As his great-grandfather had "taken hold of the thing," Tweed took hold of the aftermath to avoid being sideswiped.

Today Chip has little respect for Tweed, putting it in stronger terms to me. In an email to Tweed, he wrote, "We can only thank the divine providence that you are descended from Edith and not Alice, whose mother was Caroline Watts Haskell." He returned his medal to the Theodore Roosevelt Association.

In Brazil after the expedition, Silvio Barros, the secretary of tourism for the State of Amazonas, who got the permits for the Rio Roosevelt expedition, on the belief that publicity in the US might draw tourists to the Amazon, was aghast at the hype, exaggeration, and emphasis on the threatening nature of the jungle. He was dismayed by the lack of follow-up on the promises that Haskell and McKnight had made.

The Brazilian scientists from INPA declined to write the report for the Earth Summit, on the grounds that they hadn't been afforded the materials and opportunities to conduct the necessary research. In a long letter to New Century Conservation Trust, they detailed their discontent. "In Brazil, you have to be an idealist to be a scientist," sighed Joao Ferraz.

Fabio Netto, too, was disgruntled. He believed it would have taken a shaman to do more than he had in saving the expedition from folly, as well as saving it a great deal of money. He was hurt and financially strapped by having to bear more than $2,000 in expedition costs out of what he believed to be a more-than-fair fee for his overtime effort.

The FUNAI agent Assis sent Haskell and McKnight a letter requesting the $5,000 they had promised at the Round Table to be used for renovations to the tiny clinic at Riozinho. But with the African expedition on their agenda, McKnight replied that New Century Conservation Trust didn't have the money. Haskell passed the request on to the Public Welfare Foundation, the institution founded by his grandfather Charles Marsh.

Chief Oitamina spent a lot of time near the Serra Morena outpost, protecting his people and the environment from the effects of the dam on the Aripuaña River, he said. He was likely involved in gold mining. He sold his Bronco and bought a sports car. He and Regina separated.

Piu acquired his sawmill, located on land near Fazenda Muiraquita that had been owned by a settler until it was reclaimed by the government and turned over to the Cinta Larga. Thousands of dollars in logs came with the land, ready for the mill. Piu picked up more thousands from garimpeiros paying to dredge. It was reported that he and other Cinta Larga chiefs were charging $5,000 plus time on the water.

Sergio Prandini's beautiful vision of an eco lodge at Fazenda Muiraquita was stillborn. Rafting trips down the Rio Roosevelt with professional boatmen and guided by Cinta Larga remain a perfect dream.

I stayed in Brazil six more months, researching and writing a draft of this book, rejected because it didn't paint a pretty picture. From Rio de Janeiro, I went back to the Amazon with my friend Caju (we had rock-climbed the face of Sugarloaf together, as cadet Rondon had done in 1885). We flew to Porto Velho and rented a Volkswagen pickup truck and drove down to Riozinho, to keep part of the promise Haskell and McKnight had made to the Riozinho Indian House. After my twice nagging Charlie on the phone, he came up with $2,000, which Caju and I spent on a spree at a pharmacy, after getting a list of the most-needed over-the-counter

medicines from the nurse Judite at the clinic there. Oitamina was there for
the photo op, in T-shirt and *cocar* headdress, the meds stacked on a table
before him, with me holding a baby.

We drove into the Rio Roosevelt outpost with Tatare, to see Oitamina's
Uncle Rondon, the crazy old paje. We got lost at night, bouncing along in
dusty tangled loops of logging roads for nearly an hour. Tatare muttered
and cracked, "I'm a jungle specialist, not a road specialist." I woke up at
the outpost in a room with a rigid skinned monkey sitting up and glaring
at me from a corner, the family's food for the day.

I attended the Earth Summit in Rio, where I ran into Tatare at an event
where he shared the stage and microphone with Senator Al Gore. He'd
flown down from Porto Velho, his expenses paid by an American promoter
of an Indigenous peoples' conference at the summit. He was an eloquent
spokesman for his tribe, later representing the Cinta Larga at a meeting
attended by Ted Turner and Jane Fonda.

Some Indigenous had threatened to be no-shows at that meeting,
indignant and jealous of the Yanomami for getting all the attention; but
the promoter persuaded them to stay by offering them a shopping spree
for cowboy hats, boots, shirts, and belts, guided by some young women
from NGOs (nongovernmental organizations). The promoter accepted
being held up by Indians, fearing the embarrassment of not having them
there for Ted and Jane. I didn't ask Tatare if he got a pair of cowboy
boots out of it.

I followed Tatare from the waterfront park with the Earth Summit's
booths and displays, down a crowded Rio sidewalk, where he moved
through people like he flowed through trees in the jungle, as if his feet
were floating six inches over the concrete. I watched him disappear in the
crowd. We hadn't spoken much. He seemed casual about the trip to Rio. I
hoped he had resisted the cocaine that was available to some of the Indians,
and wondered if, like other handsome Indians, he had slept with the free-
spirited, idealistic, adventurous young women, mostly British it seemed,
who worked for these NGOs. Back home, Tatare was elected president of
Associacao Pamare, defeating Piu in a runoff.

At the Earth Summit, I regret not meeting Sydney Possuelo, head of FUNAI's *Departamento do Indios Isolados*, whom I only mention in this book in a footnote. During his time in that role at FUNAI, he doubled the size of protected Indigenous territories, to nearly 400,000 square miles, or 11 percent of the country. As the tide turned against the protection of Indians, in 2006 he was fired by FUNAI for criticizing its director, who believed that Indians had too much land that White men should be able to use for their gain.

Possuelo counts 166 Indigenous territories he has demarcated, including Roosevelt Indigenous Territory and the first territory in 1961, when he was 21, a budding activist. Today at 83, less the angry idealist he'd been for the first 50 years of his career, Possuelo continues the fight. He founded his own NGO, *Instituto Indigenista Interamericano,* to bring together Indigenous activist groups and tribal organizations like the Cinta Larga's *Associao Pamare.* In an interview in 2020, he suggested that there were still more than 20 uncontacted tribes in Brazil. "If we lose them, we will lose part of our humanity," he said.

My staying in Brazil led to a divorce (over horses). I went back to Brazil to write about the racedriver Emerson Fittipaldi, and considered staying there to lead a happy life as a bachelor freelance writer—so many stories in Brazil it spins your head. I chose to go back to Oregon and start a family, got married, had two boys, got divorced, raised them as a single dad and authored the parenting memoir, *It Doesn't Get Any Better Than This: The Dream Lives of Papa Madre and the AngloArabAsian Brothers* (available at www.sammoses.com).

CHAPTER 30

The Next 30 Years

It's as if we're living in Mad Max.
—Danicley de Aguiar, Greenpeace activist

The brutal battles between prospectors and Indigenous continue. Soon after our expedition, 20 Yanomami, including 10 children, were massacred by gold miners near the Orinoco River, after squabbles between the miners and young "warriors," as they were called by the newspaper *Folha de São Paulo*. Police had destroyed a miners' camp so the miners retaliated against the tribe. I read about it in my paper the *Oregonian*, the story by James Brooke of the *New York Times News Service*. Fifteen garimpeiros armed with shotguns, revolvers, and machetes surrounded a village while the men were gone and "killed as many Yanomami as possible," said the story. "Some of the children were decapitated with machete blows," said one survivor. Two baby girls were wrapped in their blankets and stabbed.

Nature is losing the war between environment and development. In the year of our expedition, 5,323 square miles of the Amazon were deforested, according to statistics from Brazil's National Institute for Space Research

(INPE). It doubled in the next three years, tapered for the next eight years, and spiked in 2004. It dropped for the next five years during the presidency of Luiz Inacio Lula da Silva, as gold and diamond prospecting moved in.

Oitamina and Piu made the *New York Times* in 2006, in a story titled DIAMONDS' GLITTER FADES FOR A BRAZILIAN TRIBE. Mahogany was over, the real money was diamonds. "Geologists say the diamond potential of the reservation here has barely been scratched," said the *Times*.

Oitamina (as Roberto Carlos) and Piu were both quoted, sounding exactly the same as they had speaking to me. Piu was richer but wiser. "Money only brings problems and suffering, when what we really want is tranquility," he said.

According to the *Times* reporter, "The Cinta Larga have become the most notorious of Brazil's hundreds of Indian tribes, reviled in the press as bloodthirsty savages who want the diamonds for themselves."

In 2004 the Cinta Larga executed 29 of 250 garimpeiros on Cinta Larga land. Cinta Larga girls had been raped. Cinta Larga chiefs told them to get out, but 50 refused, and 29 met the consequences, tied to trees and beaten to death with war clubs.

The long story was titled "Rough Justice," told by the brilliant Canadian investigative journal, *The Walrus.* It was like the mahogany story but darker, more sophisticated, and with higher stakes. It ended with a confrontation between the reporter, Shawn Blore, and the governor of Rondônia, who had tried to cut a deal with Piu and two other chiefs—the Cinta Larga would get a school, clinic, and paved road in exchange for the governor moving in his own diamond-mining equipment. Piu turned him down. The angry governor dropped police protections for the tribe's land, which led to the Cinta Larga's "rough justice."

For the next decade, diamond mining was stopped and started, off and on, by both the tribe and the government. In 2017, the website InSight Crime, focused on organized crime in the Americas, ran a piece that declared in the subtitle, THE CINTA LARGA IN BRAZIL ARE ON THE BRINK OF COLLAPSE AS THEY STRUGGLE TO CONFRONT ILLEGAL MINING IN ONE OF THE WORLD'S LARGEST DIAMOND DEPOSITS. This time, the story said,

"In March, there were no less than 500 armed miners who told the Cinta Larga that they would not leave the indigenous land."

It wasn't hype to suggest the Rio Roosevelt had the "world's largest diamond deposits," as the story said. The illegal diamond miners were taking an estimated $25 million per year in diamonds out of the Rio Roosevelt, but there was much more. The government's Ministry of Mines and Energy said "it might be possible to extract one million karats per year," at just one of the illegal mining operations. It was a ramshackle outlaw site with a backhoe that cut a gash 60 feet wide. An industrial operation would create a canyon.

That's what Brazil's right-wing president Jair Bolsonaro was pushing for, as he turned FUNAI into an agency staffed by people who see Indians standing in the way of wealth. He wanted their land. His argument, that 11 percent of the country is too much for 1 percent of the population, remains a popular one, echoing what Theodore Roosevelt said in the 1890s.

The BBC also found Oitamina, in 2017. In their piece titled, "The Cinta Larga and the Curse of the Diamonds," he told them, "An indigenous person without land is an indigenous person without soul."

In recent years it's been gold mining on Amazon rivers, out of control. Scott Wallace paints a vivid, grim picture in his book *The Unconquered*. "At the front of the barge, where the steel boom supporting the drill straddled a pair of rusty pontoons, a cesspool of fetid water, metal tailings, and upended trees lapped against a ravaged shore. The rig had chewed its way more than fifty feet into the embankment along a seam a hundred yards long."

In that cesspool of fetid water and metal tailings lies the mercury, used to separate gold from riverbottom sludge. A study of one Indian village found that 15 percent of the children under the age of nine had neurological symptoms from mercury poisoning. "Where rivers ran past Indian settlements downstream from gold strikes," wrote Wallace, "ulcers and suppurating sores were the order of the day. So were birth defects. The grieving nurse in Gorotire had delivered two stillborn babies in her first three months on the job. The fetuses' brains were growing outside their skulls."

The *New Yorker*, 2019: In their piece titled Blood Gold in the Brazilian Rain Forest, they said the fight between miners and Indians might "help decide the future of the planet."

Reuters, 2020: Amazon gold rush: illegal mining threatens brazil's last major isolated tribe. Satellite images showed that the number of illegal mining operations had grown from 10 to 207 in three years. It was estimated that there were 20,000 miners on Yanomami land, spreading COVID. Because of the pandemic, FUNAI agents were staying away, so no one was counting the dead.

National Geographic, 2021: indigenous communities and isolated tribes in brazil are under threat as the government moves to legalize mining, logging, and industrial farming. Byline Scott Wallace again, who wrote the book on isolated tribes when he found the Arrow People with Sydney Possuelo in *The Unconquered*. Miners in speedboats opened fire with automatic weapons on a Yanomami village. Two children drowned when they dove in the river to dodge the bullets.

In November 2021, the *Guardian* ran a story with photos of a long flotilla of gold-mining rigs on the Madeira River, just 75 miles from Manaus, poisoning the water with mercury. "I've been working in the Amazon for 25 years," said Greenpeace activist Danicley de Aguiar. "I was born here and I've seen many terrible things: so much destruction, so much deforestation, so many illegal mines. But when you see a scene like that it makes you feel as though the Amazon has been thrust into a spiral of free-for-all. There are no rules. It's as if we're living in *Mad Max*."

"Just look at the audacity of these criminals," tweeted Sônia Bridi, a Brazilian journalist passionate about the Amazon. "The extent of the impunity." President Bolsonaro looked the other way, without trying to hide his smile. He expressed no regret for the June murders of the British journalist Dom Phillips, researching a book on sustainable development, and Bruno Pereira, head of *Indios Isolados* until he was fired in 2019, as Bolsonaro dismantled FUNAI. "Bolsonaro's fingerprints are all over these murders," said one activist.

In April 2022, the award-winning Brazilian journalist and novelist Vanessa Barbara, in a powerful essay in the *New York Times*, reported that under Bolsonaro, deforestation grew 76 percent from 2018 to 2021, and boomed 69 percent in 2022. Bolsonaro admired the US cavalry, regretting that Brazil's army hadn't been as effective "as the Americans, who exterminated the Indians in the past."

After passing 593 bills to develop the Amazon in 2020 alone, Bolsonaro was now pushing further legislation to legalize logging, industrial agriculture, oil exploration, hydroelectric dams, and other projects on Indigenous lands. He also planned to legalize mining, offer amnesty to illegal loggers, and allow more than 1,000 new pesticides. Bolsonaro said he wished he could just send in his army and take the land over, the way America had.

On October 31, 2022, Barbara was able to write another opinion piece in the *Times* that began, "Four years of madness are nearly over." For the first time in the 34 years of Brazil's modern democracy, an incumbent president failed to be reelected, as Bolsonaro lost in a runoff to former president da Silva, popularly known as Lula. The killing of the Amazon, if not the planet, was stopped for now by a slim two million votes, as Lula won by 50.9 percent to Bolsonaro's 49.1 percent.

The *Guardian*, January 1, 2023, inauguration day: HOPE, JOY, EUPHORIA: BRAZILIANS TAKE TO THE STREETS TO CELEBRATE A NEW ERA UNDER LULA. It was a party to rival Carnaval, with tens of thousands celebrating in Brasilia—they called it Lulapalooza. "We feel dizzyingly unfathomable relief," said one. "We've been through four years of terror, and now we feel free."

There will be resistance from the right to this new era, driven by greed at the top exploiting ignorance at the bottom, but Lula has been clear that the Amazon must be saved. "We are going to fight for zero deforestation in the Amazon," he told journalists, in his first statement after the election. "Brazil and the planet need the Amazon alive."

He stood with his arm around 64-year-old Marina Silva, the woman who was his environmental minister when he was president from 2003–2008, and now is again. Born to illiterate rubber tappers in remote Acre, descended from native Indians, Portuguese settlers, and African slaves,

Marina, as she's known, has been an environmental activist since she learned to read at 16, and ran for president herself with the Green Party in 2014. She made a point of saying that her administration would be dedicated to the memory of the environmental activists murdered during the Bolsonaro regime. She's now like Atlas, carrying Earth on her tiny shoulders.

After rolling in his grave for half a century, like a Cinta Larga spirit Colonel Rondon now sits up and watches, pumping his fist and cheering for his caboclo sister.

Acknowledgments

First, and obviously, I'd like to thank the late Charles Haskell, and Elizabeth McKnight, along with my seventeen other teammates on the Rio Roosevelt expedition, for the exceptional experience. Especially the scientists Jose Cabral and Joao Ferraz, who translated for many of my interviews and discussions on the river. The Cinta Larga chiefs Piu, Oitamina, and Tatare, not only for sharing their story, but for allowing and accompanying us on their Rio Teodoro, the first White men and women in their history to be so privileged, excluding the unaccompanied FUNAI expedition for the purpose of demarcating the Roosevelt Indigenous Territory.

Peter Riva, my literary agent, who chose me for the job of writing this book, and whose creative idea it was to juxtapose the Roosevelt-Rondon expedition with our own. I rejected that idea 30 years ago, before I learned (with the writing of *At All Costs*, also Riva's idea) that the line between reporter and historian isn't really so broad. He had confidence in me that I lacked at that time.

When I teamed up with the Brazilian boatman Mario Peixoto to leave the expedition in the Jeep that Haskell generously made available, I didn't know how valuable his participation would become. The best and most revealing reporting in this story—and the most fun—is thanks to Mario. Memorable moments during our time together, besides the hallucinogenic trip, include glimpsing the black jaguar through the Jeep's windshield as it crossed the jungle trail, and eyeballing the rearview mirror as we raced away from Espigao d'Oeste, checking for logging company hitmen in pursuit.

I could say "as I learned 30 years later" a thousand times in this book. In the introduction of the unpublished 1993 manuscript, I quoted the scientist and interpreter Joao Ferraz, who said, "One of the reasons we have so much bullshits written about the environment and the rainforest, is it is so hard to find truth. Not because the people are asking the wrong questions, but because so little people know the exact answers, and it all must be checked maybe five times, and none of the checking agrees." Added Mario Peixoto, "The concept of information is totally different in Brazil. There is no system, no network. In the United States, information is almost a product, and truth and accuracy are goals of the system." In Brazil, the product is some sort of vague satisfaction, usually tied to an ulterior motive. Although maybe Mario is describing 30 years ago; with today's fake news, and fake charges of fake news, we've moved toward that product of ulterior motive.

Bob Brown, my editor for a few hundred stories over eighteen years at *Sports Illustrated*, saved *River Without a Cause*. I sent him a manuscript in installments that would total 130,000 words, and with his comments and criticism—no doubt tedious for him—I found the voice and path for these 84,000 words. The irascible and politically perceptive Stephen Pizzo, who also reviewed the first of those installments and rightly hated them so much he quit, mostly over my stubborn resistance at that time to using first person. The first sentence of chapter 2 is his.

Fellow automotive journalist Doug Newcomb in my hometown of Hood River, Oregon, who received the rare old copy of Alice Roosevelt Longworth's *Crowded Hours* while I was in Ecuador, and scanned and emailed the relevant pages. I guess it's his, now; I forgot to get it back and now I'm gone altogether from the USA.

I should probably thank the pandemic. This version of the book began as a lockdown project, on an island off the coast of Nicaragua. I emailed my friend and ex-wife Kim Chinnock back in Hood River, asked her to dig out the thirty-year-old unpublished manuscript from my cargo-container library, and take it to Jeremy Lazzara at PostalAnnex, who scanned the

350-or-so pages, converted them to a Word document (inevitably full of hidden bugs, which he patiently chased and fixed), and I began revising, now on the remote Colombian north coast where I was kitesurfing; then back in Hood River, then the small village of Tanah Jawa in the rainforest of Sumatra, Indonesia where I was building a house with my wife Diana, then Bali (bodyboarding), then back in Hood River to finish. I also thank my landlords and Indonesian family, namely Made, Ketut, Putu, and sweet-sixteen Michelle at the apartment hotel in Medewi with its fabulous view over the Indian Ocean.

And definitely Diana, never complaining as I spent hundreds of hours at the laptop in those places, except Hood River. We were separated six months a year for six years until we built a bamboo house in an eco-village on the island of Lombok where we now live, finally "together forever" as we vowed in our Hindu wedding ceremony.

There were friends in Brazil, where I wrote much of the original manuscript over six months in 1993, whom I regrettably can't remember. For sure I remember my rock-climbing partner Caju, so-named because he once dyed his hair and it came out green like the caju fruit; we went from Rio de Janeiro back to the Amazon together to visit the Cinta Larga for more research. I found in my box marked "Amazon" in the cargo container a warm and wise handwritten letter from "Steven," apparently an editor and/or writer friend in England; if you're still living, Steven, your kind comments and constructive criticism of the first manu-script were spot-on. You, too, urged first-person. As you said, Charlie and Beth were victims of their own goals, which they set too high. "Perhaps this should be spelled out more clearly at the end," you suggested. Hope I got it right.

Bibliography

Browder, John O. "Lumber Production and Economic Development in the Brazilian Amazon: Regional Trends and a Case Study." *Journal of World Forest Resource Management* 4(1): 1–19, 1989.

Caro, Robert A. *The Years of Lyndon Johnson: The Path to Power.* New York: Alfred A. Knopf, 1982.

Caufield, Catherine. *In the Rainforest.* New York: Knopf, 1985.

Cherrie, George. *Dark Trails: Adventures of a Naturalist.* New York: G.P. Putnam's Sons, 1930.

Conant, Jennet. *The Irregulars: Roald Dahl and the British Spy Ring in Wartime Washington.* New York: Simon & Schuster, 2008.

Cordery, Stacy A. *Alice: Alice Roosevelt Longworth, From White House Princess to Washington Power Broker.* New York: Penguin Books, 2008.

Cowell, Adrian. *The Decade of Destruction: The Crusade to Save the Amazon Rain Forest.* New York: Henry Holt & Co, 1990.

Cowell, Adrian. *The Tribe That Hides from Man.* New York: Stein and Day, 1974.

Diacon, Todd A. *Stringing Together a Nation: Cândido Mariano da Silva Rondon and the Construction of a Modern Brazil, 1906–1930.* Durham, NC: Duke University Press, 2004.

Fleming, Peter. *Brazilian Adventure.* New York: C. Scribner's Sons, 1933.

Goodland, Robert J. A., and Howard Samuel Irwin. *Amazon Jungle: Green Hell to Red Dust?: An Ecological Discussion of the Environmental Impact of the Highway Construction Program in the Amazon Basin.* Amsterdam: Elsevier Scientific Publishing, 1975.

Grann, David. *The Lost City of Z: A Tale of Deadly Obsession in the Amazon.* New York: Doubleday, 2009.

Hall, Anthony L. *Developing Amazonia: Deforestation and Social Conflict in Brazil's Carajás Programme.* New York/Manchester: Manchester University Press, 1989.

Hansen, Eric. *Stranger in the Forest: One Foot Across Borneo.* Boston: Houghton Mifflin, 1988.

Hecht, Susanna B., and Alexander Cockburn. *The Fate of the Forest Developers, Destroyers, and Defenders of the Amazon, Updated Edition.* Chicago: University of Chicago Press, 2010.

Hemmings, John. *Red Gold: The Conquest of the Brazilian Indians.* Cambridge, MA: Harvard University Press, 1978.

Kandell, Jonathan. *Passage Through Eldorado: Traveling the World's Last Great Wilderness*. New York: Avon Books, 1985.

Kane, Joe. *Running the Amazon*. New York: Alfred A. Knopf, 1989.

Kane, Joe. *Savages*. New York: Vintage Books, 1996.

Lemanski, William E. *Lost in the Shadow of Fame: The Neglected Story of Kermit Roosevelt; A Gallant and Tragic American*. Mechanicsburg, PA: Sunbury Press, 2019.

Log of Carr Clifton, 1992 Rio Roosevelt Trip.

Longworth, Alice Roosevelt. *Crowded Hours*. New York: C. Scribner's Sons, 1933.

MacCreagh, Gordon. *White Waters and Black*. New York: Grosset & Dunlap, 1926.

Mann, William J. *The Wars of the Roosevelts: The Ruthless Rise of America's Greatest Political Family*. New York: Harper Perennial, 2016. Kindle Edition.

Margolis, Mac. *The Last New World: The Conquest of the Amazon Frontier*. New York: W. W. Norton, 1992.

Matthiessen, Peter. *The Cloud Forest*. New York: Viking, 1961.

Medina, Jose Toribio, ed. *The Discovery of the Amazon*. New York: Dover Publications, 1988.

Millard, Candice. *The River of Doubt: Theodore Roosevelt's Darkest Journey*. New York: Doubleday, 2005.

Monbiot, George. *Mahogany is Murder: Mahogany Extraction from Indian Reserves in Brazil*. Friends of the Earth, 1992.

Morris, Edmund. *Colonel Roosevelt*. New York: Random House, 2011.

Morris, Edmund. *The Rise of Theodore Roosevelt*. New York: Random House, 2010. First published 1979 by Coward, McCann, and Geoghegan.

Morris, Sylvia Jukes. *Edith Kermit Roosevelt: Portrait of a First Lady*. New York, Modern Library (Random House), 2001.

de Onis, Juan. *The Green Cathedral: Sustainable Development of Amazonia*. New York: Oxford University Press, 1992.

Ornig, Joseph R. *My Last Chance to Be a Boy: Theodore Roosevelt's South American Expedition of 1913–1914*. Mechanicsburg, PA: Stackpole Books, 1994.

Patterson, Raymond M. *The Dangerous River*. White River Junction, VT: Chelsea Green Publishing, 1957.

Pineda, Cecile. *The Love Queen of the Amazon*. New York: Little, Brown and Company, 1992.

Popescu, Petru. *Amazon Beaming*. New York: Viking Press (Penguin), 1991.

Price, David. *Before the Bulldozer: The Nambiquara Indians and the World Bank*. Santa Ana, CA: Seven Locks Press, 1989.

Quammen, David. *Wild Thoughts from Wild Places*. New York: Scribner, 1999.

Rohter, Larry. *Into the Amazon: The Life of Cândido Rondon, Trailblazing Explorer, Scientist, Statesman, and Conservationist*. New York: W. W. Norton & Company, 2023.

Rondon, Candido Mariano. *Historia da Minha Vida*. Belo Horizonte, Brazil: LeBooks Editora, 2019.

Roosevelt, Kermit. *The Happy Hunting-Grounds*. Glasgow, Scotland: Good Press, 2021. Kindle Edition.

Roosevelt, Theodore. *Through the Brazilian Wilderness*. New York: C. Scribner's Sons, 1914.

Seiple, Samantha. *Death of the River of Doubt: Theodore Roosevelt's Amazon Adventure*. New York: Scholastic, 2017. Kindle Edition.

Shoumatoff, Alex. *The Rivers Amazon*. San Francisco: Sierra Club Books, 1978.

Smith, Anthony. *Explorers of the Amazon*. Chicago: University of Chicago Press, 1990.

Smith, Nigel J. H. *Rainforest Corridors: The Transamazon Colonization Scheme*. Berkeley, CA: University of California Press, 1982.

Stafford, Ed. *Walking the Amazon: 860 Days. One Step at a Time*. New York: Plume, 2012.

Stegner, Wallace. *The Sound of Mountain Water*. Lincoln: University of Nebraska, 1985. First published 1969 by Doubleday.

Stewart, Christopher S. *Jungleland: A Mysterious Lost City, a WWII Spy, and a True Story of a Deadly Adventure*. New York: HarperCollins, 2013.

Stone, Roger D. *Dreams of Amazonia*. New York: Elisabeth Sifton Books (Penguin Books), 1986.

Tidwell, Mike. *Amazon Stranger: A Rain Forest Chief Battles Big Oil*. New York: Lyons Press, 1996.

Updike, John. *Brazil*. New York: Alfred A. Knopf, 1994.

Ure, John. *Trespassers on the Amazon*. London: Constable, 1986.

Wallace, Alfred Russel. *A Narrative of Travels on the Amazon and Rio Negro: With an Account of the Native Tribes, and Observations on the Climate, Geology, and Natural History of the Amazon Valley*. New York: Ward, Lock & Co., Ltd., 1889.

Wallace, Scott. *The Unconquered: In Search of the Amazon's Last Uncontacted Tribes*. New York: Crown Publishing Group, 2011.

Zahm, John Augustine. *Through South America's Southland*. New York: D. Appleton and Company, 1916.

Index